WATERSHED

This book is dedicated to the hope that it will contribute to the dynamic that suggests, and not just to the Israelis and Palestinians, that water is one of the few truly limited resources on Earth, and that sharing of water resources is inherent to a peaceful, equitable, and efficient future for all of us.

Que n'a-t-on fait pour s'approprier l'eau? Que n'a-t-on inventé pour s'excuser de l'avoir fait? Quel crime n'a-t-on commis pour n'avoir pas à s'en excuser? Quelle raison d'état n'a-t-on invoquée pour s'en assurer la possession exclusive?

— de Laet (1992)

WATERSHED

THE ROLE OF FRESH WATER
IN THE ISRAELI–PALESTINIAN CONFLICT

Stephen C. Lonergan

and

David B. Brooks

INTERNATIONAL DEVELOPMENT RESEARCH CENTRE

Ottawa • Cairo • Dakar • Johannesburg • Montevideo
Nairobi • New Delhi • Singapore

Published by the International Development Research Centre
PO Box 8500, Ottawa, ON, Canada K1G 3H9

© International Development Research Centre 1994

Lonergan, S.C.
Brooks, D.B.

Watershed : the role of fresh water in the Israeli–Palestinian conflict. Ottawa,
ON, IDRC, 1994. xiii + 310 p. : ill.

/Freshwater/, /water supply/, /water quality/, /water distribution/, /conflicts/,
/Israel/, /Palestine/ — /groundwater/, /water consumption/, /water utilization/,
/water conservation/, /water management/, /international agreements/, /peace/,
/economic aspects/, /political aspects/, /data collecting/, glossary, bibliography.

UDC: 551.579(569.4)   ISBN: 0-88936-719-1

A microfiche edition is available.

IDRC BOOKS endeavours to produce environmentally friendly publications. All
paper used is recycled as well as recycleable. All inks and coatings are vegetable-
based products.

CONTENTS

PART II ~ THREE CRISES

FOREWORD

THE WORLD IS HEADING toward a major water crisis in the next few decades. By 2025, there will be 3 billion people living in countries exhibiting water stress or having chronic water scarcity. Water will be urgently needed not only for settlements and industries; the largest amounts will be needed to grow the food for the growing population in these countries. Given this situation, there are three main problems that await solutions:

≈ How do we cope with escalating water scarcity?

≈ What should the rules be for sharing water between upstream and downstream users?

≈ How do we overcome the barriers existing in international river basins where the interests of the riparian countries often differ?

In the face of this global predicament, the Jordan River is a highly interesting case, particularly because Israel is commonly presented as a model of sound water management. Any solution found to sharing water in the Jordan Basin will have wide relevance to other countries in the Middle East as well as other regions of the world.

No state can survive without access to life-supporting water. As a result of millennia-long cultural differences, the water problems in the Jordan River Basin are particularly complex. The problems increased with the 1946 United Nations decision specifying the borders of the new state of Israel. "Only an evil water goddess could have come up with such a solution," write the authors of this book. In other words, disputes were built into the geostrategic results of that UN decision — a fact that has made many Israelis become obsessed with the issue of "water security."

One might suggest that a central question raised by the Middle East problematique is "Who owns the rain?" The title of this book — Watershed — more or less points to that crucial question. In this book, Stephen Lonergan and David Brooks present a thorough analysis of the current situation in the Jordan River Basin, including its historical background, the environmental preconditions embodied in the local hydroclimate, the landscape topography and the hydrogeography, and the problems of past water management. The book provides some surprising insight: not even in a water-stressed country like Israel does planning start with the reasonable question of "How much water is there and how do we best benefit from that amount for socio-economic development?" Israel's politicians seem to take the same utilitarian approach to water as the rest of the world, strengthened by their dream of "making the desert bloom." Evidently, Israel's political leaders are also suffering from the well-known water blindness so widespread in Northern countries. The results are demonstrated by a water-pollution problem as great as in any other country, and a water administration as fragmented as that in any other country. Organizationally, water policy is even subordinate to agricultural policy.

Even in a water-scarce region such as the Jordan River Basin, the conventional question of "How much water do we need and where do we get it?" is paramount. As Lonergan and Brooks note, in the Israeli submission to the UN Conference on Environment and Development (the Earth Summit) in 1992, the focus was on rapidly increasing water demands and the huge water deficit that can be expected. This focus is even more remarkable as a substantial portion of the water Israel now uses — especially the groundwater that is recharged from the West Bank — is under dispute. A recent report from the Israeli state comptroller has brought these national water scarcity problems into the open, so that not only regional but also sectoral tensions over water have become very public.

This book reviews what the authors term the "three crises" of water in Israel: the water quantity crisis, which is economic in character; the water quality crisis, which is ecological; and the geostrategic crisis, which is political. They conclude with a set of regional options and policy recommendations. The analysis is limited primarily to the Israeli–Palestinian conflict — complex enough for an entire book — but Syrian and Jordanian interests are also treated on occasion. It is easy to agree with the authors of this highly interesting book that the peace process provides a real opportunity for recognition of the water entitlements of the different countries involved.

Malin Falkenmark

Stockholm, Sweden
24 November 1994

ACKNOWLEDGMENTS

WE ARE GRATEFUL to a number of people who assisted in the preparation of this book. In particular, Barb Kavanagh and Marjie Lesko of the Centre for Sustainable Regional Development at the University of Victoria, who spent countless hours typing, editing, and proofreading the manuscript; Ken Josephson and Ole Heggen of the Geography Department at the University of Victoria, who provided the maps and figures; Jim Moore of the Department of National Defence and Eglal Rached of the International Development Research Centre, who reviewed an earlier version of the manuscript; and the many researchers and residents of Israel and the Occupied Territories who provided insight and information on the issue. We also acknowledge the assistance of the Social Sciences and Humanities Research Council of Canada, which provided assistance for this project under Grant 410-93-0320.

In addition, David Brooks would like to thank Otonabee College of Trent University for granting him an Ashley Fellowship that allowed him to complete the first draft of this manuscript.

PART I

THE
SETTING

CHAPTER 1

INTRODUCTION: IMAGE AND REALITY

And Lot also, who went with Abram, had flocks, and herds, and tents. And the land was not able to bear them, that they might dwell together; for their substance was great, so that they could not dwell together.

— Genesis, 13:6

BOTH BIBLICAL AND modern Israel have been vitally concerned with water. The first explicit ecological reference in the Bible relates to the carrying capacity of pastures and water supplies that were coming under stress from growth of the herds owned by Abraham and by his nephew Lot. One of the periodic droughts of the region starts the drama that leads to the Exodus story. More recently, the challenge to "make the desert bloom" brought Jewish settlers into what was first a Turkish colony and then a British protectorate. Later projects, such as the draining of the Hula wetlands and construction of the National Water Carrier, were hailed as symbols of the potential to live productively and comfortably in an arid region — albeit at the same time they were described as "aggressive expansionist ambitions threatening all Arabs alike" (Rothman and Lowi 1992, p. 62).

Different Aspects of the Conflict

The State of Israel is commonly regarded as a model of sound water management. The reality, however, is different from the image. Israel has made appropriate microlevel choices to ensure that water is consumed efficiently at the point of use; its macrolevel choices that allocate water among alternative uses and users have been much more questionable. As a result, Israel is now confronting a water crisis — not in the future but today.

Domestic Aspects

The Israeli public has been made acutely aware of the nation's dependence on water and its vulnerability to water shortages. The whole region experienced a severe drought throughout the latter half of the 1980s, and continuing into the 1990s. Water reservoirs in Israel fell to historic low levels and, for almost the first time in recent history, restrictions on water use were imposed, particularly on farmers. The conditions were even worse in Jordan, where urban dwellers were without water for many hours a day. The drought broke with heavy rains (and snow in Jerusalem and Amman) during the winter of 1991–92, but further droughts will occur.

The concern that this situation raises is not merely an academic issue. Water is essential for irrigated agriculture, and both of Israel's main political coalitions, Labour (Avodah) and Likud, use water as a debating weapon. Neither group is averse to staged resolutions, walk-outs, or other high-profile parliamentary tactics to draw attention to their views. In general (subject to many exceptions), Likud tends to be more heavily supported by rural voters (and by the settlers), and Labour by urban voters. In 1991, when the State Comptroller claimed that favouritism toward farmers in water allocation and pricing had not only created the water shortage but was damaging the nation's fragile economy, tensions over the water issue became very public. Similar, if more moderate, tensions are also present when the Ministry of the Environment suggests that agricultural and industrial pollution are endangering sources of drinking water and that municipalities should improve their sewer systems or industries their wastewater flows.

Palestinians living under Israeli occupation did not need a drought to become aware of water shortages. As will be detailed in the following, except for the smallest and most localized sources, water in the Occupied Palestinian Territories has been fully incorporated into the Israeli water-management system, to the general benefit of Israelis and to the detriment (at least economically) of Palestinians. Indeed, given this situation, it is almost a political statement to place

Israeli–Palestinian water issues under a "domestic" rather than an "international" heading — hence our choice to place it under both. Figure 1, a political map of the region with some of the natural and constructed watercourses superimposed, shows how difficult it would be under the best of circumstances to separate domestic from international water issues. Thus, it is a gross error to discuss "Israel and 'its' water resources," as many authors do, inasmuch as many sources are common to, contained within, or underlie the Occupied Palestinian Territories.

International Aspects

Water is not solely a domestic issue. In Postel's (1992) words, the Middle East is "the most concentrated region of [water] scarcity in the world." The international aspects of Israel's water problems have four dimensions. First, the extent to which Israel's water supply originates in the Occupied Palestinian Territories is a source of much criticism both within and outside the country. Elmusa (1993a) finds that about half of the issues in what he calls the "matrix of the Israeli–Palestinian water conflict" derive from the unique problems of occupation, and about half from normal problems associated with waters that cross a border. Water is one of five topics being treated in separate multilateral peace negotiations that parallel the bilateral negotiations between Israel and each of her Arab neighbours. In the absence of an equitable and efficient resolution of Israeli Palestinian water issues, no peace agreement can last for very long.

Second, insofar as the Jordan River is concerned, Israel is a strong, downstream riparian. This is a common situation in the Middle East; Egypt is in the same position on the Nile, and Syria and Iraq on the Euphrates. As Kolars (1990) points out, over half of the population in the Middle East and North Africa, outside the Maghreb, depend upon water from rivers that cross an international boundary before reaching them, or they use desalinated water or water from deep wells. Policies and institutions established to deal with water resources shared by Israel and its neighbours are likely to play a large role in international water law — and there are literally hundreds of international water bodies (Biswas 1993).

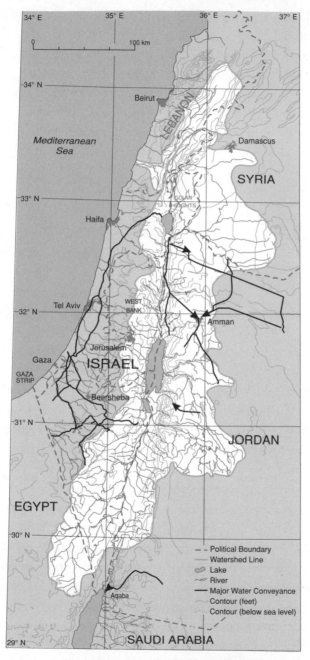

Figure 1. Base map of the Jordan River Valley
(adapted from a map provided by Spider International, Fredericton, NB, Canada).

Third, with its modern economy and western living standards, Israel exhibits a level and pattern of water demand that is currently atypical of the region. There is hardly a country in the region, however, that is not experiencing alarming growth in its demand for water, and few are instituting significant conservation programs. Apart from the impact of Israel's military occupation of the Territories (an impact with long-term consequences that should not be ignored), solutions for water problems in Israel will have relevance for other Middle Eastern countries.

Finally, as Kolars (1990, p. 57) states: "sharing of scarce water supplies is the single most important problem facing Middle Eastern populations." Kolars implies what others have stated flatly (such as Starr and Stoll 1988; Naff 1990; Bulloch and Darwish 1993): namely, in the absence of sharing, a war over water — probably the water of the Jordan River — is a real possibility. This situation makes water in this region not merely an example of environmental change and conflict but of environmental change and "**acute** national and international conflict," which is to say "conflict involving a substantial probability of violence" (Homer-Dixon 1991, p.77; emphasis as in original). Any military action would likely be as futile economically as it would be tragic for the people; "going to war over water will solve little, since the reserves of all the disputants combined are sorely inadequate" (Shuval 1992, p. 142).

A Triple Crisis

With all of these factors playing a strong role, what was once a fairly technical subject of concern to only a few people has in recent years come to be more widely appreciated, as indicated by the number of articles appearing in North American and European newspapers. At the same time, the number of references in professional journals and in the gray literature (unpublished reports, etc.) is growing rapidly. Today, the issue of water is similar to that of energy in the early 1970s: a subject of great concern and under study by a growing number of analysts, but as yet with no apparent agreement as to resolution or even for resolution.

What is apparent, even at this time, is that Israeli water problems are not limited simply to considerations of scarcity, but are a result of three interrelated and interacting crises:

≈ The first crisis is one of **water supply and demand**. Since the mid-1970s, demand has outstripped supply. Population growth through natural increases and in-migration continues to put pressure on the water system, and many proposals for economic expansion would, if implemented, augment the pressure. Yet there is no evident way to increase water supplies.

≈ The second crisis involves deteriorating **water quality**. Much of the nation's water has been, and is still being, polluted by growing volumes of industrial and agricultural wastes, and in some cases by human sewage.

≈ Finally, Israel's water crisis also has a **geopolitical dimension**. Roughly one-third of the water consumed in Israel comes from groundwater that originates as rainfall over the West Bank — on land that in any final settlement is likely to belong to Palestinians. The dependence of both peoples on the same water has led to what many have called a zero-sum game.

The first two crises are common to many countries, and even the third crisis reflects conditions that are anything but rare in the region. Rogers (1994) reports that in 1990 Bahrain, Kuwait, Libya, Qatar, Saudi Arabia, and the United Arab Emirates were all consuming much more water than their annual renewable water supply, and that Egypt, Libya, Oman, and the Sudan were fast approaching the same situation. More specifically, whatever the ultimate resolution of the Israeli–Palestinian conflict, both peoples will have to deal in the near term, in the middle term, and in the long term with water quantity and water quality problems. How they resolve these problems will have a great deal to do with the standard of living and the quality of life that each people will create.

Data: A Fourth Crisis

Concerns about data availability, validity, and reliability are common to all studies on water supply and demand. In the Middle East, however, these concerns rise almost to the point of becoming a fourth crisis.

Water is a strategic resource, vital for state security, for human well-being, and for economic development. As such, many countries in the region keep most data on water availability and use confidential. In other cases, data may be released but may be purposely misleading or too aggregate ("massaged") to permit independent analysis. In still other cases data are not available simply because the country lacks any regular monitoring program.

Problems still exist even when data are available. Inevitably, one faces problems of measurement and sampling error, and of aggregation. Moreover, just as with energy, water suppliers are few and consumers are many, so data on "consumption" are typically measured at the point of dispatch, not at the point of use. One can almost never distinguish among end-users and end-uses below the level of three broad sectors: domestic, including municipal; agricultural; and industrial. Then, too, there is a problem with complementarity, as each country typically has its own set of data and is unwilling to accept the often conflicting data from another country or from an international agency.

These problems, which make analysis of water data and development of policy options problematic at best, are all exaggerated in the Middle East. Until recently, almost all data on water in Israel were treated as state secrets, and it is still said that journalists must submit articles on water for review by military censors. Not long ago, a major university report on alternative lines of withdrawal and their effects on water security was withdrawn from circulation (even review copies had to be returned) and then "frozen." (This report was subsequently "leaked" to the press and is discussed further in Chapter 8.) Palestinians complain vehemently that they cannot gain access even to those data that are unclassified, and that any data provided to them are massaged to the point that the numbers are useless for verification or comparison (Elmusa 1993a). As well, Palestinians have been blocked from receiving some remote sensing data and satellite images because the international agencies that collect them can only release them to "states" — and neither the Occupied Palestinian Territories nor Gaza–Jericho is formally a state.

The quality and availability of water data are central to concerns at the multilateral peace negotiations. Data issues were also a primary

concern at an academic meeting of Israeli and Palestinian water specialists held in late 1992, and both sides, but particularly the Israelis,
pledged to work to improve the availability of water data as soon as possible. One now hears repeatedly of the need for some form of regional
database or regional clearinghouse for information on water that would
be accessible to all (El-Ashry 1991; Kolars 1992; Starr 1992a; Bakour
and Kolars 1994).

All data used in this report are referenced, and every attempt has
been made to check the reliability of "rumours" that seem to pervade
the literature on water in the Middle East. The issue of data is discussed
in more detail in Chapter 6.

Some Definitions and Some Terminology

The Two Peoples and Their Land

Throughout this book, we use "Israel" in two senses. From the perspective of political power, the term refers to the State of Israel, which at
this time also includes the military administration of the West Bank
and the Gaza Strip as well as those parts of the Golan Heights that
Israel has annexed. From the perspective of geography, the term refers
to land contained within the boundaries of pre-1967 Israel. The pre-
1967 borders are also implied by references to land "within the Green
Line," which is essentially where armies were when a truce was declared
in 1948. We use "Occupied Palestinian Territories," "Occupied
Territories," or "the Territories" to refer generally to areas that have, for
most of the period under study, been under Israeli military occupation
(ironically, the military authority is designated the "Civil
Administration" for most nonsecurity matters involving the Territories,
including water). Terminology is further complicated by the fact that
the Golan Heights may be occupied territory but, being part of Syria
before the 1967 war, it is not Occupied **Palestinian** Territory. Where
appropriate, we refer specifically to the West Bank, the Gaza Strip, and
the Golan Heights, and we use Gaza–Jericho to refer to land that came
under Palestinian jurisdiction in May 1994. We use Gaza Strip and
Gaza interchangeably, but Gaza City to refer to the city itself.
Information on the Gaza Strip is more limited than that for the rest of

the Occupied Territories, so in some cases we cautiously extrapolate from the latter to the former.

There is also confusion over Lake Kinneret, the major source of fresh water in Israel. The lake is also known as Lake Tiberias by the Arabs, and its Christian name is the Sea of Galilee. Since the lake lies within the undisputed boundaries of Israel, we have chosen to use the Israeli name, Lake Kinneret. This example is but one part of a larger problem of words having different spellings in different documents or publications (for example, Yarmouk vs Yarmuk, or Huleh vs Hula). There are also frequent misspellings of names in the literature, for example, many articles refer to the "Hayes" Plan, which should read "Hays," after engineer James Hays. We have tried to divert any criticism by simply using what we considered to be the most common version of names in the literature.

Semantics are even more awkward when the political jurisdiction of Palestinians is at issue. Although one can refer to the Palestinians or to a Palestinian delegation (the term can be an adjective or noun), problems arise with respect to the territory that they inhabit or represent. "Occupied Palestinian Territories" is acceptable for the land area itself, but politically connotes an interim arrangement. The terms "Judea and Samaria" are used by those who wish to indicate that the same land should be part of Israel, and "Palestine" by those who wish to indicate that it should be an independent state. To adopt either designation would immediately alienate part of our potential readership. Diplomatic documents tend to refer to the Palestinian "side" or a future Palestinian "entity" or, longer yet, a "Palestinian autonomous region." We have not been able to resolve this dilemma and, although our personal politics and our best guess for political resolution suggest that a nation named Palestine will be created from the Occupied Territories in the near future, we continue to use more awkward designations.

Water Data

Definitional problems provide additional difficulties when dealing with water data. So far as water is concerned, "consumption" is an ambiguous term. It can refer to withdrawals from natural waterways, be they on the surface or underground. Much of the water so withdrawn, however, simply runs off fields or through industrial plants and back into the waterways. In a literal sense, only that proportion of the water that is evaporated (or evapotranspirated: evaporated through the leaves of plants), drunk, or incorporated into final products is truly consumed (Seckler 1993; Pearse et al. 1985). Not only is it much more difficult to measure water consumption in this narrower sense, but even if the volume withdrawn and returned is identical there is always some degradation in water quality. In short, the physical consumption of water, just as with energy, can be measured at three points: at the point of withdrawal from a naturally occurring source, at the point of delivery to an end-user, and at the point where the water is incorporated into a product or a living organism. Depending upon the specific topic under discussion (and all too often on the availability of statistics), it is necessary to retain and use all three of these concepts.

The term "water use" is equally ambiguous. In addition to water used after withdrawal, water has flow uses (as with hydropower and dilution) and in-place uses (as with recreation, fisheries, and habitat protection), all of which have economic as well as aesthetic values (Seckler 1993; Muller 1985; Pearse et al. 1985). Except for hydropower and sometimes recreation or fisheries, almost no account is taken (and not just in the Middle East) of flow or in-place uses. Finally, there is a great deal of carelessness associated with the use of water data. For example, proportions of piped water are commonly given without specifying that the percentages may refer only to urban deliveries and not irrigation, or totals are given without recognition that local springs, rainwater collection, and direct withdrawals may affect the reported numbers.

For the purposes of this study, water consumption and use will be considered synonymous. In almost all cases, they are measured at the point of withdrawal, not at the point of final consumption. As well, we try to avoid the ambiguities we criticize in the data of other analysts. Some additional definitions readers may find useful are included in the glossary at the end of the book.

Units of Measure

The unit of measure for water in this report is generally millions of cubic metres (Mm^3) or litres (L). Each cubic metre contains 1 000 L;

1 L is equal to 0.22 imperial gallons; so 1 cubic metre is equal to 220 imperial gallons. Rainfall is measured in millimetres (mm); 25 mm of rain equals about 1 inch. A useful standard is the 500-mm line, which is the minimum for growing wheat without irrigation; below 250 mm of rainfall, almost all crops require irrigation. In addition, costs are all given in United States dollars of 1990 to 1991 value. Measurements of area are given in square kilometres (km^2) or hectares (ha; 1 ha = 2.47 acres). In reporting data, we have been as current as possible. Most tables include 1990 data; some use 1989 or 1991 figures.

Organization of this Study

The purpose of this book is to review each of the three crises outlined in the foregoing and to provide a set of regional options and policy recommendations for the future. Before delving into the crises, however, we first review briefly the geography, hydrology, and climate of Israel and the Occupied Palestinian Territories (Chapter 2). In addition, the structure of water supply and demand is discussed, as well as the infrastructure that has been developed to manage supply and demand in Israel and the Occupied Territories (Chapter 3). These preliminary chapters, which together with this chapter comprise Part I of this book, "The Setting," are required in part because they provide the ecological and institutional bases from which all options for the future must begin, and also because the interrelated nature of the three crises requires that solutions be found simultaneously for all three.

Part II of this book, entitled "Three Crises," contains three chapters that cover, respectively, each of the three crises: water quantity (Chapter 4), water quality (Chapter 5), and water distribution (Chapter 6). The conceptual distinction among the three crises begins to dissolve, however, once specific problems and policies are brought into question. It is equally difficult to draw clear lines between issues related to water and those related to economic growth or social development, to name just two other issues. Nevertheless, even if they are far from being mutually exclusive, each of the three crises has unique dimensions and they provide the most useful entry points that we have found for analyzing the existing and future role of water for Israelis and Palestinians.

The third and final part of this book, entitled "Toward Resolution," shifts the focus to the political economy of water in the region. It covers the entire period since the creation of the State of Israel, but with heavy emphasis on recent developments, including the Peace Accord of September 1993. Chapters in Part III cover regional options for water management (Chapter 7), concerns about water and security in Israel (Chapter 8), the Peace Accord and its implications (Chapter 9), and prospects for investment and institution building in the water sector (Chapter 10). Chapter 11 recommends steps that could be taken in the shorter term to improve water management in Israel and the Occupied Palestinian Territories and, we believe, to enhance prospects for peace between Israelis and Palestinians. The book concludes with an Afterword on the recent Jordan–Israel Peace Treaty.

One last word about the organization of this book: although most of the chapters deal with conditions in both Israel and the Occupied Palestinian Territories, some chapters tend to emphasize Israeli issues and others Palestinian issues. The emphasis is dictated in small part by the availability of information, but in larger part by the nature of the subject under discussion. Water control and management in Israel are highly organized; it is, therefore, convenient to discuss existing Israeli water institutions at the same time that one is discussing water supply and demand. In contrast, broad ("national") institutions for water control and management do not exist for Palestinians, and nascent structures are highly dependent on the peace negotiations; it is, therefore, necessary to focus on the options for Palestinians in a separate chapter. It is the Israelis who are, justifiably, obsessed with water security; hence, the chapter on security has far more to do with Israeli concerns and options than with those of the Palestinians.

In conclusion, it is essential to view the conflict over water between Israelis and Palestinians on two very different scales. On a small scale, what we have is the reflection of a local conflict that is engaging "two nationalist movements, each struggling for its right to national identity and national existence, while denying the adversary these same rights" (Rothman and Lowi 1992, p. 57). Appendix 1 provides a succinct summary, adapted from a recent essay by Shuval (1992), of the "claims, counterclaims, fears, and concerns" of both Palestinians and Israelis.

On a large scale, what we have in the mutual struggle for water in the Jordan River Valley and the nearby aquifers is the reflection of a global problem. Israelis and Palestinians may be acutely short of water, but their water problems are different only in degree from those faced by most nations in the world. Appendix 2 provides a short summary of results from the Earth Summit of 1992 and from the Dublin Conference on Water and the Environment, which preceded the Earth Summit by 6 months. Together, the results of these meetings show the profound attention that is now being given to the increasingly limited and increasingly polluted fresh water resources of the Earth.

We started Chapter 1 with a quotation about a Biblical struggle over water. It is fitting that we close with a modern quotation. In the words of Israeli hydrology professor Uri Shamir (as cited in Vesilind 1993):

> *If there is political will for peace, water will not be a hindrance. If you want reasons to fight, water will give you ample opportunities.*

CHAPTER 2

Geography, Hydrology, and Climate

A certain gentile asked Rabbi Joshua: "You have festivals, and
we have festivals. We do not rejoice when you do, and you do
not rejoice when we do. When do we both rejoice together?"
"When the rain falls," answered Rabbi Joshua.
— Midrash Genesis Rabbah, 13:6

THROUGHOUT THE WORLD, water is a major constraint to
further economic development. Many people argue that it is, or
shortly will be, the major constraint, and not just for economic development but for all forms of development. Satellite images have made us
aware of the small place the Earth occupies in space, and of the thin
layers of atmosphere and soil between which we live. The images are
not yet capable of showing what a small fraction of these layers is made
up of fresh water and the even smaller fraction of water available for
human use. Adapting a graphic image presented by the World
Resources Institute (WRI 1992), if we consider that the world's total
supply of all water amounts to 1 cubic metre (m³), the usable volume of
fresh water not locked in ice would amount to all of 5 teaspoons. More
than 750 litres (L) are locked in ice, mainly in the Arctic and
Antarctic. Of those 5 teaspoons, 2 1/2 occur in South America and
almost 1 1/4 in Asia, which leaves 11/4 teaspoons for North and Central
America, Europe, Australia, Africa, and the Middle East. The amount
of water that occurs across the Central African and Middle Eastern
regions is measured in drops — and, of these two regions, it is the
Middle East that is by far the more highly populated and the more
industrialized and urbanized.

Given these conditions, it is hardly surprising that water is widely regarded as the limiting resource for development, not just by Israel and the Occupied Territories, but by most countries in the Middle East. Compared with other countries in the region, the availability of water in Israel is about average: the country is less well endowed than Lebanon, Syria, and Turkey; about equivalent to the countries of North Africa; and much better endowed than Jordan and countries of the Arabian peninsula (see Figure 2, which plots countries against a set of water-stress codes introduced by Falkenmark et al. (1989); the arrows show that water availability per capita is decreasing in every country).

The Golan Heights area is relatively well endowed with water resources. So, too, is the West Bank, though much of the water in this region can only be exploited using capital-intensive techniques (Heller and Nusseibah 1991; Zarour and Isaac 1991). Gaza, in contrast, is perennially short of water and has been in a water-deficit position for a

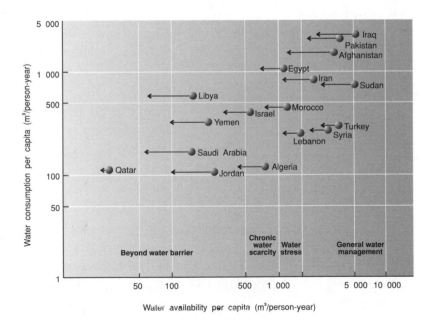

Figure 2. Water-stress codes for selected Middle Eastern countries (circles depict water stress in 1988, arrows show the changes in water availability per capita by 2020, assuming per-capita consumption remains the same).

number of years (Bruins et al. 1991; Shawwa 1992). Apart from Gaza
and the Negev, the main water problem for both Israel and the
Occupied Palestinian Territories is less total availability than it is seasonal and regional variations in availability.

Varied Geography and Topography

Lying along the eastern shore of the Mediterranean Sea, at the junction
of four ecological zones — Mediterranean, Irano–Turanian (steppe),
Sahaio–Sindic, and Sundanese (Gabbay 1992) — Israel's ecology is
more varied than that of most other countries in the region; indeed,
more than that of most other nontropical countries in the world.
Within an area of less than 21 000 km², naturalists have identified
2 600 plant species, 480 bird species, 70 mammalian species, and 90 reptilian species (Gabbay 1992). Some 130 of the plant species are indigenous to Israel, as are a few of the reptilian species.

Geographically, the area occupied by Israel plus the Occupied
Territories, exclusive of the Golan Heights, can be divided into three
zones aligned in a north–south direction (Reifenberg 1955) (see Figure
1 on p. 6). The most westerly zone is the coastal plain, 15–20 km wide,
facing the Mediterranean Sea. It lies several tens of metres above sea
level and contains most of the nation's population and industry. The
Gaza Strip is found at the most southerly point, abutting the border
with Egypt. The middle zone consists of the Judean Hills, which are
ridges formed by sloping beds of resistant limestone and dolomite. The
ridges are deeply dissected but include peaks over 800 m above sea level.
This chain forms the watershed between land sloping gradually (except
in the north) westward to the Mediterranean and land sloping much
more steeply eastward to the Jordan Valley and Dead Sea. The third
zone is the Jordan Valley itself, which forms the northern extension of
the Great Rift Valley of Africa. The West Bank includes the eastern
slope of the mountainous middle zone plus the northwestern shore of
the Dead Sea and northward for about two-thirds of the length of the
Lower Jordan River. The Jordan River is conveniently divided into two
reaches: an upper reach flowing from a number of springs in northern

Israel, Syria, and Lebanon into Lake Kinneret; and a lower reach flowing from Kinneret until it disappears into the Dead Sea.

Climate and Variations in Climate

The climate of Israel and the Occupied Territories is equally variable.
Prevailing southwesterly winds blow off the sea in the north, bringing
substantial moisture, whereas the same winds blow from Egypt in the
southern parts of the country and are devoid of moisture. The resulting
climate ranges from almost subtropical in the north (subalpine on the
upper slopes of Mt Hermon, at the northern end of the Golan Heights)
to quite arid in the Negev Desert only 500 km to the south. The climate
is also variable throughout the year, with the typical Mediterranean
cycle of hot, dry summers and mild, rainy winters. Rainfall averages
1 000 mm/year in parts of Galilee in contrast to 20 mm in the southern
Negev. Changes in rainfall occur over short distances; for example, the
Gaza Strip is only about 45 km from north to south, but rainfall averages 450 mm/year in the north and only 200 mm in the south. Periodically, during the summer months, the entire region is desiccated by
hot, dry "Chamsin" winds that blow westward from the desert for several days or longer. The processes that occur as rain falls to the Earth
and lands on soil, plants, or artificial surfaces are described in the
accompanying text box entitled "Rainfall and Human Civilization."
These different land regimes greatly affect the ultimate role of water in
society.

The ability to grow crops is not determined exclusively by rainfall;
it is also affected by the balance between rainfall and evapotranspiration, which is the phenomenon by which water is lost from the leaves of
plants and trees to the atmosphere. If evapotranspiration is less than
precipitation, the plant will grow on its own; if it is more, the plant will
have to draw water either from soil moisture or from artificially supplied .
sources. The effect on agriculture of the north-to-south variation in
rainfall is magnified by increasing differences between precipitation and
evapotranspiration, particularly during the summer months. As shown
in Figure 4, in the north of Israel, precipitation is roughly equal to
evapotranspiration over the course of a year — greater for 5 or 6 months

Rainfall and Human Civilization

From the moment precipitation hits the ground, several factors begin to affect its future use as a source of water for human consumption. Without human intervention, rain infiltrates the ground, flows on the surface, is taken up by vegetation, or evaporates. (In arid and semi-arid regions, as much as 85% may evaporate.) In forests, most of the water filters into the soil and recharges the groundwater, or is absorbed by plants and later returned to the atmosphere by transpiration; there is little runoff, although groundwater is discharged into nearby streams. In steppe or desert areas, where there are fewer plants to hold the water, runoff predominates. On the one hand, on floodplains, the amount of water entering aquifers can be large. On the other hand, evaporation may be the main water outlet in closed or semiclosed basins. In subhumid grasslands, the hydrologic cycle behaves in an intermediate manner. On average, roughly 40% of the precipitation that falls on the land areas of the Earth runs off in rivers to the ocean or to interior basins, such as the Jordan; the remainder infiltrates the soil or evaporates immediately.

When humans alter the ground surface, natural hydrological dynamics are affected. Where herbaceous crops are substituted for forest, the proportion of runoff is significantly increased. When trees are planted on a former grassland area, the opposite frequently occurs. Agriculture has a strong effect on the water balance. To grow most types of crops, land must usually be cleared of any existing vegetation to eliminate competition. For some time before the crop begins to grow, the land is bare, which drastically affects the water falling on it. Once the crop has grown, the hydrological behaviour of the area changes again. Crops pass through various stages of soil cover and height during the year. In all agricultural landscapes, the hydrological balance is strongly affected by the characteristics of the farming activities taking place.

Urbanization affects water dynamics to an even greater extent. First, a considerable portion of the ground is covered with relatively impermeable layers of various paving materials; infiltration and evaporation are almost nil and most precipitation runs off. Second, some of the land is excavated, removed, or buried under fill materials brought from somewhere else, producing significant hydrological changes. Third, many types of structures are inserted into or laid on top of the ground surface with important effects on water dynamics.

These structures can sometimes collect precipitation (roofs) or, in other cases, obstruct surface or groundwater flow.

In addition, urban design (well-planned or not) includes comprehensive water-management schemes. Storm water falling on pavement and roofs is collected in culverts, canals, and pipes and removed from the city through a conduction network.

Cities must also "import" water to satisfy the needs of their populations: water is drawn from nearby streams, lakes, or wells; treated, stored, and conducted to the residents; used for various purposes; and disposed of as wastewater. The disposal is carried out by means of another water conduction system. In some cases, water is returned to the "natural" hydrological system, treated or untreated, in a much different state than when it was originally extracted.

These processes imply dramatic changes to the environment in the urban region. Rivers are channeled or piped, their flow volumes and regimes are substantially modified, and their waters are loaded with artificially produced and "relocated" natural substances. Groundwater levels and, therefore, groundwater flow are also changed; they are usually lowered, although in some cases they may be raised.

Changes to the natural water system may occur at many stages: at the site of extraction (for example, reduction in river volume or drawdown of the water level through wells), during conduction and storage (leakage from water pipes, tanks, canals, and sewers), or at the disposal end of the system (discharge of sewage). These processes are closely interconnected. Natural and anthropogenic systems must be considered as a single unit (Figure 3).

Forests in catchment areas control the flow of water toward downstream reservoirs from which water-treatment plants receive water for homes and industries. If a forest is destroyed, the water regime in the reservoirs will change. If water is withdrawn from a river and disposed of somewhere else, the river regime downstream will change. If groundwater is pumped from an aquifer, discharge and recharge volumes to and from hydraulically connected streams will be modified and the stream regime will change. If surface water is used, related groundwater will be affected. If vegetation is eliminated, both surface and groundwater in the downstream basins will be affected.

Source: Adapted from Anton (1993)

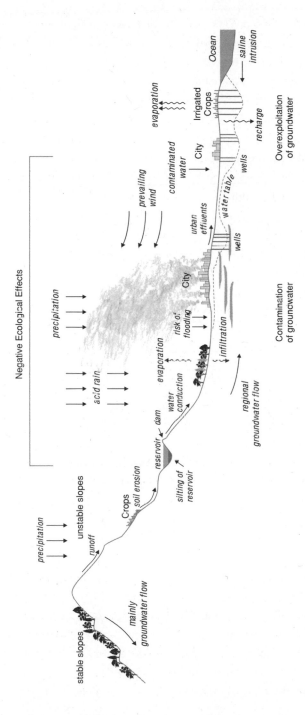

Figure 3. Hydrological processes (source: Anton 1993).

and then less for 6 or 7 months. In the middle of the country, precipitation is greater than evapotranspiration for only 3 or 4 months a year along the coast; perhaps 5 months in the mountains. In the south, evapotranspiration dominates for the entire year.

The Occupied Palestinian Territories are both better and worse off than Israel in terms of the balance between precipitation and evapotranspiration. Those portions of the Territories located in the mountains tend to be better off. As indicated in the foregoing, at any given latitude, rainfall tends to be higher in the mountains than on the coastal plain. In contrast, those portions lying in the Jordan Valley receive less rainfall than land at the same latitude but along the coast. (The measurements shown in Figure 4 are from the east bank of the Jordan River, but conditions would be the same in all respects on the west bank as well.)

Variations in climate, and particularly in rainfall, do not end with the season and location. Even greater variations occur from year to year, with the region lurching from successive years of drought or near-drought conditions to years of rains heavy enough to cause flooding and loss of life. Over just a few years, annual rainfall may vary by a factor of 10. As a result, reliable flow — defined as the discharge that could be expected 90% of the time, or during 9 years out of 10 (Foster and Sewell 1981) — may be only 5–10% of average flow in the Jordan River Basin. By way of comparison, reliable flow is 60–80% of average flow in Ontario and Quebec, and 30% in the southern Prairies of Canada.

Bakour and Kolars (1994) indicate that the entire region within which Israel and the Occupied Palestinian Territories lie (sometimes called the Mashrek) is a transition zone. To the north, the land receives more rainfall; to the south, even less. Bakour and Kolars emphasize that the dominant hydrological characteristic is the combination of aridity and uncertainty, and they illustrate the point by comparing two curves, one showing diminishing average annual rainfall and the other increasing variability in rainfall, from north to south across the region (Figure 5). As Bakour and Kolars point out, human beings adapt to many extreme conditions in part because the aridity of the desert or the cold of the Arctic are expected and planned for. In contrast, "the zone of greatest unpredictability is at the intersection of the precipitation

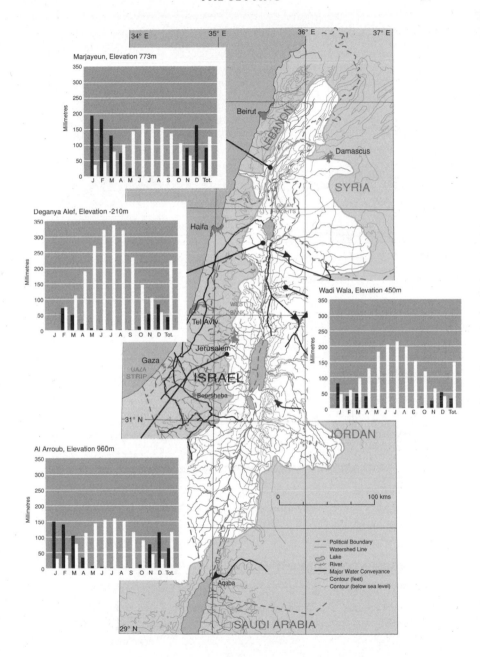

Figure 4. Average rainfall (black bars) and evaporation rates (white bars) at four locations in the Jordan River Valley (adapted from a map provided by Spider International, Fredericton, NB, Canada).

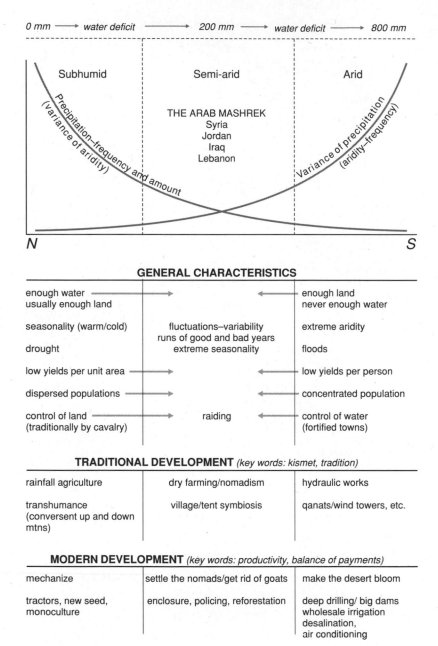

Figure 5. General characteristics of development in the Arab Mashrek
(source: Bakour and Kolars 1994).

and variance curves," which is to say in semi-arid regions (Bakour and Kolars 1994, p. 3). Whereas regions of higher rainfall sometimes suffer droughts and those receiving lower rainfall sometimes experience floods, people in semi-arid regions have to cope with both. Bakour and Kolars suggest as well that demographic and social characteristics vary systematically with these curves, at least in early stages of development. For example, people living in areas with more rainfall tend to live in dispersed communities and use farming methods that produce low yields per unit area; those living in areas with less rainfall tend to live in concentrated communities and use farming methods that produce low yields per person. As development proceeds, mechanization and the availability of modern forms of energy overcome these tendencies — populations tend to cluster, but farming systems provide high returns to both land and labour (but much lower returns to capital).

These year-to-year variations in rainfall in the Middle East have enormous implications for water planning and management. In contrast to Europe, Canada, and much of the United States, **in the Jordan Valley, and throughout the Middle East, years of extreme rainfall must be treated as normal, not abnormal, events, and water planning and management must focus on risk minimization, not maximum utilization.** For either short-term or long-term water planning, therefore, it is much more important to have a good understanding of the spatial, seasonal, and annual variations in rainfall than of annual or national averages.

Hydrological Conditions

Given this ecological and climatological situation, it is hardly surprising to find that hydrological conditions also vary, both from north to south and from winter to summer. More than 85% of Israeli–Palestinian surface water resources are located in the north. The largest river is the Jordan, which flows into Lake Kinneret and then along the border between the Occupied Palestinian Territories and the nation of Jordan until it disappears into the Dead Sea (see Figure 1 on p. 6). The Upper Jordan (that is, those reaches above Lake Kinneret) is fed from three main sources: about half of its volume comes from the Dan Spring in

Israel; about one-quarter from the Hasbani River, which rises in
Lebanon; and one-quarter from the Banias River, which rises on the
Golan Heights. The absence of full control over the headwaters of the
Jordan River plays, as will be demonstrated, a critical role in Israeli
water policy (and, therefore, its foreign policy). Just below Lake
Kinneret, the Yarmouk River, which averages about 80% of the volume
of the Upper Jordan, enters from the east and combines with the outflow from Lake Kinneret to form the Lower Jordan. The role of Lake
Kinneret and the Jordan, and the peculiar hydrology of Israel (and the
eastern parts of the West Bank), are reflected in the fact that the average elevation of the surface of the nation's water resources is 82 m
below sea level (Schwarz 1992), a geographical anomaly that has major
implications for water availability and energy use.

Despite the apparent dominance of the surface-water system, the
entire flow of the Jordan River is only equal to about one-third of Israeli
water consumption, and both ecological and political considerations
limit the amount of the flow Israel can withdraw. Most of the other
rivers in the region, such as the Yarkon in Tel Aviv and the Kishron in
Haifa, are short and flow from the Judean Hills westward to the
Mediterranean through the most populous region of Israel. Except for
headwaters of the rivers flowing westward toward the Mediterranean,
only a few permanent streams other than the Lower Jordan pass through
the Occupied Palestinian Territories. During the winter runoff, many
wadis, or streams, in the Territories carry water, but the flows do not
last much longer than the rains. The north–south ridge creates something of a rain shadow for winds coming from the Mediterranean, which
tends to make rivers flowing eastward toward the Jordan ephemeral.
Some wetlands are found near Nablus and, because of the topography,
springs are abundant. There are no permanent surface-water sources of
any kind in the Gaza Strip.

Spatial and temporal variations in water flow pose a severe distribution problem for Israel. Rainfall and water storage are concentrated in
the north, whereas demand arises primarily from the heavily populated
coastal regions and the agricultural areas in the central part of the country. To complicate the situation, water demand for both urban and agricultural uses peaks during the summer, but almost all of the rain falls

during the four winter months. The not-surprising result is maximum use of Lake Kinneret, the one natural storage reservoir in the country, and development of extensive artificial storage capacity. Indeed, some analysts argue that Israel's key water problem is not limited supply but inadequate storage.

The Yarmouk River is the final important source of surface water in the region. It forms the border between Jordan and Syria before it enters Israel and joins the Jordan just below Lake Kinneret. The Yarmouk has a very high winter flow that is currently used to dilute the increasingly saline water of the Jordan. (This salinity is not entirely natural. It results in part from the artificial diversion of nonsaline springs into Lake Kinneret where they help feed Israel's National Water Carrier.) Several plans for storing and controlling the release of Yarmouk River water have been put forward by Jordanian and Syrian officials, presumably with some allowance for use on the West Bank, but implementation has always been blocked — originally by a lack of agreement between Jordan and Syria and, more recently, by a lack of agreement from Israel. This is an issue to which we will return on several occasions.

Modern Israel would not exist if it had to depend entirely on surface water. Today (and historically) the most important sources of water are subsurface, mainly aquifers (see accompanying text box for additional information on aquifers). In central Israel, water is supplied by two large aquifers — the Coastal sandstone Aquifer and the larger Yarkon–Tanninim (or Mountain) limestone Aquifer (Figure 6). The Mountain Aquifer is actually comprised of several separate aquifers, all of which flow from west to east, under the Green Line and onto the coastal plain. A very complex structure, its hydrology is still incompletely understood, even after years of intensive study. In addition to the two large aquifers, a few small aquifers are tapped along the Israel–Jordan border in the arid Arava Valley south of the Dead Sea, and along the Israel–Lebanon border in the northern part of the country. Together, these aquifers now account for more than half of all sweet (nonsaline and nonrecycled) water used within Israel. Finally, one relatively small aquifer with a renewable flow of 125 million cubic

Aquifers

Both surface and underground water sources have a common origin: rain
or snow. The earth receives precipitation, most of which evaporates
(some 65% of that falling on land), some of which runs off into streams
and rivers, some of which is absorbed by plants, and some of which seeps
into the earth. The portion that seeps into the earth fills pores in soil,
sand, or even solid rock. As we know from oil reservoirs, many rock formations have spaces between the grains that allow the entry of water. A
rock is said to be porous if it can hold fluids, such as water or oil. It is said
to be permeable if the pores are connected, so that the water or oil can
pass through the rock.

An aquifer is a porous geological formation that contains and, if
permeable, conducts water. The aquifer can lie at any depth beneath the
surface of the Earth (down to about 5 000 m, below which the pressure of
overlying rock closes the pores). The aquifer may be composed of uncon-
solidated sand and gravel or of porous or permeable beds of rock. In addition, some of the precipitation will flow into fractures in rock formations
or, in the case of soluble rocks such as limestone, into hollowed-out caves
or even underground rivers. About half as much water is found flowing
underground as is found in rivers along the surface (WRI 1992). In arid
regions of the world, however, this ratio can be reversed, with the volume
of underground water dominating that of surface water. Human beings
living in arid regions long ago learned to tap aquifers and, in some cases,
ancient systems show remarkable ingenuity (Hillel 1991).

Underground water can be accessed through springs, where the
aquifer comes to the surface, or at wells or via boreholes that penetrate
the dry layers of soil or rock until they reach the water-bearing layer
(Figure 7). In a few areas of the world, groundwater appears in more spec-
tacular forms as geysers; more commonly, if the recharge area is at a
higher elevation than the well tapping the aquifer, water may rise to the
surface in what are called artesian wells. Groundwater is also augmented
by seepage from rivers, lakes, and swamps; in some cases, the reverse is
true and these water bodies are fed by groundwater. Groundwater can also
pass directly into the sea if the aquifer reaches the surface beyond the
coastline. The time between the original rainfall and reappearance of the
water at a spring can range from days to centuries, depending upon geological conditions (the size and depth of the aquifer, pore size, underground pressure, etc.). Except in river valleys, the water table in arid areas
tends to be deeper than in humid areas.

Generally speaking, there are three types of aquifers. The first type
involves very shallow water that has seeped through soil or sand and is
flowing on top of bedrock or some impermeable layer, such as clay. In
popular use, most so-called groundwater is of this type, and the depth of
such water determines the local water table, as shown in Figure 7.
Typically, it is this water that is tapped by the picturesque dug wells in
farmyards and gardens.

The next two types involve water trapped in or moving through
solid rock. Water that is trapped in isolated rock formations is generally

called fossil water. These aquifers can be tapped but, as with oil pools, regardless of size they are nonrenewable resources. Furthermore, they are subject to complicated engineering difficulties associated with pumping rates.

The most important type of aquifer allows water to flow through it. Such aquifers are renewable resources provided that pumping rates are not so high as to extract more water than is replenished every year. Flow rates in aquifers are determined by a large number of factors, including the permeability of the rock, and are commonly measured in tens or hundreds of metres, not kilometres, per year. In an only partly humorous comment about such slow flow rates, Arie Issar, noted hydrologist at Ben Gurion University, stated at an Israeli–Palestinian conference on water that what we are dealing with is neither Israeli water nor Palestinian water; it is Canaanite water! Flow rates can be higher when the water is flowing in channels or cracks than when it flows through pores between grains.

It is a common belief that groundwater is pure, but this may not be true. Even ignoring human sources of pollution that, along with the rain or snow, can seep into aquifers, many aquifers are naturally saline. This occurs most commonly because at some stage the water has passed over and slowly eroded soluble rocks that contain salts. Moreover, overpumping of aquifers can reduce the level of the water or the pressure in the aquifer, which in turn allows nearby saline (or, if near the coast, seawater) to flow into the aquifer.

Use of coastal aquifers always poses dangers. Because of its lower density, fresh water floats on seawater. The difference in density between fresh water and seawater, however, is only 2.5%, and the layer of fresh water that overlies seawater can sometimes be many metres below sea level. Pumping can cause upwelling of the salt water from below, but the effect may occur so slowly that it would not be discernable until it was too late to reverse the effect. Figure 8 shows the changes that occur with excessive pumping close to the margin between fresh underground water and seawater. Overpumping can also cause subsidence of the surface under certain geological conditions. Chapter 5 discusses in more detail the problems arising from both overpumping and human pollution of aquifers. Suffice it to say here that, once polluted, it is harder to clean up underground water than surface sources of water; in some cases, it may be impossible.

Finally, it is important to recognize the enormous volume of rock that must be available to serve as a source of water (Anton 1993). Consider a city with 100 thousand inhabitants, each consuming water at a rate of 100 L/day (which would be typical of the Occupied Palestinian Territories but low for Israel). Multiplication shows that this city requires nearly 4 million cubic metres of water per year. Consider now that the city is pumping from an aquifer that has an annual recharge rate of 2% of stored volume. In that case, 50 times as much stored water (200 million cubic metres) would be needed to provide for withdrawal without mining the aquifer. Assume now that the rocks in the aquifer have a porosity of 5% (that is, water makes up 5% of the volume of the geological formation). The geological formation would then have to have a volume at least 20 times greater than that of the water, or 4 billion cubic metres. This is equal to 4 cubic kilometres of rock. If the formation is 10 metres thick, the area from which the city draws water would amount to 400 square kilometres. More accurately, the city is drawing from an aquifer that extends more or less horizontally over 400 square kilometres.

Source: Leopold and Langbein (1960), Hillel (1991),
WRI (1992), and Anton (1993).

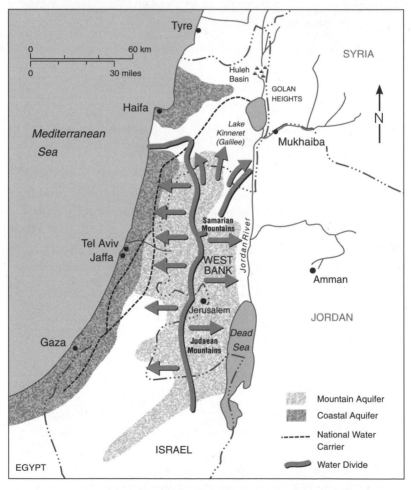

*Figure 6. Aquifers in Israel and the Occupied Territories,
and direction of flow of the Mountain Aquifer.*

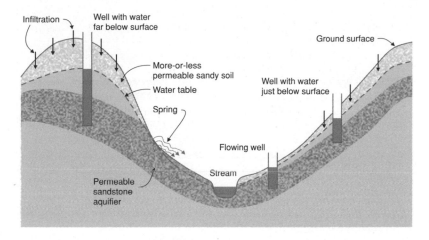

Figure 7. The underground water system (Brooks and Lonergan 1992).

metres (Mm^3) flows eastward into the Jordan Valley, but does not affect Israeli supplies (Zarour and Isaac 1991).

These few aquifers by no means exhaust the list of possible underground sources of water. Larger and deeper (and more expensive to develop) aquifers are known to exist, notably the Nubian sandstone that underlies the Negev in Israel and extends into Egypt and Libya. Most of these other aquifers are judged to be largely or entirely fossil rather than renewable, and they tend to be saline. As explained further in Chapter 3, some analysts argue that these aquifers could potentially support vigorous agriculture in the Negev (Issar 1994).

Conclusion

Geographic, hydrologic, and climatic conditions simply provide the backdrop against which the usage of water by humans is presented. In some parts of the world, these conditions allow for ample water availability, but in arid and semi-arid regions, such as those of Israel, they are ultimately limiting. As Falkenmark et al. (1989) have emphasized, such regions are vulnerable not only because of water scarcity and intermittent droughts, but also because they are particularly susceptible to stresses engendered by humans through misuse of land (leading to

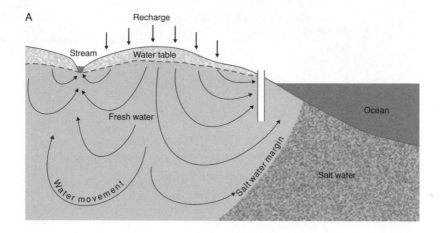

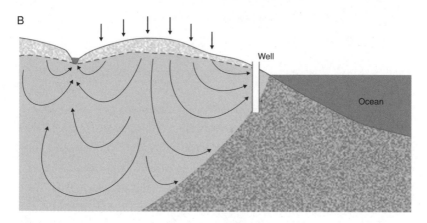

Figure 8. Pumping of aquifers and salt-water intrusion: A, before extensive pumping; B, after extensive pumping (Brooks and Lonergan 1992).

"landscape desiccation") and through population growth. What is even more problematic is that appropriate ways of dealing with these problems are generally small in scale and locale specific, and typical approaches to them have "a frontier philosophy, manipulating natural systems to whatever degree engineering know-how would permit" (Postel 1993, p. 23). Accordingly, we now turn to the specific ways in which water resources are used and managed in Israel.

CHAPTER 3

WATER SUPPLY AND DEMAND

*And We send down water from the sky according to
measure, and We cause it to soak into the soil, and surely
We are able to drain it off.*

— Koran, Sura XXIII, 18

WATER, OR A LACK THEREOF, has been the historic resource problem of the entire Middle East. Neither local nor regional politics can be understood anywhere in the region, and certainly not in Israel or the Occupied Palestinian Territories, without reference to water (surface and underground); nor can patterns of water supply and use be understood without reference to internal and external politics (Hosh and Isaac 1992; Lowi 1992) and to culture (Rothman and Lowi 1992).

The region has long suffered from misuse of both land and water resources (Reifenberg 1955). Hillsides have lost their vegetative cover, streams that were once perennial now dry up shortly after a rain, and the productivity of fields and orchards has declined. A secular trend toward lower rainfall may account for part of the degradation, but the greater part appears to be anthropogenic. Since the creation of the State of Israel, enormous efforts have been made to restore the land to earlier, more productive conditions (Hillel 1991). The same kind of attention, however, has not been paid to the water resources that interact with land, nor has the same kind of attention been devoted to land and water lying across the Green Line in the Occupied Territories.

In Israel, the structure of supply and demand for water, the infra-structure of water management, and the geopolitics associated with water are all interlinked. This situation is to be expected. For one thing, the boundaries of surface water supply sources do not necessarily coin-cide with political boundaries and, in many parts of the world, control over lakes and rivers is a cause for dispute. The same is true of ground-water, and in this case the problem is compounded by the absence of any agreed upon body of international law (Hayton and Utton 1989; see Chapter 7). For Israelis and Palestinians, the difficulties are com-pounded by the remarkably close overlap (as shown in Figure 6 on p. 32) of the geological position of the Mountain Aquifer and the politi-cal boundaries of the West Bank. Throughout the region there is a major reliance on megaprojects to couple regions of high demand with those of ample water availability, and such projects involve either inter-national effects on resources or international sources of capital — or most commonly both.

Consumption

Most modern analysis of natural-resources management begins with an examination of consumption rather than production or resource poten-tial. The end-uses are the objective or output of the management process, and it is a peculiar (if common) reversal of management meth-ods to start with the inputs and vary consumption accordingly.

Consumption in Israel

Water consumption in Israel by sector for the years 1958–91 is depicted in Table 1 and Figure 9. Broad comparisons to Canada (a water-rich country by any standard) and to Jordan (a water-poor country) are pre-sented in Table 2. As these tables show, the most glaring difference is between nonagricultural water use in Canada and in either Israel or Jordan — a reflection of differences in both climate and life-style. Less obvious differences, however, are also relevant. Nonagricultural water use in Israel is twice that in Jordan, a result of, among other things, greater resource availability and Israeli use of water to provide a high quality of urban life. Both nations are comfortably above the

Table 1. *Fresh water consumption (Mm³) in Israel by sector from 1958 to 1991.*

Year	Domestic	Industry	Agriculture	Total
1958	196	46	1 032	1 274
1964–65	199	55	1 075	1 329
1969–70	240	75	1 249	1 564
1975–76	305	95	1 328	1 728
1979–80	375	90	1 235	1 700
1980–81	367	100	1 212	1 679
1981–82	385	103	1 282	1 770
1982–83	401	103	1 255	1 759
1983–84	419	103	1 356	1 878
1984 85	422	109	1 389	1 920
1985–86	450	103	1 434	1 987
1986–87	424	111	1 025	1 560
1987–88	447	123	1 179	1 749
1989	501	114	1 236	1 851
1990	482	106	1 157	1 745
1991	445	100	875	1 420

Source: Israel, Central Bureau of Statistics (1985, 1988, 1992).

100 L/person-day (36.5 m³/year) generally regarded as the minimum for an adequate quality of life.[1] (As will be discussed, this is not the case for the Gaza Strip.) If only those needs for human health and hygiene are considered, total use can be considerably lower. Agenda 21 (see Appendix 2) recommends a global target for the year 2000 ensuring that every urban resident has 40 L/day (14.6 m³/year).

Striking differences occur in the use of agricultural water. Despite similar crops, Israel uses less than half as much irrigation water per hectare as Jordan, the difference being the result of more advanced (and more capital-intensive) technology. Given the difference in climate, the data also suggest that irrigation is more efficient in Israel than in Canada.

Israel's annual fresh-water demand has recently approached 1 900 Mm³ (although it is much lower in drought years; Table 1).

---

[1] Each cubic metre contains 1000 litres (L), so litres per day can be roughly derived from cubic metres per year by multiplying by 3 (more accurately by 2.74 = 1 000/365). At the extreme, Bedouins may use less than 15 L/person-day.

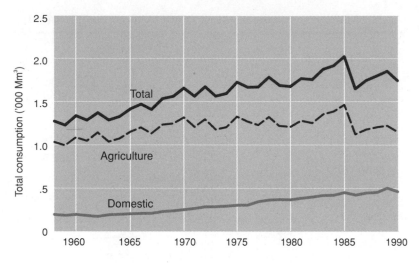

*Figure 9. Water consumption in Israel from 1958 to 1990
(source: Israel, Central Bureau of Statistics 1988; Fishelson 1992a).*

*Table 2. Comparative data on water consumption:
Israel, Jordan, and Canada.*

	Israel	Jordan	Canada
Population (1990) (millions)	4.8	4.2	26.6
GDP[a] (1990) (million US$)	53 200	3 330	543 700
Irrigated land (1989) (million hectares)	215	56.4	920
Water use (Mm^3) per year (1990)			
Total	1 745	822	42 210
Irrigation	1 157	534	3 559
Other	588	288	38 651
Water use (m^3) per capita-year	368	196	1 587
Water use (L) per US$ GDP per year	32.8	246.8	77.6
Nonirrigation water use (m^3) per capita-year	114.6	68.6	1 510
Irrigation water use (m^3) per irrigated hectare-year	5.4	9.5	3.9

Source: Israel, Central Bureau of Statistics (1992) and WRI (1992).
[a] GDP, gross domestic product.

Another 150 Mm^3 of saline water is used in agriculture, and 30 Mm^3 in industry. Some other estimates have reported total consumption to be as low as 1 700 Mm^3 and as high as 2 100 Mm^3 (in 1989), differences that exemplify the difficulty in deriving accurate water balances for the region. The primary consumer is the agricultural sector, and the dominant use is irrigation, which takes approximately 1 200 Mm^3 of sweet and recycled water every year (just over 70% of total consumption if saline water is included; just under if it is not). Domestic and municipal uses, which include everything from households and hotels to urban gardens and fire protection, account for just under one-quarter of total use. Israeli industry accounts for less than 7% of total use.

Most of Israel's consumption occurs within the Green Line, but 40–50 Mm^3/year are taken directly by Israeli settlements in the Occupied Palestinian Territories (Zarour and Isaac 1991; Lowi 1992). Demand for water in the settlements has been rising faster than the population, a result of increasing per capita demands for both irrigated acreage and domestic amenities, such as grass and swimming pools. (Swimming pools are almost insignificant in terms of the total consumption of water, but they are dramatically visible symbols of the difference in living standards.) The amount of irrigated land being farmed by settlers has reached 4 700 ha (Elmusa 1993a), accounting for about three-quarters of the water used. Only a small fraction of Jewish settlers are farmers, but they have been lobbying the government to increase their allotments of land and water (both of which the Palestinians regard as having been confiscated). If their demands are met, which seems unlikely under the current Labour government, water use could continue to increase even if the number of settlements does not.

Within Israel proper, water use per capita and per dollar of output has fallen dramatically over the past 30 years because of improved efficiency (Hillel 1991; Gabbay 1992). Drought-enforced reductions in allocations to the agricultural sector are responsible for much of the drop in consumption since 1989. Despite these changes, absolute consumption remains high because of continued population growth and increases in economic output, and water supply problems are evident almost every year and magnified during times of drought.

Consumption in the Occupied Territories

Water consumption data for the Occupied Palestinian Territories is difficult to obtain. Estimates for the Gaza Strip by Bruins et al. (1991) for the early 1990s include figures of 28 Mm^3/year for household use (excluding garden watering) on the basis of 100 L/person-day and a population of 510 thousand refugees and 275 thousand residents. (The consumption of some 3 000 settlers was subtracted from the figures given by Bruins.) In addition, about 100 Mm^3 is used for agriculture. Even the demand for drinking water may exceed the estimated renewable flow of 25–50 Mm^3 in the freshwater aquifer. Perhaps most troubling is the point raised by McDowall (1989) that official population estimates for the Gaza Strip underestimate the true population by about 16%. Some two-thirds of the population are refugees, and half are under 15 years of age.

In addition, McDowall (1989) estimates the population of the West Bank to be 860 thousand (excluding 130 thousand residents of East Jerusalem). Three-quarters of this population lives outside the cities and towns, either in villages or refugee camps. In both the West Bank and Gaza, most of the camps are organized as small townships. In McDowall's words (1989, p. 20), these camps are "highly and densely populated areas like towns, but lacking in the other attributes of civic life, such as infrastructure, civic services, and employment opportunities."

Estimates of water consumption for the West Bank suggest that annual consumption for all purposes at the time of the 1967 war was approximately 100 Mm^3, with 90% being used for irrigation and the rest for household purposes. Estimates in 1984 put consumption at 119 Mm^3. These figures reflect Palestinian consumption and exclude that consumed by Jewish settlers. They also exclude an unknown but sizable quantity of water pumped directly onto fields from the Jordan River. Except for modest increases to allow for population growth, consumption would not be much different today: 125–130 Mm^3/year. Because its growth was artificially restricted, irrigation use would be down to about 75% of the total (about the same 100 Mm^3/year as was used in 1967), with the rest being used by households (23%) and industry (2%).

The World Bank (1993a) report on the West Bank states that 62% of residents have access to piped water, and another 33% to courtyard cisterns or taps. A later report by the World Bank states that in 1991, 90% of households in the Occupied Territories had safe water, up from 15% in 1970 and 47% in 1980 (World Bank 1993b). It is not surprising that the Israeli government cites these figures as evidence of its contribution to the Palestinian economy. Nor is it any more surprising that some Palestinian sources challenge these figures and suggest that no more than half of the population receives piped water in their dwellings. The earlier World Bank report states that Mekorot, the Israeli water company, supplies water to 16.5% of the population of the Territories, but Elmusa (1993a) says the figure is closer to 25% and that another 25% is supplied by the Municipality of Jerusalem and by other municipal agencies. However, the general quality of service is poor, with limited quantities supplied and frequent interruptions in service (World Bank 1993a). Regardless of the actual numbers, the situation in the Occupied Territories compares unfavourably with that in Jordan, where nearly all villages are served by piped water and per capita use (for domestic purposes) is twice that of the Territories (Elmusa 1993b; World Bank 1993a).

Figures on water consumption in the West Bank are also somewhat confusing. A United Nations (1992) report estimates that 27 Mm^3 are consumed annually for household use. If this figure is divided by a population of 840 thousand, the result is a per capita use of only 88 L/person-day. Elmusa (1993a) gives an even lower figure, but this may include Gaza. Unless these data include only water for direct household use (that is, excluding garden watering and nondomestic municipal uses), they seem too low. It may be that the data exclude local collection, such as through rainwater catchment schemes (which are widespread in the West Bank). Even a figure of 88 L/person-day, however, would be adequate, if only marginally so.

In summary, piped water is most widely available in the urban areas of the West Bank, with almost 250 towns being served. There is only minimal service in rural areas. It is probably true that additional villages could have opted for service but that the inhabitants were reluctant to tie into the Israeli state water system because of its implicit

acceptance of Israeli control over what they see as their water. The high
prices that Mekorot charges Palestinians (see Chapter 6) no doubt also
play a role in creating this situation.

Availability: Principal Sources

Israel exploits three natural sources of fresh water for its needs: Lake
Kinneret (and the sources of the lake); large aquifers, notably the
Yarkon–Tanninim (or Mountain) Aquifer, which extends from the
West Bank into Israel, and the Coastal Aquifer; and smaller aquifers
and streams within its own boundaries.

Surface Water

It is estimated that Israel's renewable water resources are approximately
1 400 Mm^3/year, with an additional 360 Mm^3 added through reuse programs and some 60–100 Mm^3 from the collection and storage of storm
runoff (McDonald and Kay 1988; Beaumont 1989; Kolars 1992a)
(Table 3). Total surface flows account for over one-third of the total,
with almost 90% of that coming from the Jordan River. Northern
tributaries to the Jordan River, which deliver approximately 540 Mm^3
to Lake Kinneret (Kolars 1992a), come from Lebanon (the Hasbani
River), Israel (the Dan Spring), and the Golan Heights (the Banias
River and Hermon Spring). These flows combine with local runoff and
precipitation to represent the total inflows to the lake, which has a total
storage capacity of approximately 4 000 Mm^3. The National Water
Carrier, which is the main distribution system for water from Lake
Kinneret south to the Negev (see Figure 1 on p. 6), draws 500 Mm^3
from the lake annually. Roughly 70 Mm^3 of water passes out of the lake
to the Jordan River, which then combines with the Yarmouk River, the
Zarqa River, various salt springs, and precipitation/runoff for an annual
flow of 697 Mm^3 (and a salinity level of 2 000 ppm) by the time it
reaches the Dead Sea (Figure 10 provides a schematic diagram of the
Jordan River's water flow). No major additions to surface water are
expected in the future except through greater use of recycled wastewater, water harvesting, and desalination of brackish water in special
areas.

Table 3. *Water supply in Israel in 1972 and 1990 (Mm³).*

Source	1972	1990
Total groundwater	830	840
Sandstone aquifer	240	230
Limestone aquifer	590	610
Total surface water	610	650
Jordan watershed	570	570
Flood and storm water	40	80
Total recycled wastewater	39	360
Domestic	35	300
Industrial	4	60
Total saline water	NA[a]	180
Agricultural	NA	150
Industrial	NA	30
Total desalinated water	1.0	40
Grand total	1 480	2 070

Source: McDonald and Kay (1988), Beaumont (1989), Kolars (1992a), and Lowi (1992).

[a] NA, not available (but negligible).

Underground Water

As indicated in the foregoing, the majority of fresh water in Israel is derived from underground sources. Israel has long tapped the Coastal and Mountain aquifers, and these remain the principal sources of supply. Total renewable groundwater potential is estimated to be 840 Mm³/year (Table 3), although discharge figures vary from about 650 to 900 Mm³/year (Lowi 1992). Well over twice the volume is taken from the Mountain Aquifer as from the Coastal Aquifer. The West Bank is also underlain by aquifers that flow in several directions. The Gaza Strip, however, has only a single, relatively shallow freshwater aquifer that some Israelis claim is cut off from other parts of the Coastal Aquifer. A larger and deeper aquifer in Gaza is too salty for direct use. Even before the 1967 war, Israel was exploiting two of three aquifers under the West Bank, and since the war the third source has been tapped for an additional 66 Mm³ annually (Anderson 1988).

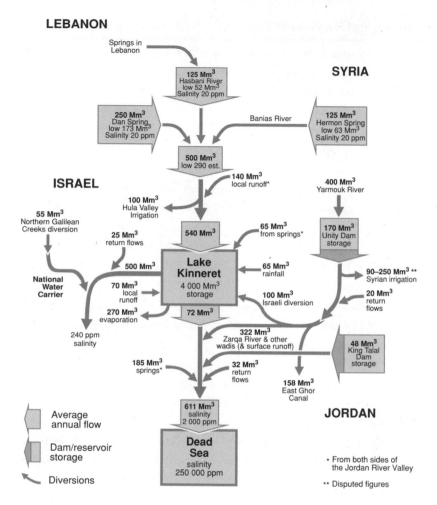

Figure 10. Water flow in the Jordan River Valley (ppm, parts per million).

All aquifers are vulnerable to declines in water levels as a result of excessive pumping, which reduces the water level and permits the intrusion of salt water from nearby saline aquifers or from the Mediterranean. Already, some 10% of the wells tapping the Coastal Aquifer yield water that exceeds the national limit for chlorine salts, and the percentage is increasing each year. Maintaining the level and quality of water in the Mountain Aquifer is a prime objective of Israel's water policy.

Recharging Groundwater

Artificial methods for directing surface water to augment or accelerate natural flows into aquifers is a third alternative to methods that seek to increase supply and methods to promote conservation. Recharge techniques generally involve the use of either spreading basins and pits or the use of wells. Basins and pits (distinguished only by their depth) collect water that then seeps into the aquifer. Wells can do the same thing, but more sophisticated systems inject water under pressure. Among the advantages of artificial recharge are the absence of evaporation, long-term storage, increased pressure, and "self-distribution." For all systems, but for wells in particular, water quality considerations are critical, and the practice of injecting partially treated wastewater (used in Israel) is questioned by some authorities (*Israel Environment Bulletin*, Winter 1993).

Artificial recharge has been used in Israel since the 1950s and now has a capacity of 150–200 Mm^3/year, including systems for recharging treated sewage in the Dan Sewage project and fresh water to the Coastal and Mountain aquifers. Jordanian systems are capable of recharging as much as 400 Mm^3 in a rainy year. Assaf (1994) suggests that similar systems have a high (and noncontroversial) potential in the Occupied Palestinian Territories. One system is already in operation in Gaza, but opportunities are limited there until the quality of surface water can be improved, which depends upon more systematic approaches.

Availability: Supplemental Sources[2]

Conventional surface and groundwater sources are no longer adequate to meet the demands of a growing population and an expanding economy. There are, however, other sources available. By the year

---

[2] Research for this and the following sections was aided immensely by a report prepared by the International Water Engineering Centre at the University of Ottawa for participants in the Multilateral Working Group of the Middle East Peace Process (IWEC 1993). This report divides technologies into five groups: augmentation of surface flows, water treatment and reuse, groundwater, desalination, and large-scale regional applications. The database on which the report is based is in the process of being transferred to the MINISIS system and will be housed at the University of Jordan, Amman, Jordan.

2000, Israeli water use is expected to be 150 Mm³/year higher than in 1990, entirely from expansion in the use of treated wastewater, saline water, and water gathered by harvesting methods (Gabbay 1992). At that time, it is expected that 52% of the water used will come from aquifers and springs, 31% from the Jordan River and its tributaries, 12% from treated wastewater and saline water, and 5% from harvested rain-water. This section will review some of these supplemental sources. Techniques aimed strictly at the treatment of wastewater will be ignored, as will techniques, such as desert dams, that seem less likely to be applied by Israelis or Palestinians. The focus is on relatively simple technologies with wide application; more complex and larger scale technologies, such as desalination, are reserved for the next section.

Recycled Wastewater

Recycled wastewater and water harvesting (collection, storage, and later use of storm runoff) are two water sources that can now be treated as conventional, even though their application is still uncommon outside the Middle East, China, and a few cities in Latin America and southern California. To be more accurate, controlled reuse of treated wastewater is uncommon; uncontrolled local use of raw sewage, however, is all too common in many parts of the world, and is a source of typhoid, cholera, and other diseases. According to Vesilind (1993), a cholera outbreak in Aleppo in 1989 was blamed on parsley grown with untreated sewage water.

Israel is among the world leaders in recycling sewage, and it now accounts for almost 18% of Israel's total water supply, up from 3% two decades ago (see Table 3). Some 70% of the wastewater collected in sewers is being reused, mainly from sewage systems in the Tel Aviv and Haifa areas (Avnimelech et al. 1992). According to the Ministry of Environment, recycled sewage effluents "constitute the most readily available and cheapest source of additional water, and provide a viable solution to Israel's water scarcity problem" (Gabbay 1992, p. 60). By the end of the century, recycled wastewater could provide 400 Mm³ of water per year for irrigation, and according to Shuval (1992), by early in the next century it will provide one-third of the total water supply for both Israelis and Palestinians. Former Water Commissioner Meir Ben

Meir goes further; he has said that irrigated crops in Israel will eventually receive only recycled wastewater. Currently, however, with adequate rainfall, on the one hand, and an expanding sewage-treatment system, on the other hand, Israel appears to have a surplus of treated wastewater, which is being discharged to the sea.

Jordan also recycles close to 40 Mm^3 of wastewater from its two largest cities (Amman and Zarqa, which contain 90% of the population) by conveying the outflow from the Alsamra wastewater treatment plant to the King Talal Reservoir and then to farms in the Jordan Valley. Only one wastewater-for-irrigation project has been designed for the West Bank (near Bethlehem), but informal use of wastewater is fairly common. It is only reasonable to assume that, in the near future and under independent control, the potential of wastewater will be realized throughout the Occupied Palestinian Territories, with 25–50 Mm^3 of recycled water becoming available in each of the Gaza Strip and the West Bank.

Recycled wastewater is mainly used for the irrigation of nonfood crops and animal fodder, and secondarily for recharging aquifers. A small amount is also used for urban landscaping and, outside the Middle East, industrial cooling or toilet flushing. Most of the cotton grown in Israel, for example, depends upon reclaimed rather than fresh water. After secondary treatment and storage for a time in an aquifer, however, some recycled water is chlorinated and released for unrestricted use in irrigation. Even so, recycled water must be used with caution because of the potential for toxic chemicals and heavy metals, which cannot always be completely removed by conventional wastewater treatment, to enter the food chain. Workers in fields irrigated with recycled water must take special precautions, but the occupational hazard is reduced if the water is conveyed in pipes rather than in open canals or ditches. Finally, aquifers can show adverse effects from continued use of reclaimed (or brackish) water because of seepage from the surface. Many analysts believe that the use of recycled water should be prohibited in areas that drain into aquifers unless the seepage rate is very low and the water highly treated.

All use of recycled water in Israel requires a permit from the Ministry of Health, which follows, and for certain crops and urban uses exceeds, standards proposed by the World Health Organization (WHO). In particular, as implied earlier, Israel distinguishes between restricted and unrestricted uses of recycled water: the former refers to the use of lower quality water for specific nonfood crops grown under controlled conditions in some areas; the latter refers to more highly treated effluents that can be used for food crops that are cooked. Israel's national report to the 1992 Earth Summit states that continuous monitoring has indicated the safety of recycled wastewater provided treatment levels are high enough (Gabbay 1992). It is not clear whether this claim refers only to organic components or also includes heavy metals.

Despite technological viability, recycling water is not inexpensive. Among other things, recycled water contains contaminants not found in natural sources and, being aimed mainly at irrigation, systems must be sized to permit high rates of use in the summer and negligible rates in winter. Recycling water for irrigation adds about $0.13/m^3$ to conventional secondary treatment and disposal costs (excluding transportation; Shelef 1991), making it less than the cost of new fresh water but equal to what farmers have been paying. Alternative and relatively low-capital treatment systems, notably the use of reeds growing in marshes and swamps as biofiltration systems for household and even some industrial wastes, may be particularly applicable to conditions in the West Bank, but they are just beginning to be investigated. The additional cost to treat wastewater sufficiently to make it potable would be nearly $0.85/m^3$, well above what is acceptable and possibly above the cost of desalinated water.

Israeli practices for recycling water are now well established and are being adopted or adapted by other countries in the region (Aboukhaled 1992; Khouri 1992). The US Environmental Protection Agency has also produced a set of guidelines for water reuse (EPA 1992). As of now, however, no international quality standards apply to recycled water and, perhaps as a form of nontariff barrier, the European Community has recently moved to prohibit importation of produce irrigated with recycled wastewater. Although not yet accepted by all members, this could affect widespread use of the technique. Currently, no crops exported from Israel (except those from certain fruit trees) are irrigated with recycled water, so the initial impact on the Israeli economy of such a policy would be small. The policy would, however, affect plans to use more recycled water in agriculture. Only if such bans limit the use of recycled water in agriculture or if there is a long-term surplus of reclaimed water should Israelis and Palestinians contemplate the costly option of dual distribution systems (that is, one system carrying potable water and the other nonpotable water, mainly for toilet flushing). Such systems are appropriate for islands and other constrained communities, such as Hong Kong, but not generally for regions with intensively managed agriculture, such as Israel and the Occupied Palestinian Territories.

Water Harvesting

Water harvesting is the general name applied to gathering rain that falls over a broad area and bringing it to a much smaller area so that it can be used productively. As described in an article by Vesilind (1993), if a field receives only 150 mm of rain per year, crops will fail. If, however, the water from one half of the field could be moved to the other half, the total of 300 mm of water on that half would be adequate to support crops. Actual techniques to achieve this include construction of small, typically microscale, dams and trenches to gather rainfall and storm runoff. Some create temporary ponds, others increase soil moisture or direct water to crops, and still others recharge aquifers or fill cisterns. The contour terracing that is seen in many parts of the world is designed, in part, for water harvesting. It was their deep knowledge of water harvesting that permitted the Nabateans and other desert dwellers to establish rich civilizations in the desert 2 000 years ago (Hillel 1991; Evenari et al. 1982). Even today, low rock or earthen dams can be seen across intermittent streams throughout the Middle East, commonly in series one after the other on tributaries to the main wadi, some dating from ancient times and some of much more recent origin.

Water-harvesting techniques are now being rediscovered and, with the aid of computers and highly sensitive mapping, adapted to make optimal use of every drop of rain that falls. Their main applications in Israel have been for growing trees and shrubs in areas where rainfall is less than 300 mm/year, for halting desertification at the northern edge of the Negev, and for directing rainwater into channels so that it recharges aquifers rather than evaporating. Perhaps the most important new application is known as savannization (Gabbay 1992), an application of water harvesting that permits the growth of widely spaced trees in a carpet of grasses to exploit both winter rains and deeper soil moisture, while protecting the soil and the aquifers. Surface cover plays a key role in controlling runoff, soil moisture, and salinity. Similar, and in some cases even more sophisticated, techniques are being studied in Jordan.

Simple water-harvesting systems have been used for centuries in what is now Israel and the Occupied Territories, and there is every reason to believe that the higher technology extensions would be equally applicable. Because the applications are widely distributed to avoid the need for reservoirs or transportation, it is difficult to estimate their true potential. The increases in water supply provided by water harvesting are largely invisible.

Rainwater Catchment Systems

Rainwater catchment systems are a form of water harvesting applied to the built environment. A simple example once common in North America was the rainspout coming off the roof and leading to a barrel. With better designs and growing demand, rainwater catchment is making a comeback. Many systems still operate without mechanical equipment, although pumps are used in larger systems or those with deeper reservoirs.

Rainwater catchment systems can be built on a range of scales from household to neighbourhood. In contrast to ground harvesting, these systems have the advantage of starting with a prepared surface. If the surface is at street level, the resulting water can only be used for irrigation or perhaps industrial cooling. If the surface is a roof, however, it is entirely possible to gather and store potable water. The main problem lies not in capturing potable water, but in keeping the stored water clean. In properly covered containers, the water remains potable and is generally purer than water obtained from other sources. The cost of rainwater catchment systems is remarkably low; commonly cited figures range from $100 to $300 per family, depending mainly on storage capacity. (Lower cost systems store only enough water for drinking and cooking.)

Rainwater catchment systems were formerly seen in Israel but are no longer widely used. In contrast, they are ubiquitous on roofs in the West Bank. They are rare in the Gaza Strip, however. The surface area and volume of the catchment system and the annual rainfall determine the amount of water collected (assuming no losses and no leaks from storage). The systems in the West Bank typically supply 100–150 m³/year, quite adequate to meet a family's household consumption requirements. Systems designed for Gaza would likely supply less water because of lower rainfall, and would serve as supplemental sources — adequate in some months but not in others. As with water harvesting, the potential of rainwater catchment is only slowly becoming known with any degree of certainty. Moreover, if structures with larger roof surfaces, such as commercial buildings or greenhouses could be used, quite substantial amounts of rainwater could be captured, perhaps enough to meet annual demands for drinking water.

Captured Flood Runoff

Still another form of rainwater harvesting involves capturing winter runoff and floodwater. In some years, winter rains in Israel and the Occupied Palestinian Territories are intense and cause sharp flow peaks that cannot be handled by the storm sewers. In other years, winter flows are all but negligible. A small source of supplemental water supply can come from construction works that capture these high flows when they occur. Depending upon the terrain across which it has flowed, the runoff may be relatively fresh or contaminated. The highly intermittent nature of winter peaks and runoff, and the fact that collection systems must be sized for these high flows, mean that the cost per cubic metre of water captured can be quite high. Moreover, because peak flows tend to be erosive, they carry a high sediment load with the result that dams become filled within a few years.

Israel has developed several methods to capture winter runoff, either directing the water to a reservoir or using it to recharge aquifers. Recharging aquifers is increasingly favoured because it is less sensitive to water quality and because it avoids the need to purchase land, which is at a premium in the region. Approximately 40 Mm^3/year are recovered using this approach. No significant projects of this type are found in either the West Bank or Gaza; one project was initiated but not completed in Gaza City.

Use of Brackish Water

Most saline aquifers are isolated and thus nonrenewable, and the cost of pumping them is high. The potential to increase their use exists, however, particularly in the sandy soils along the coastal plain. As indicated in the foregoing, Israel is already using approximately 180 Mm^3/year of saline water for agricultural and industrial purposes. Total renewable supplies are estimated to be 300 Mm^3/year, but much larger quantities can be found in nonrenewable fossil aquifers (Vengosh and Rosenthal 1994).

Brackish water contains some salts but is less salty than seawater (which is 3.5% salt or 35 g/L). From aquifers, it can be used for irrigating salt-tolerant crops, which Israel is working to develop. Citrus trees, for example, cannot tolerate salty water, whereas olive, fig, and date trees can. Broccoli, tomatoes, spinach, beets, and other vegetables can also be grown in salty water — but only if capital-intensive, drip-irrigation methods are used. Some fruits, such as pears, can also be grown in salty water. The range of salinity that can be tolerated by different crops varies greatly; the most sensitive field crops require water that has less than 500 mg/L (0.05%), only a little more salty than drinking water, whereas the least sensitive can tolerate more than 2 000 mg/L (0.2%). According to the World Bank (1993a), forest plantations have been established on deep sandy soils in Abu Dhabi using saline groundwater containing 10 000 mg/L. The level of salinity is mitigated by soil conditions and the composition of the salts, with some plants more tolerant of chlorides and others of sulfates. On some farms, the saline water is buffered by adding gypsum to the soil.

The largest potential source of brackish water in Israel lies in Nubian sandstones that underlie the Negev and the Sinai. This aquifer was discovered in 1967 but remains totally unexploited. Although the aquifer is fossil and is thus nonrenewable, it is huge in size (70 billion cubic metres (Gm^3) below the Negev alone) and only mildly salty (about 600 mg/L). There is also another aquifer below, which is deeper and saltier. Arie Issar (1994) is a strong proponent of the potential value of this aquifer, although he admits that considerable research would be required to determine optimal pumping patterns and rates and to verify the feasibility of alternative extraction techniques. Shafts and tunnels, rather than wells, have been suggested because the rock containing the water is not very permeable. Issar also refers to a dual water system to make these aquifers viable, with one part containing fresh water and the other salty water. Cost estimates for this project are variable yet generally quite high, but Issar maintains that these brackish aquifers represent Israel's only option if it is to expand onto the Negev — the last frontier left open to Israel and its growing population.

Submarine Springs

Finally, it is worth noting that submarine fresh water springs occur along the coastline of Syria, Lebanon, and northern Israel. These are springs like any other, except that they discharge under the ocean, in a few cases in quantities large enough to be well known to fisherfolk and sports divers.[3] Despite some studies, knowledge of submarine springs is meagre. For example, estimates of the total undersea discharge off the Lebanese coast vary from 200 to nearly 2 000 Mm^3/year. Even the lowest estimate is greater than that of all but the largest rivers in the region. As yet, however, no one has found a way to recover this fresh water and bring it to shore in commercial quantities. Nevertheless, submarine springs must be regarded as a potentially important resource for the future.

Availability: Higher Technology Options

There are higher technology, more capital-intensive alternatives for new water supplies — notably cloud seeding and desalination of seawater or brackish water. We will discuss what appear to be the most important of these options in this section.

---

[3] These submarine springs occur because sea level was much lower in the recent geological past, and the mouths of many riverbeds, some with karstic passages, flowing to the sea were later drowned as sea level rose. They now lie 40–50 m below the surface.

Cloud Seeding

Cloud seeding is practiced in Israel, Jordan, Libya, Syria, and Saudi
Arabia. Based on the fact that clouds contain a large amount of water
that does not fall as rain, the technique consists of dispersing from
ground generators or from aircraft a chemical agent that causes the tiny
water drops to form ice crystals (nuclei), which gather more water until
they are heavy enough to fall.

Cloud-seeding experiments have been going on in Israel for more
than 30 years, and a regular program in the northern part of the country
in operation since 1976 is believed to have increased winter rainfall in
that area by at least 10% (Benjamini and Harpaz 1986). The resulting
water costs $0.04–0.05/m^3, and agricultural benefits range from $12 to
20 million/year. Tahboub (1992) reports even greater increases in rainfall and thus lower water costs for northern Jordan. These results are
generally consistent with those in other countries with favourable climatic conditions, and they suggest that comparable results could be
achieved in the northern end of the West Bank and in the Golan
Heights. Even larger increases in rainfall should be possible with jointly
managed regional programs, provided that research is carried out to permit rapid identification, tracking, and seeding of appropriate clouds
(not all clouds are susceptible to seeding) wherever they appear.

Desalinating Seawater

Israel and its neighbours have looked longingly at desalination for 30
years or more. Its appeal is easy to understand. One might say that
desalination is to water what nuclear power is to electricity — a promise
of unlimited supply coupled with the curse of high costs, environmental
problems, and megaproject fragility. The most common techniques for
desalination involve either multistage flash distillation (repeated evaporation of the water until the salt content is greatly reduced) or reverse
osmosis (forcing the water through a membrane that extracts the salt).
Israel previously had a number of small desalination plants that used a
variety of technologies to desalinate seawater and brackish water,
mainly in the Negev and at Eilat and Ashdod. By the mid-1980s, however, all of the seawater desalination plants had been closed because of

high costs. About 4 Mm³/year of fresh water are still produced by desalination, but all use brackish water feedstock (Glueckstern 1991). At least half of this desalination currently takes place in the new plant at Eilat. Given its landlocked location, seawater desalination is not an option for the West Bank. It has been discussed for years, however, as a way of resolving or reducing water deficits in the Gaza Strip, but to now only one small plant operates in a refugee camp. As discussed in Chapter 6, Palestinians have been wary of desalination.

Most studies have found that the high cost and energy requirements for desalination make its future as a major source of supply questionable. Production costs for large, modern plants (start-up in the late 1980s) that start with seawater are typically reported to be $1.00–1.50/m³ (Wade 1991; for the methodology used to calculate these costs, see Leitner 1991). The process requires enormous quantities of energy, so it is not surprising that 60% of the world's total desalination capacity, and the great bulk of its seawater-desalination capacity (around 5 Mm³/day or 1.8 Gm³/year), is located in oil-exporting countries of the Arabian peninsula, half of this in Saudi Arabia alone (Wangnick 1991).[4] Even with low oil prices, reported production costs for desalinated water are three to five times what urban dwellers pay for delivered drinking water and enormously more than what farmers pay.

A few analysts believe that the figures cited in the foregoing exaggerate the cost of desalination. Hoffman (1992), from a firm called ADAN based in Tel Aviv, has suggested that a combination of reverse osmosis and low-temperature, multieffect distillation can reduce both operating costs and initial capital requirements, so that final (plant-gate) costs would be $0.65–0.70/m³. These two technologies contain an independent power system and can be matched with a turbine generator that discharges steam to the distillation plant and electricity to the reverse-osmosis plant, a "total energy" scheme that Hoffman believes can achieve overall thermal efficiencies of 80% or more. These plants would be deliberately designed to be relatively small

---

[4] Neither is it surprising that, prior to its evacuation, Iraq did its best to destroy Kuwait's six desalination plants during the Persian Gulf War. Kuwait has no stable supply of fresh water; four of the desalination plants are now back in operation.

and modular — 40 Mm^3/year at a capital cost of $143 million (including the 25-MW steam turbine). Most people who have looked at seawater desalination for Israel or Gaza find it difficult to believe such low cost figures. The consensus is that operating costs alone (costs exclusive of interest on and return of capital) are not less than $0.80/$m^3$. Thus, Glueckstern (1991), an engineer with Mekorot, cites costs closer to those given by Leitner (1991), 40–60% higher than those given by Hoffman (1992), but for plants of similar size. Glueckstern (1991) also gives other figures as low as those cited by Hoffman (1992) based on "very preliminary designs," but only for very large plants (200 000 m^3/day). Even Hoffman's cost figures are twice those of conventional water supply in Israel, and they do not include delivery from the plant. Seawater desalination should, therefore, be seen as an option for the longer term, and only then if lower cost options for demand management and structure shifts are ignored.

Desalinating Brackish Water

Brackish water containing 500–5 000 parts per million (ppm) of total dissolved solids can be desalinated for $0.40–0.60/$m^3$, about one-half the cost of desalinating seawater (Glueckstern 1991; WRI 1992). Water for Eilat at the southern tip of Israel has for many years been supplied by a plant that desalinates brackish water pumped from an aquifer. A number of other small plants were built at remote locations not served by the National Water Carrier. Even those plants seldom operate for more than a few hours a day because of high operating costs.

For many years, the favoured method for desalination was distillation. In recent years, reverse osmosis, which involves the use of high pressure to force water through a membrane that filters out 90–98% of the solids plus most organic constituents and recovers 60–80% of the input water, has become the favoured technology. This is at least partly due to the lower energy requirements — and hence less sensitivity to fluctuating energy prices — of reverse osmosis (Wade 1991; Wangnick 1991). Reverse-osmosis plants now account for about one-third of world desalination capacity.

Hoffman (1994) argues that marginally brackish water (up to 1 250 ppm) is better treated by nanofiltration, an alternative membrane

process that operates at low pressure and, therefore, has energy requirements under 1 kWh/m^3 (3.6 MJ/m^3). He cites capital costs for a plant
that could produce 100 Mm^3/year to be just over $100 million, with the
desalinated water costing $0.25–0.27/m^3. (Just as with seawater desali-
nation, Glueckstern's (1991) cost figures are 40–60% higher.) In combination with brackish water reverse osmosis, Hoffman (1992) also argues
that the process could be used to reduce salinity levels in sewage for
municipal use or for recharging the Coastal Aquifer (where purification
would be completed). An added benefit would be the reduction of water
hardness so that the use of detergents and water softeners could also be
reduced.

If desalination is to be viable in the near future, it is more likely to
be based on brackish water than on seawater. More than 40% of the
world's desalination capacity now uses brackish feedstock, and that proportion is growing (Wangnick 1991). Costs of this procedure are less
than twice those of conventional supply, and further decreases can be
expected. Large reserves of low to moderately brackish water occur in
aquifers throughout the Middle East, and most can be tapped with conventional drilling equipment. Just as with the huge reserves under the
Negev and the Sinai, much of these reserves contain fossil water that is
nonrenewable; however, if reserves are large enough, it is possible to
amortize a sizable plant.

Canals to the Dead Sea

An alternative to stand-alone plants for desalination in the near future
lies with the renewed interest in Med–Dead or Red–Dead proposals to
bring seawater from either the Mediterranean Sea or the Red Sea and
convey it by means of tunnel and canal to the Dead Sea (see Figure 1
on p. 6). Because of the 400-m difference in elevation, the projects were
originally conceived as a means of generating electricity (and replacing
water in the rapidly diminishing Dead Sea basin). Although part of the
electricity generated would be required to pump water across the Judean
Hills (in the case of Med–Dead) or along the Jordanian border (in the
case of Red–Dead), the plans alleged that enough would remain to
power a substantial agroindustrial complex and thus make the projects
viable. Plans for the Med–Dead Canal have now been reconceived so

that all of the electricity generated would be devoted to desalination, thus reducing by about two-thirds the external energy requirements (Gur 1985). Viability would be enhanced by the supply of fresh water to potential agricultural land and industrial plants. The estimated cost of this project is $2 billion, with a series of hydroelectric stations (costing $340 million each) generating electricity and producing desalinated water at half the current cost (Moore 1993). The Italian government has expressed interest in participating in the project.

Although recent discussion has focused on the Red–Dead Canal (Kally 1993), each of the two routings has advantages and disadvantages. The Red–Dead Canal would be twice as long and have to climb twice as high before beginning its descent, but would avoid populated areas and the need to tunnel through the Mountain Aquifer. Although the Med–Dead route has a perceived advantage for some, because it could be built largely or entirely within Israel, others find the Red–Dead Canal appealing because it would have to be binational and, therefore, could solidify a peace treaty with Jordan. As a practical matter, either project probably requires agreement among Israelis, Palestinians, and Jordanians because the Jordan River and the Dead Sea are shared international waters. Jordan has clearly indicated its preference for the Red–Dead option (*Mideast Mirror*, 31 March 1994, p. 12). Israeli Foreign Minister Shimon Peres also seems to favour the Red–Dead option (*Mideast Mirror*, 29 June 1994). Both nations see it as a key to developing their southern frontier regions from the Red Sea along the Arava Valley to the Dead Sea.

Currently, a variation on the Med–Dead Canal, known as the "Gur Plan," has been attracting the most attention. According to this plan, fresh water from springs feeding the Upper Jordan River would be diverted to recharge the Coastal Aquifer to restore its original level and quality. This water would be replaced by desalinated water, which would be pumped back up to Lake Kinneret and would have the added benefit of improving water quality in the Lower Jordan (which is now too saline even for most agricultural uses).

Another variation of the Med–Dead Canal is suggested in Annex IV of the September 1993 Peace Accord, which lists a "Mediterranean Sea (Gaza)–Dead Sea Canal" as one of a number of possible regional economic development projects. Proponents of the Red–Dead Canal are also becoming active as Israeli–Jordanian relations improve. Among the elements of bilateral cooperation envisaged in the Israeli–Jordanian "Common Agenda" (a document released by Jordan just after the signing of the Peace Accord) are plans for the Rift Valley, including water, energy, and environmental development. If designed as an international pump-storage system, with reservoirs and power stations optimally located on both sides of the border, Kally (1993) argues that Red–Dead would be cheaper than Med–Dead. He calculates that the Red–Dead system could be built for under $1.5 billion (1988 dollars), would generate 800 MW of power (during 8 peak hours per day), and deliver 5 Mm^3 of water every day to the Dead Sea. In the Jordanian announcement on 7 June 1994 of progress in talks with Israel, reference was made to several transboundary projects, including a highway from Jordan through Israel to Egypt, a heritage park in the Jordan Valley, and — almost inevitably — the Red–Dead Canal.

While one or another of these desalination proposals surfaces from time to time, any routing or diversion would cost billions of dollars and raise very important environmental questions. No such plan is likely to be implemented within a time frame that is relevant to a discussion about current water problems. Although all of the routes are clearly technically feasible, the Gur Plan is probably the most integrated and the most sensitive to environmental concerns. Even so, just as with the other plans, it would require a large block of initial capital and a megaproject approach to problem-solving at a time when the world is short of capital and increasingly skeptical of megaprojects.

Infrastructure, Management, and Planning

As a result of the importance of fresh water, a great deal of emphasis has been placed on developing a comprehensive water management and monitoring scheme for Israel (Beaumont et al. 1988). All water resources in Israel belong to the state. Management decisions on water quantities, production, and the supply system rest with the Water Commissioner, who reports to the Minister of Agriculture. Few powers escape the Water Commissioner. The few exceptions

include: responsibility for water quality in natural resources, which
resides in the Ministry of Environment; responsibility for the quality of
drinking water, which is under the Ministry of Health; and control of
water-delivery systems and billing, which is shared by the Ministry of
the Interior, local authorities, and a few other bodies (Gabbay 1992).
This situation centralizes decisions affecting water supply and, in many
sectors, water use. It also ensures an integrated and highly engineered
water supply and sanitation system, comparable to that found in
California and other water-deficient regions of the industrialized world.
At the same time, the locus of power within the Ministry of Agriculture
puts a particular cast on decisions and engineering relevant to water.
Obviously, the institutional design of the Israeli water system reflects
the strong linkage between agriculture and water. Less obviously, it
symbolizes the conviction that water policy is a subordinate element of
agricultural policy.

The Water Commission has two main operational arms: Mekorot,
the national water authority, and Tahal, the water planning company.
Mekorot is a public corporation owned jointly by the government, the
Jewish Agency, and the National Federation of Labour (Histadrut). It
owns much of the water supply infrastructure, including pumping stations, wells, irrigation projects, and the National Water Carrier, and it
is responsible for overall water quantity and quality management, distribution of water to users, conservation and efficiency of water use, and
water supply development. Tahal is a government corporation
(although, according to Moore (1993), it was on the government's list
to be privatized, a move that has been delayed under the Labour government) with responsibility for overall water planning, research, and
design. Both Mekorot and Tahal must grant permission before any new
wells are drilled in either Israel or the Occupied Palestinian Territories.
Of the two organizations, Tahal has more independence but Mekorot
has more power — mainly because it can raise money independently for
which it is accountable only to the Minister of Finance. Neither unit,
however, is open to much public review. There is no general "right to
know" under Israeli water law, although the Water Commissioner must
file an annual report with the Knesset Committee on Economics to
review activities during the year (Laster 1993).

A third agency reporting to the Water Commissioner is the Hydrological Service, which maintains a large network of water monitoring stations (surface and underground), and maintains a computerized database of water information. The Hydrological Service also monitors the wells used by settlers, and receives from the Civil Administration Water Authority information on other wells in the Occupied Palestinian Territories.

Israel's water-supply system includes an extensive transportation and distribution network, most of it operated by Mekorot. The main component is the National Water Carrier, an integrated system of large-diameter pipes and reservoirs that carries water from Lake Kinneret to the central and southern regions of the country (see Figure 1 on p. 6). Completed in 1964, the Carrier, which has been described as a means of transforming the Jordan River from a border to an internal river, can transport more than a million cubic metres per day. The National Water Carrier carries almost 80% of Israel's surface water (supplemented by some pumping in the south) and provides access to water for almost all the nation's people.

Later sections of this book will emphasize water in the Occupied Palestinian Territories. Suffice it to say here that prior to 1967, the Natural Resources Authority of Jordan was responsible for water resources and water-supply/distribution systems in what is now the West Bank; Egyptian and Syrian agencies played similar roles for Gaza and the Golan, respectively. After the 1967 war, responsibility for water resources and water management was taken over by the Israeli military. Initially, the Civil Administration delegated its powers to a "water officer," who was in turn responsible to the Water Commissioner. In 1982, responsibility was transferred directly to Mekorot (Elmusa 1993a). Since then, Mekorot and Tahal have operated in the Territories, although they collaborate only minimally with local Palestinian authorities. Regardless of the mechanism or agency employed by the Civil Administration, all activities are subject to military orders, which, in the case of water, have been extensive. As early as August 1967, ultimate control over water resources in the West Bank was granted to the military commander (Military Order No. 92), and a few months later publication of information on water was prohibited (Military Order

No. 158). The Civil Administration continues to operate a Water Department (using mainly the Palestinian staff of the former Jordanian Agency) to monitor water for quantity and quality; the information is then sent on to the Israeli Hydrological Service and, in the absence of appropriate computers and software, the Water Department has no further access to it.

Before the 1967 war, a great deal of the water supply and sewage management, including planning, was undertaken by municipalities and district councils, particularly in what is now the West Bank. Some of these institutions still exist, notably in Bethlehem and Jerusalem, but since 1967 their responsibilities have been limited to the operation and maintenance of existing systems. The West Bank water companies and municipal agencies read meters, collect water fees, and administer certain rules, but they do little more. They have no ability to raise funds and have no independent sources of revenue. Elmusa (1993a) points out that they have not hired even one hydrologist since 1967. (Some technical functions have been taken over by nongovernmental organizations (NGOs), such as the Palestine Hydrology Group.) To allow for development and implementation of technical solutions to water problems in both the West Bank and the Gaza Strip, a significant financial investment would be required. For the most part, Israel has refrained from such a commitment. Between 3 and 6% of Israeli government expenditures in the West Bank go toward water projects, with most of this money being used to maintain existing systems. In absolute figures, one estimate suggests that $10 million a year is spent for both maintenance and development.

In summary, the institutional structure for managing water in Israel is diffuse, and in the eyes of some it succeeds in managing the water system more through "friction" than cooperation (Galnoor 1980). Israel's water institutions, however, are less diffuse and no more fractious than those of most other countries. The institutions are efficient at what they do, even if they are slow to react to changing needs. Put another way, it is the failure of the water institutions in Israel to meet the special responsibilities of an occupying power, on the one hand, and to provide the flexibility needed for a changing domestic economy, on the other, that make them appear so inefficient today.

Development and Diffusion of Irrigation Technology

In parallel with its development of a management scheme and institutional structure for water, Israel has made a great effort to develop and implement technologies appropriate for arid and semi-arid environments. For example, Israelis have extended geophysical techniques in the exploration for water and improved drilling methods to permit extraction of water from deeper aquifers. For this study, it is more important to focus on end-uses rather than production technologies, and of these the most important by far have been aimed at irrigation.

For all practical purposes, agricultural use of water is in the form of irrigation. Other uses, such as washing, rinsing, and local sanitation, are insignificant by comparison. Roughly 18% of the world's cultivated land is irrigated (a total of over 350 million ha) but it produces one-third of the total harvest. Globally, irrigation expanded slowly from less than 50 to nearly 95 million ha in the first half of this century, but then exploded to 250 million ha by 1990 (WRI 1992). Although that rate of increase is now slowing down, the figure could still reach 300 million ha by the turn of the century. In other words, the amount of irrigated land doubled in the first half of this century and could triple again in the second half.

Drip Irrigation

Today, irrigation is a highly complex technique with variations for different crops and different climates (Shady 1989). Israel has always been concerned with efficiency in irrigation, but it was only when Israeli researchers developed the drip-irrigation technique that it became a world leader in irrigation technology. During the first two decades of independence, Israel managed to reduce average water use for irrigation from about 8 000 to 7 000 m^3/ha, although total use went up significantly because Israel was simultaneously increasing the amount of land under irrigation. With the advent of drip irrigation in the mid-1960s, specific water use fell by one-third to two-thirds, depending upon the crop. As a result, total water consumption for agriculture was stable over the next two decades, and this was before the cutbacks imposed by the long drought at the end of the 1980s.

Drip irrigation is a technique by which relatively small amounts of water are delivered directly to the roots of growing plants by means of perforated plastic piping (Gabbay 1992). When fully developed so that the flow of water is controlled by sensors linked to central computers on large farms, efficiencies (that is, the proportion of water that reaches the roots) can reach 95%. Yields are increased further by "fertigation," which is a colloquial expression for introducing fertilizers directly into the irrigation water. Despite high capital costs for installation ($1 500–3 000/ha (Postel 1993); perhaps one-third less if farmers use their own labour for installation), nearly half of all irrigated land in Israel is now under what is more broadly called microirrigation (Gabbay 1992). Only Cyprus has a greater share of land under microirrigation, but its actual acreage is only one-quarter that of Israel's.

Drip irrigation has been widely adopted by Jordanian farmers on the East Bank of the river, and all indications are that it has a high but largely unrealized potential in the Palestinian portions of the West Bank. Indeed, Wishart (1989) argues that the transfer of drip-irrigation technology — sometimes legally, sometimes illegally — to Jordan and other Arab states was one of the main reasons why conflicts over water in the region did not escalate into violence. Currently, few Palestinian farmers in the Occupied Territories can secure a large enough allocation of water to make drip systems worthwhile. Given larger allocations, they would still need good credit terms and secure tenure, neither of which is assured even under an autonomous government. Technology is the least of the problems; both Israeli and Jordanian factories can manu-facture the equipment, and both Israeli and Jordanian advisors can assist with installation and maintenance.

Palestinian farmers may also want to look beyond their immediate neighbours for ideas about drip irrigation. In some of the more arid areas of Latin America, such as Peru, less technologically advanced forms of drip irrigation have apparently been in use for centuries and are now being adapted to modern conditions for growing vegetables and trees (Paredes 1993). The key to the success (and the low cost) of these sys-tems is that, in contrast to the Israeli system, they do not have to be operated under pressure. These "primitive" systems use a series of cheaply fired but rugged ceramic pots that are either filled using a funnel or that receive water through plastic hoses and exude it through pores (in the same manner as desert coolers used for drinking water). When the target crops need water, a negative pressure (suction) is created in the surrounding soil, which in turn determines the rate at which water is exuded from the pots — a simple but elegant approach! Apart from pots and hoses, the main cost is the labour required to install and maintain the system — at least after research has determined optimal pot spacing and filling rates for local crops and conditions.

Reducing Water Losses

Water losses in Israel have been further diminished by the adoption of techniques to reduce seepage and evaporation. The most common technique to reduce seepage involves lining canals and shallow reservoirs with an impervious layer, either clay materials or plastic sheeting, asphalt, or ferrocement. Natural materials are cheaper but also less effective, and they generally require more attention to maintenance (Shady 1989). A variety of techniques have been tried to reduce evaporation in small reservoirs, but none has proved to be both successful and cheap. A simple method is to site reservoirs, wherever possible, at higher elevations to avoid the hottest temperatures; however, this implies that higher pumping costs are incurred.

The best way to reduce both evaporation and seepage is to replace canals and ditches with pipes. Not surprisingly, a large share of the plastic irrigation pipe required is produced in the region. By shifting from open canals to piped water, the irrigated area expanded by 38% on farms on the Jordanian side of the Jordan River, and farm incomes also increased (Abu-Sheikha 1984). Even with piping, leakage is seldom reduced below 10%. If the leakage is into the cropped area, however, it is not a total loss. Seckler (1993) emphasizes this point and challenges the notion that much irrigation water is being used inefficiently and can be diverted to other uses. He argues that what appear as "microinefficiencies" of parts of the system are made up of "macroefficiencies" created by natural recycling in the ecosystem as a whole. Seckler is correct up to a point. As he recognizes, however, degradation of water quality also occurs in this recycling process, and it is commonly more important than he admits. As well, the lost water is not being used as efficiently (again, at the microlevel) as it might be and, in arid and semi-arid areas, all these microinefficiencies result in high losses to evaporation, which **are** consumptive. Finally, in areas near the coast or the Dead Sea, the runoff can be lost completely.

Water losses can also be reduced by techniques that limit the loss of soil moisture. Perhaps the most common technique, particularly for vegetables, is mulching. At one time, organic materials were the dominant forms of mulch, and they are still used by poorer farmers. Now, however, a farmer with a small amount of capital uses plastic mulch (large sheets that cover exposed soil between rows of growing plants), so much so that the plastic sheeting is a major source of waste that all too commonly fouls water courses and despoils the countryside. Another technique is to plant windbreaks or erect physical barriers that retard air circulation. In a few cases, it is also possible to develop crop plants, such as cacti, that evolved under desert conditions and have very low rates of transpiration (Evenari et al. 1982).

Ecological and Economic Gains

Microirrigation techniques have the further advantage of reducing adverse environmental impacts typical of land under continuous irrigation. Notably, drip irrigation can avoid or reduce the salinization that tends to occur on irrigated land in an arid climate. Flood irrigation also leads to high levels of runoff. If Canadian data for the southern Prairies can be taken as an indication, three out of every four units flow back to watercourses, but typically laden with pesticides, fertilizers, and chemicals (Pearse et al. 1985). Despite drip irrigation, agricultural runoff remains a major environmental problem in Israel (see Chapter 5).

Taken together, efforts to increase the efficiency of water use in Israeli agriculture have been highly successful. Agricultural output has increased using the same amount, or even reduced volumes, of water (Heathcote 1983; Hillel 1991). Water consumption per hectare has declined from nearly 6 400 m^3/ha in 1975 to 4 500 m^3/ha in the late 1980s. Over the same period, the volume of water consumed per dollar of agricultural output has declined from 1.6 to 0.75 m^3 (Fishelson 1994). In parallel with, and in part as a result of, the shift to capital-intensive irrigation methods, Israel has also encouraged farmers to shift their planting toward crops that have higher unit values in the market, mainly fruits and vegetables.

Municipal and Domestic Demand

Urban growth and municipal water consumption account for a growing proportion of water use around the world, so it is worth digressing briefly to look at the structure of Israeli and Palestinian cities. Throughout the world, more people are coming to live in urban areas, and cities are getting larger. The Middle East is no exception to this trend. Israel is already more than 90% urbanized. Indeed, that part of Israel lying along the coast between Tel Aviv and Haifa, as well as the Gaza Strip, are among the most densely populated regions of the world. (Apart from this one statistic of people per hectare, we do not mean to suggest that conditions in northwestern Israel and the Gaza Strip are at all comparable.) On the one hand, Jordan is nearly 70% urbanized and, although data for the West Bank are confusing, that is probably a good estimate for the Occupied Palestinian Territories. On the other hand, Israeli and Palestinian cities are rather small by international standards. Even Tel Aviv has well under half a million people, and it is by far the largest city in the region. With the exception of Gaza City, whose population is artificially inflated by refugees, no city in the Occupied Palestinian Territories has more than 150 thousand people.

Urban areas vary widely in water use per capita — from 100 to 500 L/person-day, based on deliveries from municipal companies to individual consumers and small industry (Anton 1993). Although statistics are not readily available on a municipality-by-municipality basis, Israeli and Palestinian cities rank quite low in terms of water use per capita, at around 120–200 L/person-day. Nevertheless, their water systems share a number of characteristics with those of other cities. For example, the importance of groundwater, formerly of little concern except in cases of island cities, is increasing throughout the world. Also growing is the use of wastewater for irrigating gardens in the city or farms near the city; for example, some 90 000 ha of land in Mexico City is irrigated with wastewater and 2 000 ha in Lima (Anton 1993). Cities in Israel and the Occupied Palestinian Territories, along with many other cities throughout the world, have neglected their water and sanitation systems, a situation that has become worse as they have grown. Problems stemming from deficient sewage systems in both Israel and the Occupied Palestinian Territories are discussed further in Chapter 5.

Finally, the cost of delivering water to urban areas is increasing in Israel and the Occupied Palestinian Territories, as it is around the world. Although data specific to the immediate area are difficult to obtain, more general data clearly indicate that cities in the Middle East already suffer from the highest costs for water in the world. The median cost for connecting one new household to the system reached $300 in 1985 (twice the cost in North America), and that figure would be much higher today (World Bank 1993a).

Finally, there is at least one way in which the urban areas of Israel and the Occupied Palestinian Territories differ sharply. Poorer residents of Israeli cities and villages receive water at essentially the same price and through the same delivery systems as their more affluent neighbours. This is not necessarily the case in the Territories, where low-income persons may have to buy water in small quantities from private companies or vendors who sell it by the litre. The result, which replicates a depressing pattern found in many parts of the world (World Bank 1993a), is that the cost of domestic water supplies are highly regressive. Per litre of water consumed, low-income people pay much higher prices than middle- and upper-class people. Almost any form of centralized system of delivery and billing will alleviate this problem, and the more appropriate pricing structures (notably, increasing block rates) can create a progressive system in which the poor pay less, not more, for their water (Brooks et al. 1990; World Bank 1993a; see Chapter 4). As will be emphasized in the following, such systems depend on accurate water metering and regular billing, but both are universal in Israel and in those parts of the Occupied Palestinian Territories served by piped water delivery systems from Mekorot.

Energy: The Hidden Input

For all countries in the Middle East, water is the key input and, ulti-mately, the factor limiting development. In contrast, these same nations vary dramatically in their access to energy. Thanks to oil (and to a lesser extent natural gas), some Middle Eastern countries are among the most energy rich in the world; others are among the most energy poor. A few, notably Jordan, are simultaneously at the extreme low-water and low-energy poles. Moreover, there are distinct linkages between water demand and energy use.

Energy is required to make use of all but the most local surface and shallow underground water. Most importantly, today energy is used for pumping water, both vertically from underground sources and hori-zontally from place to place. Farms tend to be located in valleys, which limits pumping costs, but this is not true of cities. For centuries, based on military, cultural, and environmental considerations, cities have his-torically been placed on hills or mountains, which increases pumping costs. Furthermore, wastewater must be removed (in this case, the ele-vation of cities is a minor advantage) and treated, both of which require energy. Wastewater treatment can refund some of that energy through the recovery of methane, but in most cases only enough is captured to operate the treatment plant itself. If water must be treated further before it can be used, still more energy will be required. As indicated in the foregoing, if desalination is contemplated, energy and capital costs become the dominant variables.

Currently, Israel uses 12% of its electricity just to pump water (Schwarz 1992). In Jordan, the proportion is almost 20%. The proportion of electricity used in Israel to pump water used to be 20% but has declined as a result of increases in total electricity use. Most of this electricity is used to pump water up from Lake Kinneret, which lies 209 m below sea level, to the National Water Carrier, which operates at and above sea level. Detailed figures are not available, but estimates suggest that as much as one-third of urban electricity use is for water treatment and pumping. In contrast to the Israeli population, which is concentrated along the coast, the Palestinian population is, with the exception of Jericho, concentrated in the highlands, which increases net pumping costs. In Israel today, it takes 1 kWh (3.6 MJ) to deliver each cubic metre of water; at the margin it can take 3 kWh (Kally 1993). For the worst case in the region (that is, pumping over the longest distance and to the highest elevation), direct use of electricity for pumping is moving toward 10 kWh for every cubic metre delivered. For the region occupied by Israelis, Palestinians, and Jordanians, which has little in terms of indigenous energy supplies, this situation necessitates the expenditure of foreign exchange.

Conclusion

Despite all of the investment in infrastructure, improvements in efficiency, and the increased use of recycled and saline water, water supply has not kept pace with demand in either Israel or the Occupied Palestinian Territories. The threat of water shortages persists. Population growth rates are close to 2% per year, and immigration could significantly increase the population in both Israel and the Occupied Territories. Growing demands for higher standards of living and a better quality of urban life are exacerbating the situation. Clearly, Israel's water planning must now attempt to address demand problems by developing a less water-intensive economy, and promoting efforts to reduce losses and inefficient use. Reducing losses and inefficient use is equally important for the Occupied Territories, but it is less evident whether Palestinians could or should move to a less water-intensive economy.

PART II

THREE CRISES

CHAPTER 4

WATER QUANTITY: THE ECONOMIC CRISIS

For the Middle East has undergone an amazing decline from former times of more numerous populations, higher standards of living, much better agriculture, and more general irrigation of farm lands, and better practices of soil conservation.
— W.C. Lowdermilk
(introduction to Reifenberg 1955)

BEFORE THE 1967 WAR, water use in Israel had reached both its physical and economic limits. The war greatly increased the nation's access to water, but patterns of usage were maintained and over time the new sources of water also came to be used up to, and beyond, their limits. Since the mid-1970s, water use in Israel has been at or near 100% of the resource potential. According to Israel's Ministry of Environment (*Israel Environment Bulletin*, Spring 1991), consumption exceeds available capacity (the amount of water one can tap before "mining" occurs) by some 200 Mm³/year. Moreover, the deficit in the reservoir system (that is, the gap between current levels and what is considered a safe operational reserve) had reached 1 430 Mm³ by late 1991. Faced with increasing standards of living (air-conditioning, etc.) and renewed immigration, on the one hand, and several successive years of low rainfall, on the other, Israel was finally forced to ask how to augment water supply or reduce water demand without affecting the economic growth of the state or the quality of life of its citizens. True, the answer was deferred when the latest drought ended in the winter of 1991–92, completely recharging Lake Kinneret and increasing water levels in the aquifers. Other droughts, however, will occur.

Water is an economic problem from both short- and long-term perspectives, and in terms of both micro- and macro-options. In the short term, there are immediate costs and returns as seen by conventional economic accounts; in the longer term, population growth and global change may result in significant impacts. This section will attempt to examine the implications for regional politics in the context of both perspectives. Throughout, the recurring theme will be the potential of shifting from supply-side to demand-side approaches. The need for such a shift is well stated in the report of a World Bank mission to the region looking at opportunities for water conservation (World Bank 1993b, pp. 1–2):

> [As] uses for water have changed and expanded, and as more accessible resources have been fully exploited, so the costs of further supply-side options have increased dramatically. Even water-rich countries are finding it increasingly expensive, in some cases prohibitively so, to resort to large-scale infrastructural solutions for providing water to meet increasing demands. Furthermore, in addition to direct investment costs, issues related to resettlement of population, and to adverse effects on the natural environment have become more difficult and more expensive to overcome. Such concerns add weight to the need for major changes in the approach to water resources management, if the challenges of imbalances between usable water supplies and demands are to be overcome.

Effects on the Economy

Roughly two-thirds of all the water Israel currently consumes is used for agriculture, which is close to the world average (WRI 1992). Many countries in the Middle East use more than 80% of their water supplies for irrigation. Although the value added in agriculture per unit of water has more than doubled in the past two decades, even a 70% share does seem disproportionate compared with agriculture's importance in the economy of Israel. Agricultural employment now accounts for less than 4% of the labour force, 2.3% of the gross domestic product (GDP), and 5.4% of Israel's export earnings (Tables 4 and 5).

In terms of the declining proportion of employment in agriculture and the decreasing importance of agriculture in the national economy, Israel appears to be only a few years ahead of other countries in the region; only in Turkey and Sudan is agriculture's contribution to total output relatively constant (Beschorner 1992). Where Israel differs from many other Middle Eastern nations is in the extent to which its economy is increasingly oriented toward services, design, and manufacturing

Table 4. Export earnings and employment in Israel, selected sectors, 1990.

	Value of exports (million US$)	Employment ('000 employees)
Agriculture	656.2 (5.4)[a]	58.9 (3.9)
Chemical and oil products	1 449.7 (12.0)	18.6 (1.2)
Metal products	691.0 (5.7)	46.0 (3.0)
Electrical and electronic equipment	1 637.0 (13.6)	43.8 (2.9)
Transport equipment	596.5 (4.9)	23.9 (1.6)
Total (all sectors)	12 079.0	1 491.9

Source: Israel, Central Bureau of Statistics (1992).
[a] Percentage of total in parentheses.

Table 5. Economic characteristics of Israel and the Occupied
Palestinian Territories (OPTs), 1990–91.

	Israel	OPTs West Bank	Gaza	Total
Population (millions)	5.059	1.005	0.676	1.681
GDP[a] (million US$)	59 127	1 643	536	2 179
GNP[b] (million US$)	58 112	2 138	839	2 977
GDP per capita (US$)	11 687	1 634	792.9	1 296
GNP per capita (US$)	11 487	2 127	1 241	1 771
Sector contribution (%)				
Agriculture	2.3	22.2	16.7	20.6
Industry	21.8	5.7	11.8	7.2
Employment in agriculture (%)	3.5	12.2	18.5	14.5
Exports (million US$)	18 024	175[c]	63	
Imports (million US$)	27 287	700[c]	423	

Source: Israel, Central Bureau of Statistics (1992). Data for Israel are for 1991; for the OPTs, 1990.
[a] Gross domestic product.
[b] Gross national product.
[c] Estimated from 1987 data.

in the "high tech" sectors. Indeed, Israel has one of the highest ratios of research to GDP (3.9%) of any country in the world, and only a small fraction of that research is devoted to agriculture. The leaders of the nation clearly do not perceive a prosperous future in farming — yet they have not made that fact evident through water policies.

It would appear that reductions in water use by the agricultural sector could alleviate water problems in Israel at little or no economic cost. This conclusion is reinforced by Fishelson (1992b), who notes that, because the direct economic role of agriculture in the Israeli economy is so small, any further decline as a result of lower water allocations would be almost negligible. He also notes that the proportion of water costs in the total consumption expenditures of households and industrial firms is relatively minor, so that an increase in price would have little effect on the quantity demanded by these sectors.

Current Misallocation

The evidence strongly suggests that Israel's water quantity crisis is more a result of misallocation than absolute scarcity. As many analysts have noted, a shift of water away from agriculture toward urban and municipal uses, or even toward less water-intensive crops, would enormously reduce or even eliminate problems of relative water scarcity. Rough calculations show that a one-third reduction in irrigated acreage, together with modest improvements in end-use efficiency, would be sufficient to bring Israel's water consumption and its renewable water supply into balance. According to Beschorner (1992), who had access to Tahal documents, transferring about this quantity of water from agricultural to domestic use "is part of all stated policies and plans."

Plans are, however, just that; they may or may not be implemented. Given the strength of the farm lobby in Israel, any plan to shift water out of agriculture would not be implemented easily. Even an allocation scheme that would maximize the value added per unit of water used in agriculture (which, given the vagaries of agricultural markets would favour poultry, dairy, roughage, and melons at the expense of other fruits, field crops, and citrus) would help solve the water-supply problem, at least in the short term. But it must also be noted that, although the direct economic costs of reducing water allocations to the agricultural sector may be quite small, indirect costs, such as displacement of people and dissolution of some kibbutzim, may be much higher. No detailed study of these welfare costs has been conducted, although Fishelson (1992b) has indicated that they may represent a problem. We tend to disagree, and feel that even with the indirect costs included, the overall economic cost of reducing water allocations to agriculture would still be minor.

In saying that indirect costs would not be excessive, we do not mean to ignore that the "value" of water to Zionists and to the State of Israel is more than the economic value of water as an input to production; it also has political, social, and ideological (and security) importance. These noneconomic interests have often dominated any consideration of the most efficient economic use of water in the country. Nevertheless, it is important to note that in dollar terms water has been, and may still be, the most valuable input to production in the Israeli economy. An economic analysis conducted using interindustry flow data for Israel for the years 1976 and 1983 demonstrated that for these 2 years, water was the most essential input — in economic terms — to the Israeli economy (Lonergan and Brooks 1994). This analysis included a ranking of economic sectors that demonstrates where constraints on the availability of resources would have the greatest potential for limiting aggregate economic output. In each of these years, water is ranked number one by a wide margin.

The core of the problem in Israel, as in so many countries, is that farmers pay far less than the full cost of the delivery of irrigation water. Most farmers cannot afford to pay a very high price for water if their crop is to be sold profitably (Muller 1985). Within the Green Line, farmers typically get water for agricultural use at $0.16/m^3$ (roughly 80% of the water used for irrigation costs $0.125/m^3$ and the remaining 20% is priced at $0.20/m^3$), compared with anywhere between $0.70 and $1.65 for household consumption. (For a household, the first 18 m^3 in a 2-month period — more than enough for a family to have basic services — is priced at the lowest rate, so as to provide for both equity and efficiency.) The prices paid by households are on an increasing block-rate structure: the more water consumed, the higher the price. Approximately one-third of Israeli households pay the top price of $1.65/m^3$; industrial users pay $0.15/m^3$. Zarour and Isaac (1991) estimate that the actual cost to supply water in Israel is $0.36/m^3$ (0.036 cents/L). Other estimates (such as in Fishelson 1992b) are slightly lower, but none are less than $0.30/m^3$. Urban dwellers, therefore, are paying more than the full average costs (though not necessarily marginal costs), which range from about \$0.40 to well over \$1.00/m^3 for advanced technologies. Farmers and industrial users, however, are highly subsidized. Prices are the same for Arab and Jewish communities in Israel, but differ in the Occupied Palestinian Territories. Gideon Fishelson (1992a), of Tel Aviv University, estimates that only about half of the water devoted to agriculture in Israel has a marginal value greater than its cost. This estimate is supported by Schwarz (1992), who reports results from a survey indicating that 25% of high-yield farms and over 60% of low-yield farms exhibit a lower value per unit of water used than the average cost of water per unit. Fishelson (1992a) estimates that appropriate market pricing of water would transfer 300 Mm^3 from inefficient agricultural uses to nonagricultural uses — enough to eliminate the overdraft on Israel's water system and provide, in addition, another 2 million people with 100 L/day. In August 1994, the Government of Israel announced that, as part of a complex reform budget for fiscal 1995, prices for water to farmers and to industry would go up and subsidies would be reduced.

Although it is true that the level of subsidy received by farmers in Israel for water is modest by regional standards (Khouri 1992), the low marginal economic productivity of the water used in agriculture strongly suggests that some water should be reallocated away from irrigating crops toward industrial and household uses. Perhaps growing flowers and some fruits and vegetables that are exported fresh to Europe could cover the full cost of water, but grains and most field crops cannot.

Water is expensive because even conventional water-supply systems are capital intensive, especially per dollar of revenue (Rogers 1986). According to the World Bank (cited in Starr 1992), the Middle East–North Africa region has the highest capital costs associated with water supply in the world. Operating costs are also high. As indicated in Chapter 3, Israel uses 12% and Jordan 20% of their electricity just to pump water. If conventional systems are capital intensive, nonconventional supply alternatives are even more so. This is particularly true in the case of desalination. Water-saving techniques, such as installing drip irrigation, lining canals, and eliminating leakage, are also capital intensive. About the only options that are not capital intensive are conservation measures achieved through improved management and better housekeeping.

The Potential to Reallocate Water

The emphasis on agriculture in Israel and the subsidies agriculture receives are well out of proportion with the sector's total economic importance to the nation. A partial restructuring of the Israeli economy away from agriculture and toward light industry, services, and information technologies would save not only water, but energy as well. The contribution of the light industrial sector to GDP is almost 30 times greater per unit of water used than the contribution of the agricultural sector (Naff 1994). From this perspective, the point so often raised — that Israel is one of the world's most efficient users of irrigation water — misses the main point. The main point (and it is not exclusive to Israel) is that, as river basins and aquifers come to be more highly developed, options for improvements in efficiency come more from reallocation of water among users than from improvements in use by any one user. Furthermore, uses and users become highly interconnected and linked to broader aspects of government policy. This situation is indicated in the accompanying text box, entitled "Lessons from Closing Water Systems," which identifies the kinds of changes that occur as a water resource basin becomes fully used (or, in the World Bank's terms, "closed").

The strongest attack in many years on water use in Israeli agriculture has come from Miriam Ben Porat, the State Comptroller. Ben Porat emphasized the misallocation problem, and she clearly saw the close linkage between the Water Commissioner and the Minister of Agriculture as part of the problem. She put most of the blame for the water crisis on low prices and poor management, which have stimulated demand for water and reduced incentives to conserve (Shuval 1992). As the subsidized water is commonly used for export crops, the benefit is effectively passed on to foreign consumers. Accordingly, Baskin (1992) ironically states that it would be cheaper to import oranges from Europe than to grow them in Israel, and he suggests that exporting oranges is equivalent to exporting water. More formally, the State Comptroller charged that, in contrast to an illusion of contributing to the nation's

---

Lessons from Closing Water Systems

A water system, for example a river basin, is said to be "closing" when water use and reuse exceed water entering the system. In a perfectly closed system, water will progress through many use cycles until it evaporates or reaches a salt sink. The result is a "water-multiplier" effect, which can be calculated. When a water system is closing:

≈ Users become increasingly interdependent as water reuse increases;
≈ Efficiency of water use and reuse becomes a public issue as well as a private one;
≈ Water management improvements have system-wide consequences;
≈ The widespread consequences of improvements in water use efficiency or water quality allow costs to be shared among users;
≈ Conjunctive use of surface water and groundwater increases in importance;
≈ System-wide management requires flexible operations; and
≈ Reallocation of water becomes increasingly important, with possible consequences for establishing rights and users.

Source: Peabody (1992)

---

economy, subsidized prices for irrigation water actually caused "recognizable economic damage in Israel." In making this point, she has merely added her conclusions to a list of consulting reports dating back at least 15 years that make essentially the same point (Kneese 1976). She has also added her voice to earlier calls to remove water management from the Ministry of Agriculture and place it under an independent state authority that would make judgments on overall national priorities.

During the recent drought, pressure to reduce water allocations and subsidies to farmers became too great to resist. Water allocations to the agricultural sector have declined since 1986, at first by marginal volumes but by 37% by 1990 and 50% by 1991 (Lowi 1992). During the drought, promises were made that the lower levels would be in place for at least 5 years. After abnormally heavy rainfall in the winter of 1991–92 raised the level of Lake Kinneret and recharged aquifers, however, water allocations to agriculture were again increased. Yet it has been estimated that these rains provided Israel with only 1 year of additional water supply.

The reductions in water allocations to agriculture should have provided a great deal of information on the ways in which farmers adjust crops, cropping patterns, and operations for lower water consumption. Unfortunately, a literature review commissioned by Canada's International Development Research Centre (IDRC) in 1992 found no studies on how farmers and others actually coped with potentially permanent reductions of this magnitude. Data do show, however, that the land under drip irrigation declined by 18% and total irrigated land by 15% during the drought (Postel 1993). Fishelson (1992a) reports that output was down by about one-third at the peak of the drought, but this figure compounds secular and cyclical effects and is too aggregate to be truly instructive. Detailed information on adjustment patterns, which is likely available in the Israeli Ministry of Agriculture, would be very useful in determining the timing and extent of water reallocation that could occur without causing undue hardship and economic loss for farmers who have, quite understandably, invested in infrastructure and developed management systems on the assumption that water would continue to be available in large volumes at low prices.

In the longer term, permanent reallocation of water away from agriculture — whether directly, through reduced allocations, or indirectly, through higher prices — is inevitable. This creates a dilemma for the nation. On the one hand, conversion to more efficient farming methods to reduce water demand could be expensive and, in effect, dilute the dominant role of the agricultural sector in Israel's politics and economy (Frey and Naff 1985; Starr and Stoll 1988). Although this role may be out of proportion with the sector's economic significance, it also has a long history related to the Zionist ideology of a Jewish proletariat working (and, therefore, justifying possession of) the land and to national pride in "making the desert bloom." Finally, for Israel (as for every other country in the Middle East), military security is based in part on a domestic food supply sufficient to feed the population in times of emergency.

On the other hand, agriculture is decreasing in significance in Israel's economy. This situation parallels international trends toward slower growth in irrigated agriculture, with most gains in production now expected to come from existing rather than new supplies of water

(Postel 1991; WRI 1992). The eventual resolution of this dilemma appears to lie with the full substitution of reclaimed wastewater for fresh water in agriculture, provided that high enough standards are applied to the water; salt-tolerant, high-value crops are selected; and appropriate irrigation methods are used.

Projections of Water Use

Projections of future water use in Israel vary significantly. One set of projections implies steady growth in consumption to 2025 (Gabbay 1992). According to Gabbay's (1992) report, which was a component of Israel's national report submitted to the Earth Summit, the greatest absolute and relative growth in water consumption is projected for the agriculture sector; only the industrial sector shows no significant growth in water use. These assumptions assume increasing availability of water in the region, a condition that is highly unlikely without major water-sharing agreements and importation of water. It is also a scenario that would be very costly to the Israeli economy.

A rather different, and more realistic, set of projections has been prepared by Tahal as part of a water master plan. Although the Tahal projections show substantial growth in water use by the domestic and industrial sectors to the year 2000, agricultural consumption is expected to remain constant. (These projections refer to fresh water; brackish and recycled water are excluded.) Tahal's projections include Ministry of Agriculture plans to maintain agricultural water consumption at 1 300 Mm^3 annually. These projections seem the more reasonable because, in the wake of reduced allocations and higher prices, agricultural water consumption in 1991 fell below 1 000 Mm^3 for the first time since the 1950s.

Projections of water use in the Occupied Palestinian Territories are surprisingly rare, presumably because water use is so restricted by the Israelis. Rogers (1994), for example, combines data for the West Bank with those for Jordan, and most others refer to increases in only general terms. Awartani (1994) and Moore (1992) represent exceptions to this trend. Moore (1992) deals with the political uncertainty by postulating two scenarios — one in which no final settlement has occurred and the status quo continues, and the other in which a Palestinian State is

created with some measure of cooperation. Based on projected population growth and possible expansion in each of the three main consuming sectors, he comes up with the projections of water use presented in
Table 6. For comparison, his projections for Israel, identical for the two
scenarios, are also shown.

Awartani (1994) uses a somewhat more disaggregate approach in
allowing for tourism, for water losses, and for improvements in irrigation
efficiency. His projections assume some kind of peace settlement, but
not necessarily an independent Palestinian State. Awartani's population projections for the year 2000 (his full analysis goes to 2005) are
comparable to those of Moore's independence scenario — about 10%
below Moore for Gaza but about 10% higher for the West Bank. His
expected aggregate water use for both parts of the Occupied Palestinian
Territories together, however, is only 371 Mm^3 (497 Mm^3 in 2005),
33% below what Moore projects.

Published projections of water use may summarize (or deliberately
conceal) most of the underlying research. It is, nevertheless, remarkable
that all of the projections available are, to one degree or another, top-
down, aggregate forecasts in which water use is econometrically related
to sector growth, population, and a few other variables. With the partial
exception of Awartani's (1994) approach to irrigation water, the

Table 6. Projected annual water use in Israel and
the Occupied Territories, year 2000.

	Population (thousands)	Total water use (Mm^3)	Per capita domestic water use (Mm^3)
Scenario 1: No final settlement			
Israel	7 040	2 044	104
West Bank	1 330	150	50
Gaza	921	50	
Scenario 2: Independent Palestinian State			
Israel	7 040	2 044	104
West Bank	1 737	476	80
Gaza Strip	1 202	80	

Source: Moore (1992).

alternative of working from the bottom up with disaggregated, end-use specific projections does not seem to have been considered. Bottom-up projections require a large database, as end-uses of water must be defined as finely as possible, and then technical, economic, and social forces impinging upon each end-use must be taken into account. Although both types of projection have their uses, over the longer term bottom-up approaches have proven far superior in the case of energy (Robinson 1990), and it is likely that they would also be better for water. Among other things, bottom-up methods are more capable of identifying turning points, and they are less constrained by history. They also tend to bring out, rather than bury, conservation opportunities. For all of these reasons, bottom-up projections would be particularly applicable to water futures in Israel and the Occupied Palestinian Territories.

Quite a different approach to the problem of projecting future requirements is suggested by Shuval (1992). He believes that peace depends upon "the principle of a sufficient, fair, and equitable allocation of essential baseline water for domestic, urban, industrial and fresh food use, much of which would be from sources within the territory of each partner" (1992, p. 41). Shuval then suggests that the basic allocation for all uses except fresh food should be 10 m^3/person-year, and that another 25 m^3/person-year should be allocated for growing fresh food. Other agriculture would depend upon recycled water. Based on these assumptions, he calculates "baseline needs [for fresh water] to assure water security" as shown in Table 7.

These demands for fresh water are much more modest than those usually projected. Although Shuval admits that they are attainable only

Table 7. Population and water-consumption projections (years 2005 and 2020) under a Water-for-Peace Plan.

	Population (millions)		Water use (Mm^3/year)	
	2005	2020	2005	2020
Palestinians	3	5	375	625
Israelis	7	10	875	1 250

Source: Shuval (1992).

if "coupled with sound measures of water conservation," they, nevertheless, provide a more manageable target, and one less threatening to either political or ecological stability. In effect, Shuval has taken the "equitable and reasonable utilization" formula that appears in so many model treaties for water and has stated that in the case of domestic use it means "equal." Only once the minimum water requirements are met (and Shuval believes that they alone will pretty well exhaust supplies for the Israelis, Jordanians, and Palestinians) can more sophisticated interpretations of those formulae come into play.

Shuval's suggestion for a baseline security approach is intermediate between the use of projections and the use of scenarios in identifying possible water futures. A similar approach is suggested by Elias Salameh, a noted Jordanian hydrologist, who is quoted (in Vesilind 1993, p. 59) as saying:

> We should take what we need for domestic purposes first, and then use the rest for irrigation, not the reverse. We have a crisis because we are not able to put enough investment into industrialization, so we rely on agriculture, which needs less investment and more water.

Salameh is talking about Jordan, but his words apply equally well to Israel and the Occupied Palestinian Territories. A still more radical approach called the "soft-water path," which starts with scenarios rather than projections, is described in Chapter 7 with other aspects of planning.

Implications for the Political Situation

Although our main discussion of water and the Israeli–Palestinian struggle appears in Chapter 6 and Part III, it is appropriate to add a few paragraphs here to identify some of the political implications of the special role that water has played and continues to play in Israel's economy and social structure. The fact is that current levels of water use in Israel, both in urban and in rural areas, would be totally unsustainable were Israel not currently drawing just over 35% of its total fresh-water supplies and 50% of its drinking water from sources that originate in the West Bank (Benvenisti and Gvirtzman 1993). Most of that water continues to be drawn, as it was in the pre-1967 period, from wells within Israel proper. That is, vertical wells are drilled within the Green

Line to reach the Mountain Aquifer and bring water to the surface for irrigation and other uses. Israel draws roughly 450 Mm^3/year from these wells, which is about three-quarters of what the aquifers can supply on a renewable basis. Such wells are consistent with international law but, as will be discussed later, some of the provisions applied on the Palestinian side of the Green Line to ensure maximum flow into the aquifers are legally and morally questionable.

Israel would undoubtedly face immediate water shortages and significant curtailment of its economic development if it lost control of West Bank water-resource supplies in a sudden or disruptive manner. The West Bank, then, has become a critical source of water for Israel, and some observers argue that this fact may actually outweigh other political and strategic factors in its continued occupation (Anderson 1988). It is important to realize that these problems arise strictly from consumption within the Green Line; they have little or nothing to do with consumption by the settlers, which is, in principle, a separate issue.

Although a more complete discussion of the Israeli's supposed "hydraulic imperative" (Calleigh 1983) is included in Chapter 8, it is apparent even at this stage that the same steps outlined in the foregoing to rationalize the economy's use of water could also reduce or eliminate the need for Israel to transfer water from the West Bank for consumption elsewhere in the country. To date, Israel has clearly given priority to its own water needs at the expense of those of the Palestinians. Reductions in water allocated to Israeli agriculture could be coupled with increases to the Occupied Palestinian Territories. Such action is indicated as much by economics as by justice. The West Bank remains far more rural than Israel, with agriculture accounting for almost one-quarter of its gross domestic output and one-eighth of its employment (see Table 5 on p. 75). Comparable figures for Gaza are just under 20% for both output and employment. Moreover, whereas Israel already has 95% of potential irrigable land under irrigation, that same proportion for the West Bank is variously estimated at only 20–30%, and for the Gaza Strip at 55% (Elmusa 1993b).[5] (Land irrigated by Israeli settlers in

---

[5] Lesch (1992) states that only 6% of West Bank land is irrigated. The difference seems to arise because Elmusa divided the area irrigated by the area estimated to be irrigable; Lesch divided by the total area farmed — another example of the care that must be taken with statistics in this region.

the Territories is excluded from all of these figures.) Put more formally, the marginal-value product of a cubic metre of water in Palestinian agriculture is much higher than in Israeli agriculture.

Ironically, then, while Israel needs to transfer water out of agriculture, Palestinians need to transfer water in. Such a transfer, however, is feasible only if the Palestinians have access to a greater share of both surface and underground water, which is the subject of Chapter 6. Before confronting distribution issues, which represent the third and culminating crisis of Israeli water policy, we must complete our examination of the crisis facing water quantity by considering forces that could reduce water use (mainly conservation) and forces that could increase it even higher (mainly population growth and global climatic change). In addition, we must review the ecological crisis, which is treated in Chapter 5. Only then can we adequately address the question of the "equitable and reasonable" sharing of water between Israelis and Palestinians.

End-Use Conservation

Contrary to the typical approach, demand management (including pricing) and not supply augmentation should be the first topic discussed when developing water plans or strategies. In many ways, Middle Eastern nations have implicitly observed this principle for many years. Centuries ago, the peoples of the desert learned how to make use of every drop of water. Today, with the exception of the agricultural sector, nations in the Middle East are remarkably sparing in their water use. Per-capita withdrawals in Israel are only about 25%, and in Jordan only about 17%, of those in the United States or Canada. Nevertheless, all of the countries in the region are using much more water than they need to, and enormous potential exists to increase efficiency in the use of water and to stimulate greater conservation.[6] The problem, to quote

---

[6] "Efficiency" and "conservation" are commonly used synonymously, but, strictly speaking, the former refers to minimizing inputs to achieve a given output whereas the latter includes changes in the output. Less formally, efficiency deals with how you accomplish a task; conservation includes changes in the task. Demand management (or demand-side management) is the general name applied to measures or inducements aimed at reducing water use, whether by increasing efficiency or altering habits and patterns of use.

Thomas Naff, is not that these nations are inefficient but "that they are
not as efficient as the crisis and the scarcity requires them to be" (Naff
1990, p. 170).

In the first chapter, reference was made to the difficulty of defining water consumption, because much of what may appear to be consumption returns to a watercourse. That reference was in terms of the
physical definition of consumption; equally difficult, and more important for this chapter, is the economic definition. Water requirements
are often stated as if they were fixed quantities. Except for those minimum amounts needed for human survival (which are a tiny fraction of
water use), "requirements" are highly conditioned by the technical
options available, the availability of other inputs (labour, capital), the
quality of the water, and, most importantly, by water policies and by the
price of water. In other words, what appear to be requirements really
reflect specific short-run conditions of particular end-users at particular
points in time. The more appropriate term in economics is "demand,"
which is less a technical coefficient than it is a complex relationship in
which the amount of water demanded by end-users is seen as a function
of price and other economic variables against a background set by government (and possibly international donor agency) policies and programs. Depending upon those other variables, end-users may shift inputs
to increase or decrease the efficiency of water use, alter their patterns of
water use, or conceivably even shift out of water-intensive activities.

The need to reallocate water was discussed in the foregoing. This
section will demonstrate that, even in the absence of reallocation, there
are many ways to promote greater efficiency and conservation in water
use. Water efficiency in Israel and the Occupied Territories lags behind
the best practices achievable except in irrigation. Appropriate policies
and programs will be discussed under the subheadings of alternative
price structures for water and then conservation in, respectively, residential uses, commercial and industrial uses, and municipal systems.
Because it has been discussed in Chapter 3, irrigation will not be treated
here. Apart from irrigation, farms consist of households (analogous to
residential uses) and processing plants (analogous to industrial
operations).

The following subsections barely introduce a subject that is the topic of an extensive body of literature, and no attempt is made to deal with the range of policies, education and awareness campaigns, training schemes, incentives, and other features that must be included in a full water-conservation program. Suffice it to say that neither water supply nor water conservation should be approached as exclusively technical problems. They do have technical dimensions and economic dimensions, but in many instances the most important dimensions are social or institutional (or both) (Brooks and Peters 1988; Postel 1993; Sadler 1993; World Bank 1993b). Many well-conceived, demand-side management programs have failed because of a lack of attention to institutional and social dimensions. Furthermore, except for changes in prices and price structures, none of the measures discussed in the following will be very effective if governments at all levels do not insist — and insist very strongly — on higher levels of water conservation and water efficiency, and if they do not demonstrate their resolve by highly visible conservation in their own operations.

Alternative Price Structures for Water

Because water is the highest valued input to the Israeli economy, many feel it should be priced accordingly. This means a number of things. Most obviously, those who use water should pay the full cost, capital as well as operating, to extract, treat as necessary, and deliver water. Less obviously, price structures should reflect what economists call the long-run incremental or marginal cost, which is the cost of supplying the last unit of water demanded. In this way, users will be forced to recognize the cost their demand imposes on the water-delivery system. When the system is operating correctly, the same principles mean that prices will also reflect opportunity costs, or the value of water in alternative uses. Although an exception to full opportunity cost pricing may be made on the grounds of equity for direct household consumption (analogous to lifeline rates for electricity), the quantities needed to provide everyone with enough water for basic needs are so small relative to other uses that they have little effect on final results.

The same principles that argue for pricing water as an input also argue for charges for disposing of wastewater. Appropriate charges would vary by volume and toxicity of the discharge — with some credit offered for those wastes, such as sewage, that have value in themselves. As with water, the objective is to ensure that households, industrial firms, and farms take account of the cost their operations impose on the system. Unfortunately, charges cannot be applied very effectively to nonpoint sources of wastewater, such as runoff from farms. Farmers, however, can pay a fee to reflect the degradation in quality that occurs before the runoff reaches a watercourse or aquifer.

The rationale for pricing water in a way that reflects its true cost has been expressed in many reports and is supported by a great deal of evidence (Pearse et al. 1985; Brooks et al. 1990; Postel 1993). The essential point is that, beyond the amounts needed for basic human and household needs, water demand is elastic, and notably so in the case of irrigation. If water is cheap, more will be used; if it is expensive, less will be used. If discharge is cheap (or unregulated), wastewater flows will be high; if expensive, flows will be reduced. Neglect of the elasticity of water demand in current pricing structures makes the whole water system inherently inefficient from an economic perspective. The low prices create excessive demand for water supply or discharge; force up government expenditures to provide infrastructure to meet this demand; and inhibit conservation and recycling efforts.

An ideal pricing system for water includes two elements: one is a charge per cubic metre consumed; the other is a fixed charge per month (Pearse et al. 1985). The fixed charge covers hook-up costs and other overhead needed to operate the system. The charge per unit used can be set in many ways but ideally equals the marginal cost of water supply. Assuming increasing costs of supply, which is the case throughout the Middle East, most economists would favour a price structure in which unit charges for water increase with consumption, commonly referred to as increasing block rates (Brooks et al. 1990). Although not necessarily appropriate for lower income communities where households have to share water taps (Whittington 1992), as in parts of the Gaza Strip, increasing block rates would certainly be appropriate for all users in Israel and many users in the cities of the West Bank. The price structure can be made to reflect marginal costs even more closely by increasing prices during the summer when demands tend to peak and supplies come from more limited and expensive sources. Alternatively, charges could be reduced for users who can use water during off-peak periods or who can accept lower quality water that requires less treatment.

Any approach to efficient price structures for water requires that meters to measure water volume, and other meters to measure at least the volume of wastewater, be installed at every billing point. Fortunately, water meters are ubiquitous in Israel and in those parts of the Occupied Palestinian Territories served by piped-water systems. They are found on a unit-by-unit basis within apartment buildings and (for control if not billing purposes) on a process-by-process basis within some industrial plants. Farms are also metered for water use, but the low prices for water mitigate the effect. Wastewater meters are less common, and charges for wastewater disposal are only now being considered.

No matter how well designed the price structure, and even if price levels are set high enough to cover all costs, supplemental policies and programs will be necessary to capture the full range of conservation and efficiency options. The supplemental measures are necessary in part because of market failures, in part because of a lack of information on conservation measures or a lack of capital to pay for them, and in part because the market system is only one of the signals to which consumers respond (Brooks et al. 1990; Sadler 1993). The Department of Water in Jerusalem is becoming something of a model in its use of a variety of incentives to induce consumers to reduce water use. The most common supplemental measures include information services, technical assistance, and financial incentives or disincentives. In most cases, the key is to find those measures that will not only reduce water use but will also be attractive and convenient for the water user to adopt. In the jargon of economics, this implies that they have "low transaction costs."

Full-cost pricing of water, however, may not be the panacea that many make it out to be for the Middle East. To date, there has not been a detailed study undertaken on the social, cultural, economic, and environmental impacts of full-cost water pricing. Any move toward higher water prices — particularly in the Occupied Territories — must be accompanied by a comprehensive impact assessment, which would include issues of competitiveness and social impacts (including impacts on woman and the disenfranchised).

A Note on Discriminatory Pricing — Much has been written about the discriminatory pricing policies (as well as the restrictions on allocations, drilling of wells, and so on; see Chapter 6) of the Israelis with respect to the Palestinian population in the Occupied Territories. The water prices in the Territories vary considerably, depending on whether consumers are supplied from local sources or are linked to Mekorot's system. Prices range from a low of $0.25/m^3 in small households in Jericho District, which are supplied by local production sources, to a high of over $3.00/m^3 in Nablus District (outside the municipality) for larger consumers. Mekorot charges municipalities in the Territories 1.8 New Israel Shekels (NIS) — about $0.90/m^3 — and 2.1 NIS for individuals, whereas it charges Israeli settlements only 0.5 NIS/m^3 (and 0.3 NIS in Gaza). These prices are reflected in the per-capita water consumption figures for Israeli settlers and the Palestinians; settlers consume roughly 8–10 times more water than the Palestinians. The issue is not the absolute price that Palestinians pay for water, which may indeed reflect real costs. The issue is one of blatant and formalized discrimination on the part of the Israelis.

Conservation in Residential Uses

Residential uses of water tend to be less price elastic than other uses, partly because these uses are essential for life and partly because (except for the poorest people in developing countries) water does not account for a very large part of household budgets. The major uses for water in housing with internal plumbing are toilet flushing, clothes washing, and showers/baths. (Again, excepting the poorest of the poor, the proportion of water used for drinking and cooking is all but negligible.) None of these end-uses is individually large compared with agricultural or industrial use of water, but significant overall gains are attainable from simple technologies and minor changes in habits, even with housing that is already efficient (Brooks and Peters 1988). For example, low-flow household faucets cut use to 0.5 L/min without sacrificing performance, a saving of up to 85%; low- and variable-flow toilets can cut water use by 40%.[7] For those housing units with external space, lawn and garden watering typically dominates total water use, but is more responsive to price than other uses (Brooks et al. 1990). If hot water is saved, the gains are multiplied: energy as well as water.

Total residential water savings from conservation (again on a North American basis) with existing technology is one-third to one-half, with the higher levels applying to hot water. The potential for a citywide retrofit of plumbing fixtures has been demonstrated by the experience of Phoenix, Arizona, in the United States, which is also located in a water-deficient region with characteristically subsidized water prices. Based on a 50-year planning program, 3% of total water use could be saved with the benefit–cost ratio for the water utility exceeding 2.6 and that for the community reaching 15.5 (data cited in World Bank 1993b). Even more striking are results for Perth, Australia, where a citywide retrofit of toilets with 6-L/3-L dual flush systems would cut domestic water use by more than 10% (Sadler 1993).

High-quality service at what appear to be modest rates of consumption can be found in Singapore, where domestic use is only 160 L of water per person-day, despite high incomes and, except in times of drought, an apparent absence of direct controls (Sadler 1993). Singapore does, however, add a conservation levy onto water rates for all households using more than 20 m³/month (roughly the equivalent of 160 L/day in a four-person family). Domestic use in Perth, Australia, which has a climate similar to that of southern California, is about three times that of Singapore. When Perth was faced with drought conditions, residents dropped their consumption by 40% and, even after the end of the drought, per-capita use remained 30% below what it had been (Sadler 1993).

Market failure from misplaced incentives is common in the residential sector. For example, firms or agencies building housing units do not, in general, continue to own or manage them. Given market and

[7] Although these savings are based on comparisons in North America, which might overrate savings in Israel because of higher existing standards of water efficiency, this will not always be true. Daniell (1993) reports that toilets in Jerusalem commonly use 9 L per flush, which is high by any standard.

political pressures to build at a low unit cost, builders will not likely include more water-efficient plumbing or drought-resistant landscaping if it is significantly more expensive. Housing, therefore, is the sector where regulations for minimum efficiency standards for equipment that utilizes water are most appropriate. In the case of Israel, where pressure exists to build housing for newly arriving immigrants, the need for such regulations is that much greater.

If the experience with energy can be taken as a model, regulations not only change purchase patterns but also stimulate manufacturing research so that the equipment available is improved over time. This impact is enhanced if only end-use efficiency is mandated (for example, water flow per minute or per flush) and manufacturers are left free to determine how best to achieve that level. Regulation is usually most effective if coupled with information programs for every part of the market: producers, designers, builders, financiers, and residents. For example, the Australian Water Resources Council promoted a labeling scheme for plumbing appliances with three simple categories: A for an acceptable level of efficiency; AA for a level 25% lower than A; and AAA for a level 25% lower than AA (Sadler 1993). Other measures can also be considered, as with design awards.

Special forms of government intervention are required to stimulate improvements in the water efficiency of existing housing, which is large and typically well behind state-of-the-art techniques. As a rule, it is more expensive to retrofit existing systems than to build new ones. In this case, regulation can help by insisting on changes at the time property is sold, and information programs can stimulate building owners to install some of the less costly measures themselves. Some form of financial incentive for conversion to more water-efficient systems may also be appropriate for existing housing. Even then, total potential savings are only about two-thirds as great as with new housing (Brooks and Peters 1988).

Conservation in Commercial and Industrial Uses

Commercial and industrial use is heavily concentrated in a few sectors, and each sector is significantly responsive to price signals. Office and retail buildings generally have relatively low levels of water use, but restaurants, hotels, and certain commercial establishments, such as laundries, use a great deal of water, much of it hot. Most of the technologies appropriate for residences are equally appropriate for the hospitality industry, and others, such as self-closing valves, can be added. In North America, savings of 10–25% have typically been obtained simply by better management and very low-cost adjustments to the system. Savings of up to 50% have been achieved with more substantial retrofits, such as dual water systems (one for fresh water and one for recycled water (Okun 1991)), which have paybacks of a year or less at current water prices. It is not possible to estimate what the savings might be in Israel, but even casual observations indicate wide differences in water efficiency at different hotels.

Industrial use of water varies widely both between and within sectors. The largest single industrial use of water by far is for cooling, mainly for thermal (coal, gas, or oil-fired or nuclear) electrical generation. (The huge, truncated, conical structures seen near electrical power plants are cooling towers.) Because of the availability of residual oil (heavy oil left at the end of the refining process) or low-grade crude oil, generating stations in the Middle East are generally fuelled by oil. Israel is an exception; for security reasons, coal is the preferred fuel. In many parts of the world, cooling results in high rates of water use. (For example, Ontario Hydro coal-fired stations use a "once-through" cooling system that requires about 14 m^3 of water per megawatt of capacity for every hour of operation. All but a small volume of the water is returned to the watercourse, warmer but otherwise unaltered.)

In Israel, electrical generating stations have been located along the coast to use seawater for cooling — an expensive option (because the corrosiveness of seawater requires the use of special materials), but one that avoids the use of fresh water. Plants constructed in Gaza could follow the same practice. Any electrical generating plants Israel builds further inland, however, and any plants built on the West Bank, would have to adopt alternative cooling systems. The choice of a cooling system is complex, involving engineering, economic, and ecological considerations. For example, systems are available that require much less water throughput but that result in higher rates of evaporation and, therefore, losses. As well, some cooling towers create plumes of vapour or are noisy and can be a hazard to migrating birds. Suffice it to say that any new electrical stations, on either side of the Green Line but distant from the coast, should adopt designs that minimize water losses consistent with other objectives.

Among manufacturing industries of importance in Israel, the food and beverage sector and the chemical, petrochemical, and refinery sectors are large water users, although they undertake a great deal of recirculation to minimize total water requirements. (They are, unfortunately, less careful about wastewater discharge.) Government policy, which required that specific (per unit of production) water-use norms be established for every industrial sector, and which enforced these norms by quadrupling the price of water for amounts consumed in excess of the norms, was highly instrumental in effecting major gains in industrial water efficiency (Whitman 1988). Further savings were effected as industry found ways to use brackish water; today, more than one-quarter of the industrial water used in Israel is saline (Schwarz 1992).

Again, in the absence of sector-by-sector information about output and water use, which is not published, it is difficult to compare existing efficiencies and potential savings in Israeli industries compared with those in other countries. Such techniques as process metering, mapping of pipes, timers, pressure reductions, and heat recovery (to eliminate the need for cooling water), but not including recirculation or process change, have yielded savings of 30–50%; if recirculation and process change are included, savings have reached 90% (Brooks and Peters 1988; Postel 1993). Although higher savings could be expected when dealing with the water-inefficient plants in North America than with the relatively water-efficient plants in Israel, it must also be remembered that the required investments were determined to be cost effective at prices well under those in Israel. Japan, not particularly water rich, has cut its industrial water use by nearly one-quarter, and increased its output per litre by $3 1/2$ times, over the last 25 years (Postel 1993). In summary, there is no longer any question that industrial water consumption is significantly elastic to price and also responsive to government policy.

Currently, industrial water use in the Occupied Palestinian Territories is small and, given the limited access to capital and technology over the past 25 years, likely rather inefficient in its use of water. Electricity in the Gaza Strip is largely supplied by Israeli generating systems and in the West Bank, by Israeli and Jordanian systems. (No disaggregated data have been found on this sector.) If economic development proceeds as hoped under autonomy, investments would be expected in food processing, mineral processing, and possibly cement. It will be essential that such investments pay particular attention to water use and water efficiency. Fortunately, those involved with the nascent Palestinian industrial sector are fully aware of the limitations imposed by water.

Except for large buildings, where policies and programs similar to those for residential uses are appropriate, it is difficult to generalize about policies appropriate to commercial and industrial uses. Each sector needs to be studied on its own. The one thing that is clear is that higher prices and more carefully designed price schedules will have a strong effect. The effect will be even stronger if supplemented with information and possibly low-cost financing aimed at smaller industrial and commercial establishments. Owners typically lack both information and capital, and they may not even know how they are using water, or to what extent they are degrading its quality. A program to provide water (and energy) audits at cost might prove highly effective.

Conservation in Municipal Systems

Municipal use of water includes a great variety of end-uses, such as fighting fires, street cleaning, irrigating parks, public swimming pools, etc. Opportunities for conservation and use of recycled water are evident. The most important aspect of the municipal system, however, is the system itself: reducing pressure, valve maintenance, and, above all, repairing leaks. Losses of 10–15% of the water in municipal systems are quite common in industrialized countries. With older systems, and in the cities of developing countries, including those of the Occupied Palestinian Territories, losses can exceed 50%. The water-supply system is either twice as large as it needs to be or it could serve twice as many people. These cities suffer all the problems of those in industrial countries and must cope with many more illegal connections, anti- quated billing systems, and half-completed construction.

Identification and repair of leaks in municipal water distribution systems are not cheap, but they are generally one of the most cost- effective ways of increasing the supply of water. Cities in all parts of the world have found it possible to reduce losses using techniques that range from labour-intensive tracing of systems and measuring water flows from place to place to the use of technology-intensive instruments that can sense leaks and pinpoint where repairs will be most effective. Typical water savings from leak-detection/repair programs in cities of develop- ing countries have been on the order of 20% in Manila, 15% in São Paulo, and 30–50% (estimated) in Bombay (World Bank 1993b). Singapore, with a population of under a million, maintains a staff of 50 people for continuous leak detection and waste prevention (World Bank 1993b).

Other forms of municipal water conservation are less important for their absolute savings than for their highly visible effects. Water- saving urban design and landscaping are good examples of uses where the selection of drought-resistant species and use of water-efficient equipment can be seen by almost everyone (Sadler 1993). Less visible but equally effective are moisture sensors in soil that indicate exactly how much water is needed. In Israel, most municipal landscaping already uses recycled water but the efficiency of use could still be improved.

There is little point in talking about policies for municipal sys- tems. For the most part, all of the necessary tools are within the control of city officials. Senior levels of government can help by providing tech- nical and, probably most important, financial assistance. Once an effort is made, savings can come quickly. Jerusalem cut its water use by 14% between 1989 and 1991 through a combination of water-saving devices, leak repair, pressure reduction, and more efficient irrigation of city parks despite an increase in population (Daniell 1993; Postel 1993). If private companies are involved in water supply, the same kinds of measures can be applied to reduce "unaccounted for" water. For example, the pay- ment owed to private companies can be reduced in proportion to the water lost in the system, and norms can be established below which the companies risk losing their rights to deliver water. Finally, municipalities have at their disposal numerous means to influence public attitudes and to instruct people of all ages about ways to increase water-use efficiency.

Longer Term Prospects for Changes in Water Balances

Water scarcity in Israel becomes more acute when one considers demand and supply in the context of future socioeconomic and ecological changes that may occur. The socioeconomic factor with the greatest potential impact is population growth; the ecological factor of greatest concern is global climatic change.

Demographic Change

Israel's current population is just over 5 million; population growth is 1.6% per year in Israel, and the government maintains a pronatalist policy. Immigration of Soviet and Ethiopian Jews to Israel will likely increase the population over the next few years, if not the natural growth rate.

The Palestinian population of the West Bank (including East Jerusalem) and Gaza is about 1.7 million (Israel, Central Bureau of Statistics 1992). The rate of population growth is close to 3% per year. A Palestinian state on the West Bank could draw back an additional 750 thousand to 1 million people (Israel, Central Bureau of Statistics 1992), most of them from refugee camps (which currently house close to 800 thousand Palestinians in the West Bank and Gaza, Jordan, Lebanon, and Syria). The numbers could increase with new conflicts within the Arab world, which provides a home for much of the Palestinian diaspora. Lesch (1992) suggests that 20 thousand new housing units should be built in the eastern highlands of the West Bank in each of the first 5 years after an independent Palestinian entity is created. The objective would be to house the 600 thousand people currently living in substandard conditions in refugee camps in Israel and

Jordan. Although not all of this housing would result in a net increase
in population, the improved quality of life would certainly be reflected
in greater water use than at present.

Finally, to complete the picture, although Jordan and Syria are
relatively lightly populated at present, growth rates of 3.8% are exhibited by both countries. Even present population levels strain the available resources (in Jordan) or the existing infrastructure (in Syria).
Population growth can only increase pressure on water (and other)
resources. The results of these rates of population growth are shown in
Table 8.

Combining these rates of population growth with projections that
assume no changes in water policies, technology or consumption patterns yields truly frightening deficits. By 2020, the existing Israeli water
deficit of 200–250 Mm^3/year could grow to around 500 Mm^3/year in the
absence of immigration and to twice that figure if one assumes an additional million immigrants (Fishelson 1994). Palestinian immigration
and natural population growth would, under these assumptions, roughly
double the current water deficit in the Occupied Palestinian Territories
of 100 Mm^3/year.

In addition to internal deficits, problems of water supply and
demand in Israel must be placed within the broader regional context.
Jordan is projecting a water deficit of 350 Mm^3/year or 2–2.5 times this
amount based on its rate of population growth and immigration. Syria
and Lebanon are the only countries that could continue to expand
water use for some time in concert with population and economic

Table 8. Population (millions) of selected Middle Eastern countries
from 1960 to 1990, and projected to 1995 and 2025.

	1960	1970	1980	1990	1995	2025
Israel	2.1	3.0	3.9	4.8	4.9[a]	6.9
Jordan	1.7	2.3	3.2	4.2	4.7	9.9
Lebanon	1.9	2.5	2.7	2.9	3.0	4.7
Syria	4.6	6.3	9.0	12.3	15.0	34.1

Source: WRI (1989), Fishelson (1992b), and Israel, Central Bureau of Statistics
(1992).

[a] Israel's population already exceeds 5 million.

growth, although both countries already face local shortages in urban areas.

Deficits of the size and duration suggested above are not sustainable. Furthermore, it might not even be possible to supply sufficient water except during an occasional year of high rainfall. Projections, however, should not be treated as predictions. Their main purpose is to emphasize the impossibility of a business-as-usual scenario and, by implication, the need for changes in policy, technology, and consumption patterns.

Global Climatic Change

Magnifying demographic pressures on the water system is the spectre of global climatic change that could reduce the amount of water available to the region's rapidly growing population. Anthropogenic emissions of certain gases, most notably carbon dioxide (CO_2), methane (CH_4), chlorofluorocarbons (CFCs), nitrous oxides (NO_x), and water vapour, all contribute to a general process known as the "greenhouse effect," or global warming. The term "greenhouse gas" has been applied to atmospheric gases that are relatively transparent to incoming shortwave solar radiation but that absorb the long-wave radiation from the surface of the Earth and re-emit it downward, warming the surface of the Earth and the lower atmosphere. Emissions of these gases are increasing primarily as a result of increased fossil fuel combustion. The focus to date has been on CO_2, released from the burning of coal and other carbon-based fuels and from the burning and decay of the world's forests.

Since 1958, when measurements of CO_2 in the atmosphere began, its concentration has increased from 315 to 353 ppm. A doubling of CO_2 from preindustrial levels, expected sometime next century, could result in global temperature increases on the order of 1.5–4.5°C (and much greater in the high-latitude zones of the northern hemisphere). Concentrations of the other greenhouse gases, currently at much lower concentrations than CO_2, but more potent in their ability to promote heating and thus potentially cause more damage, are increasing even more rapidly. CH_4, which is emitted from wetlands, rice paddies, livestock, and warming permafrost, is increasing at the rate of 1% per year (compared with 0.4% per year for CO_2). CFCs have been increasing at 5% per year, although with the Montreal Protocol, which set international limits on the emissions of CFCs, concentrations of this gas should decrease over the next two decades.

Global warming, if it occurred, would affect the water supply situation in Israel in three ways (Lonergan and Kavanagh 1991; Hillel and Rosenzweig 1992). First, temperatures in the region would likely increase between 15 and 30% over current levels. This would increase evaporation rates by 5–20%, increase the amount of energy needed for space cooling (which would prompt a demand for more electricity, although it would not, necessarily, affect water demand or supply directly), and likely increase the demand for drinking water and water for recreational uses. Second, and more importantly, precipitation would likely decline (although climate models are not consistent in their precipitation projections for the region). This would have obvious implications for the amount of water supplied to replenish streams and recharge aquifers. Third, the variability of precipitation might change, resulting in longer and more severe droughts.

These three potential effects on water availability in the region resulting from global warming are not to be taken lightly. Increased rates of evaporation could have major implications for surface water flow and storage; the seasonality of water availability and water needs throughout the region poses additional problems. Marginal changes in precipitation and evaporation during the rainy winter months are likely to have little effect (except on water storage and recharge), whereas the same changes that are expected during drier months would create problems. More important, however, is the general acceptance by climatic impact analysts that the magnitude and frequency of extreme events are likely to change with global warming. Even if regions are able to adapt to the relatively slow changes in temperature and precipitation patterns, more frequent, and more severe, droughts can also be expected, which would be catastrophic for the region. Given the importance of water to the economies of all countries in this region, it is surprising that so little attention has been paid to the longer term issues of climate change and water availability.

Summary

Water quantity problems in Israel are not so much ecological as economic in origin: from a supply perspective, there is plenty of water available provided you can pay for it; from a demand perspective, the cheaper water is, the more abundantly and wastefully it will be used. By common agreement, the core of the problem in Israel is misallocation of water. Most people, and particularly farmers, pay too little for water. As a result, water conservation is more a slogan than the imperative it should be. To exacerbate the problem, there is a possibility that less water will be available in the future, through a combination of increased variability in precipitation and higher rates of evaporation. Very high rates of natural population growth, coupled with significant immigration, will further strain the water-supply systems. These facts and their connection to declining water availability are becoming more widely known, and the time is likely not far in the future when permanent reallocation of water and new pricing structures for water will be instituted in Israel, which is not to say that either will be accomplished without spilling a great deal of political blood and without insistence on change from the public.

The need to shift from supply-side to demand-side approaches to deal with water resource problems is not just an Israeli-Palestinian or even Middle Eastern issue; it is worldwide. The World Bank has already indicated that the cost per cubic metre of water for tomorrow's supply projects will typically be two to three times today's cost (Biswas 1993). Thus, it is hardly surprising that Mohammed El-Ashry (1991, p. 234), head of the World Bank's Environment Department, concludes that:

> The traditional strategy of responding to water shortages by increasing water supplies through capital-intensive water transfer or diversion projects has clearly reached its financial, legal and environmental limits. Attention must now shift from development to management.

El-Ashry's view reflects a major shift in the World Bank's approach to water resources management, one that is bound to reverberate throughout the entire international-aid community. Where the World Bank goes, others are sure to follow.

CHAPTER 5

WATER QUALITY:
THE ECOLOGICAL CRISIS

Waters wear the stones.

— Job, 14:19

THE SECOND COMPONENT of Israel's water crisis is less ancient but equally pressing: water quality. This component is part of a growing environmental problem that has been described as a "sharpening struggle" by Brooks and Shadur (1991). Water-quality problems are a result of many factors, three of which deserve to be highlighted: overpumping of aquifers, pollution of watercourses, and the limited size and protection of ecological preserves.

Overpumping of Aquifers

Overpumping of wells causes a decline in the water table. During the recent drought, when aquifers were pumped particularly hard, water levels in aquifers in Israel and in the Occupied Palestinian Territories were typically falling by 10–40 cm/year, a situation that everyone recognized as unsustainable. The term "mining" is used to reflect the fact that a renewable resource was being used in a way that made it nonrenewable.

A decline in the water table has several adverse effects. At a minimum, it adds to pumping costs and increases the amount of energy needed for pumping. More importantly, a lower water table reduces pressure in the aquifer and permits lower quality water to flow inward and contaminate the fresh water of the aquifer. The Coastal Aquifer in its natural state is 3–5 m above sea level, a level that, with the force of gravity, creates an outward pressure that blocks the inflow of seawater. Pumping, or more accurately overpumping, has lowered the fresh water

level below sea level so that this effect is reversed, and salt water from
the Mediterranean can now be found 1–3 km inland. This situation
changed recently with the unusually high rainfall during the winters of
1991 and 1992; it is believed, however, that this is temporary. An indirect effect of overpumping could also become apparent near the Dead
Sea, which is receding as almost all of its fresh-water sources are
diverted to other, mainly agricultural, uses on both sides of the Israeli–
Jordanian border. With the fall in its level below –400 m, pressure
could be so reduced in aquifers flowing into the Rift Valley that the out-
flows and losses of good-quality water from those aquifers will be
increased.

The inflow of seawater magnifies the effects of using and reusing
water for irrigation, resulting in 10% of the wells tapping the Coastal
Aquifer producing water that is too salty for domestic use. This loss of
potable water is growing at a rate of roughly 20 Mm^3/year (*Israel
Environment Bulletin*, Winter 1993). If World Health Organization standards for drinking water were observed in Israel (less than 250 mg of dissolved solids per litre), many more of the coastal wells would be
declared unfit as sources of drinking water (*Israel Environment Bulletin*,
Spring 1991). And this situation is getting worse. Israel's Hydrological
Service estimates that one-fifth of the wells will soon be too salty even
for agricultural irrigation (Gabbay 1992). Worse yet, intruding salty
water corrodes the limy portions of the porous sandstones that make up
the aquifer, so that they become blocked and are reduced in capacity or
even destroyed. Some Israeli hydrologists have begun to argue that,
given population densities along the Israeli coast and in Gaza, there is
no possibility of keeping the Coastal Aquifer free of pollution.
Accordingly, sources of drinking water should be sought elsewhere, with
the Coastal Aquifer being devoted exclusively to agriculture and
industry.

In the case of the Mountain Aquifer, which is the main source of
drinking water for Israel, the problem is not seawater but nearby saline
aquifers that can seep into the overpumped zones. Each of these zones
contains some brackish water. Because it is composed of channels in
limestone ("karst" structures), water (and pollutants) flows more quickly
through the Mountain Aquifer than through sandstone aquifers with

small pores. The Ministry of Environment has proposed that a Mountain Aquifer Authority be established along the lines of the Kinneret Authority, but, to date, the response from the government has been noncommittal.

Water Pollution

Israelis have taken steps toward controlling air pollution, primarily because of the assertiveness of the Ministry of Environment (until 1988 the Environmental Protection Service) in an area where no other ministry had prime responsibility (Whitman 1988). This was not the case with water, where the ministries of Agriculture, of Industry, of Health, and of the Interior have constantly demonstrated support for vested interests and a lack of enthusiasm for protecting water quality. Dumping is common, sometimes directly into watercourses and sometimes into wadis, which allows contaminants to seep into the aquifers with the next rainfall. Cleaning a polluted river is difficult; cleaning a polluted aquifer is infinitely more so and, in some cases, not possible (Goldenberg and Melloul 1992). Only in 1991 were jurisdictional issues over water resolved, with the Ministry of Environment receiving responsibility for toxic and hazardous substances, pest control, and the prevention of nuisances. Some of Israel's major water pollution problems are discussed below.

Agricultural Runoff

Around 400 000 ha of land is being farmed in Israel (about a million acres or 10 times the size of Prince Edward Island). Roughly half of the land is irrigated and half is rain-fed, and 95% is sprayed with pesticides and fertilizers (see text box entitled "Irrigation and the Environment"). Annual inputs include about 875 Mm^3 of water (down from 1 300 in 1984), and 90 000 t of fertilizer (4 400 m^3 or 0.235 t/ha on average) (*Israel Environment Bulletin*, Spring 1993). Given these data, it is no surprise that agricultural runoff is a major nonpoint source of many pollutants, including sediment, phosphorous, nitrogen, and pesticides. The per-hectare use of pesticides and fertilizer in Israel is among the highest in the world, and runoff is correspondingly high. To date, regulations on

Irrigation and the Environment

It is easy to understand why irrigation is popular among farmers. Roughly 18% of the world's cultivated land is irrigated (a total of more than 350 million ha), but this land produces only one-third of the total harvest. Yet, it is becoming increasingly realized that irrigation also produces an array of environmental problems.

Irrigation systems interact with the surrounding environment in many ways, with some effects being positive and some negative, and some impacts flowing from the land to the water and some flowing from the water to the land. Irrigation systems withdraw water from a surface or underground source, affecting the downstream or downflow hydrology. As well, in the construction process, land is normally leveled, either by terracing or by remoulding. Depending upon the design of the irrigation system, water may seep into, or out of, the system, creating problems that are discussed in this section. The most profound problem with irrigation, however, is the tendency, particularly in arid areas, for waterlogging and salinization of soils. Salinity now seriously affects productivity on 7% of the world's irrigated land (20–30 million ha), and this level is thought to be increasing at a rate of over 1 million ha/year (El-Ashry 1991). In the worst cases, large areas of formerly productive land have been rendered sterile, but more commonly the productivity of the land is simply reduced. Similarly, any pollution carried by the irrigation system will flow onto fields when the water is distributed, and pollution from surface (or less commonly underground) sources, pesticides, and fertilizers can flow into the irrigation system. The passage of waterborne pathogens is also commonly encouraged, if not directly spread, by irrigation systems. Inevitably, partly because of the irrigation system itself and partly because of the cultivation patterns it supports, there is a change in ecology, with the replacement of some species of plants and animals by others.

The popularity of irrigation and the increasing size of irrigation systems has forced planners to take more seriously the associated environmental implications. In one such attempt, the International Commission for Irrigation and Drainage has compiled a checklist of some 53 possible impacts of irrigation systems divided into eight categories: hydrology, pollution, soils, sediments, ecology, socioeconomics, health, and ecological imbalances (Mock and Bolton 1991). The purpose of the checklist is to help planners to anticipate (in the case of new irrigation systems) or to diagnose (in the case of existing systems) the type and extent of possible damages and then to adjust the design to reduce the adverse impacts.

pesticide use have been quite relaxed and all but nonexistent for agricultural runoff. Even some irrigation water, for which acceptable standards are well below those of drinking water, is now so contaminated with residues that it is unfit for use. Such problems are anything but inevitable. Practices such as conservation tillage, contour planting, terracing, and filter systems, among others, can control soil erosion and reduce phosphorous and nitrogen runoff by up to 60% (WRI 1992).

Pesticide residues are an added problem. As stated in the *Israel Environment Bulletin* (Spring 1993, p. 8): "The agricultural community represents, for all intents and purposes, a large group of exterminators — but a group which is exempt from the licensing and training requirements of pest-control operators." The entire system for controlling pesticides is complicated by overlapping jurisdictions among (and differing interests of) the ministries of Agriculture, of Health, and of Environment. An official from the Ministry of Environment emphasized that the government controls only pesticide registration and labeling; beyond this, there is no regulation. In contrast, an official from the Ministry of Agriculture claims the ability to trace "almost every molecule that is released" and states flatly that "there is no residue problem" (*Israel Environment Bulletin*, Spring 1993). Both of these statements may exaggerate the situation. On the one hand, new regulations on spraying and disposal came into effect in 1991; they outlaw spraying within 300 m of a water source and prohibit any emptying or rinsing of pesticide containers near watercourses. On the other hand, there are no standards for permissible levels of pesticide residues in drinking water, and food destined for Israeli and Palestinian consumers is known to exceed permitted levels (*Israel Environment Bulletin*, Spring 1993). The Ministry of Health is responsible for monitoring and testing food for local consumption but does so only irregularly. In contrast, food products destined for export are rigorously monitored.

Comparing the tests on food consumed locally with those on exported produce would certainly be instructive. Even tests done on local products, however, are seldom available to the public. Only occasionally do relevant stories make the news; the example of the Ministry of Environment making public its discovery that pesticides were being stored in water-pumping stations on some farms is a rare one. In the past year, the ministries of Environment and of Health seem to be working toward closer collaboration, which might improve the situation (or might just indicate a political alliance against the Ministry of Agriculture). It is still the policy of the Ministry of Health, however, that the results of its water-quality tests are not available to the public. It is for this reason that the Israel Union for Environmental Defense and other public-interest groups have joined in a coalition to secure passage of a Freedom of Information law in Israel.

Two additional problems are unique to the Occupied Territories. First, even if the labeling (which includes directions on use and cautions) is adequate for Israeli farmers, there is no requirement that labels be bilingual, a disadvantage for Arabic-speaking farmers, most of whom live on the Palestinian side of the Green Line. Second, there is a great deal of evidence that pesticides banned in Israel are moved across the Green Line or are exported directly to the Territories, adversely affecting human health and leading to the contamination of watercourses.

The situation is not much better in terms of fertilizer residues than in terms of pesticides. Over the past two decades, nitrate concentrations in the Coastal Aquifer (from both fertilizers and recycling of sewage effluents) have doubled (Gabbay 1992). A 1991 survey by the Hydrological Service of Israel found that one-third of the wells in the country contained nitrates at levels "that would exclude them from drinking purposes according to European standards" (45 mg/L) (*Israel Environment Bulletin*, Spring 1993), a statement that implies that many, if not most, of these wells continue to be sources of drinking water. On the coastal plain, the intensive use of nitrogen fertilizers is responsible for 70% of the nitrates found in the groundwater. The problems are magnified in greenhouses, which are widespread in Israel and in the Occupied Territories. Greenhouses are periodically rinsed with as much as half of the fertilizers going directly into the soil. If built appropriately, the greenhouse can be removed from contact with groundwater and it is possible to reuse the rinse water, but this practice is not yet common. In addition, the widespread poultry-raising operations create their own set of runoff problems. In this case, the water carries manure with a high organic content that should be, but seldom is, recycled.

The growing use of brackish water can increase soil salinity, a problem that is already evident in certain parts of the country (Gabbay 1992). Washing out the salts with fresh water can alleviate local problems, but this is done at the expense of allowing the salts to drain into watercourses or aquifers, potentially causing longer term problems. Regulations have yet to be developed to deal with this problem (except for limitations on the use of brackish water just above sensitive parts of the Coastal Aquifer).

In an otherwise technical article, Vengosh and Rosenthal (1994, p. 389), from Israel's Hydrological Service, condemn the lack of concerted attention being given to the contamination of Israel's water supply by saline sources:

> The newly established groundwater flow regimes have facilitated the migration of saline water bodies, their participation in the active hydrological cycle and the progressive contamination of fresh groundwater. These processes which were not anticipated by planners and water resources managers emphasize that large-scale groundwater exploitation was undertaken without giving sufficient consideration to the occurrence and subsurface migration of saline water and brines.

Drinking Water and Sewage

Piped drinking water and sewer systems are extensive throughout Israel, as is piped water in urban areas of the Occupied Palestinian Territories. With the support of a World Bank loan, the water and sewage system in Israel expanded rapidly in the 1970s and early 1980s. Today, 93% of municipal wastewater within Israel is collected in sewers, and nearly 80% receives secondary treatment. As a result of several billion dollars in grants and loans from Japan, sanitation systems are also being extended in the West Bank and Gaza.

These apparently positive statistics, however, obscure serious problems. As is the case in many North American cities, most of the sewage collection and treatment systems have either begun to deteriorate or cannot handle growing demand. Only about one-third of the sewage is treated to a high standard, about 10% ends up in septic tanks, and another 10% receives no treatment at all. The city of Jerusalem still discharges half of its wastewater untreated into dry riverbeds.

Fortunately, the city's high elevation allows wastewater to be highly aerated by in-stream turbulence and thus considerably improved in quality by the time it falls to the level of the coastal plain. A new wastewater treatment plant has been approved to stop this pollution. In an interview shortly after he was appointed Minister of Environment in early 1993, Yossi Sarid identified pollution from sewage and rehabilitation of Israeli rivers as his second and third priorities, respectively (solid waste was number one). In his words: "If people truly understood the nature and extent of the problem, they would shudder" (*Israel Environment Bulletin*, Spring 1993, p. 3). Minister Sarid's position was immensely strengthened by powers granted to the Ministry of Environment to intervene in local sewage disposal decisions.

The Ministry of Health tests extensively for bacteriological contamination, and quality standards for drinking water were tightened in 1989. A small percentage of tests shows excess contaminants, mainly because of antiquated and leaking sewage pipes in the northern part of the country. Older systems are being replaced, but progress is slow because of budget constraints. In addition to Jerusalem, new treatment plants have been planned for the expanding cities of Carmiel, Netanyah, and Ashdod, with the last planned as a demonstration solar-powered plant. The Dan Region plant for the Tel Aviv area (already the most modern in Israel) will also be expanded to handle peak storm loads.

Not surprisingly, Israeli investment in water supply is concentrated within the Green Line. Mekorot has connected Palestinian towns and larger villages close to the Green Line and within the Gaza Strip to the National Water Carrier (Bruins et al. 1991). Nevertheless, drinking water quality is generally poorer on the West Bank and significantly poorer in the Gaza Strip, where many residents routinely drink contaminated or saline water or a mixture of both (Zarour and Isaac 1991; Shawwa 1992). Half of Gaza's sewage (which totals 20–22 Mm^3/year) goes directly into the Mediterranean Sea with no treatment; the other half goes to settling ponds, where it gets only primary treatment and aeration.

Today, 20% of West Bank villages still have no regular water supply (Al-Khatib 1992), and many residents are experiencing health problems because of inadequate (or nonexistent) sewage disposal. It is hard to think of any excuse for this situation. Water-supply and water-treatment systems for small communities are well known, if expensive (per person served). Israel has extended water-supply lines to cover just over 60% of the households of the West Bank and is now beginning to extend sewage lines (Sbeih 1994). For example, a sewage project is being built to serve Bethlehem, Beit Sahour, and Beit Jala in the West Bank (Zarour and Isaac 1991). The new sewage projects, however, come with a trade-off: Israel gets the sewage, which it then reclaims for its own use. The same wastewater could make a much greater addition to output if directed to Palestinian farms, which have limited irrigation water (Zarour and Isaac 1991) and cannot generally afford to install the capital-intensive irrigation techniques that characterize Israeli agriculture. This may be the reason why Nablus has not been able to build an adequate sanitation system despite repeated requests to Israeli authorities.

In both the Gaza Strip and the West Bank, conditions tend to be worse in the refugee camps. This is partly due to levels of population density: many camps have close to 50 thousand people per square kilometre; some have even higher levels. Most of the water and sewage systems in the refugee camps have been financed by United Nations agencies, and the systems deliver on average less than 100 L/person-day — in some camps less than half that amount. In recent years, however, camps near cities have been connected to the water supply networks and, in such cases, service is equivalent to what other residents receive. Sewage still remains a problem, with many camps served only by open canals.

A further problem for Palestinians stems from the neglect of adequate sewage treatment in some settlements in the Occupied Territories, particularly those along Hill Ridge, south of Tulkarm. Being located at higher elevations, the sewers simply discharge into wadis or onto Palestinian fields. It has been alleged that funds were provided to the settlements for sewage systems but that they were diverted to other purposes.

As noted in Chapter 3, some 70% of municipal sewage in Israel is recycled as irrigation water. This process is critical to Israel's water balance. Reuse of sewage, however, has its own problems; two-thirds of the reused water receives minimal or no treatment and even that which is treated contains high chemical loads (*Israel Environment Bulletin,* Spring 1991; Gabbay 1992). This fact creates contamination problems for farm workers and, in some cases, for crops.

Chemicals

It is difficult to know the extent of contamination of Israeli surface and underground water. Mekorot does sample water for quality from more than a hundred wells each year on a rotating basis, covering some 1 000 wells in all. More than a hundred tests are done on these samples, but the results are not generally made public. Moreover, the test wells are keyed to agricultural needs and may not catch the worst industrial pollution. Spot checks by the Ministry of Environment have found concentrations of specific contaminants at levels that are a few to 100 times the allowable levels in other industrial countries. Some 70% of Israeli industry is located along the coast, and sections of the Coastal Aquifer near Ramat Hasharon and Holon, both in the Tel Aviv area, are badly contaminated with heavy metals from industrial waste. Some wells are now closed, but this is a minor problem compared with the fact that "contamination [of the aquifer] by heavy metals is nearly irreversible except by very expensive methods" (*Israel Environment Bulletin,* Winter 1993, p. 9; see also Goldenberg and Melloul 1992).

As late as 1989, it was estimated that only about half of the hazardous waste produced in Israel was arriving at the Ramat Havav disposal site south of Beersheba, and that figure does not take into account domestic harzardous wastes (Narkis and Kornberg 1990). Solvents, petrochemicals, gasoline products, and other wastes (some of them known or suspected carcinogens) are routinely dumped by municipalities and industries into any nearby watercourse. For example, the Kishon River in Haifa receives 10 000 m^3 of industrial wastewater every day — so much that parks along its banks are considered dangerous to human health (Hirschberg 1991). Olive oil mills, an otherwise excellent way to increase the value added from farming and to provide employment in rural areas, have both solid and liquid residues. The former can generally be put back on fields, but the latter has such a high BOD — or biological oxygen demand — that it is generally dumped.[8] No data on the extent of this problem have been found for Israel or the Occupied Territories, but the impact of some 40 mills in Jordan is equal to that of a city of one million. Contamination by heavy metals and synthetic organic chemicals is still reported to be low and limited to industrial areas, but more serious problems are expected in the future (Gabbay 1992). Thousands of tonnes of waste lubricating oil are also estimated to reach watercourses each year, but new regulations prohibiting the pouring, burning, or dumping of waste oil should reduce the problem significantly.

The Ministry of Health is just now considering whether to establish standards on maximum levels of organic and inorganic compounds ("micropollutants") in drinking water. The Ministry of Environment has proposed regulations to deal with industrial dumping and is moving to establish new regulations to deal with toxins. Still, Israel is a long way from a "polluter pays" principle. The country's one official toxic waste disposal site (Ramat Hovav) was so poorly designed and so limited in capacity that disposal pools have overflowed after heavy rains and contaminated nearby reservoirs (Whitman 1988). Worse yet, evidence suggests that toxic wastes have been seeping downward into the aquifers that are vital to Israel.

Nature Reserves

Although Israel has a higher proportion of its land (about 18%) in national parks and nature reserves than most other countries, the protected areas are necessarily quite small. Freshwater areas come under intense pressure, particularly during the hot summer months, from both domestic recreational use and international tourism. They are also subject to encroachment, as illustrated by the proposal to build an industrial park close to Kabri Springs (a plan that was blocked by legal action).

---

[8] Biological oxygen demand (BOD) is an indication of the oxidizing power of the waste stream. Liquid wastes with a high BOD draw all of the oxygen from water so that other forms of life, both animal and plant, suffocate.

Moreover, in its effort to assure adequate and growing supplies of water, Israel has regularly violated its usual concern for the protection of nature and the Biblical landscape (Brooks and Shadur 1991). Waste now contaminates many beaches, and those near Herzliyyah and Netanyah, among others, are regularly closed to bathers during the summer. Flow in the Jordan River has been reduced to a fraction of its former volume. There is a plan to dam (albeit for electricity rather than, directly, for water) the last free-flowing stretch of the Jordan River. Ironically, the plan is being advocated by a kibbutz. In contrast, site-specific regulations defined as part of the Mediterranean Coastal Plan differentiate carefully between those river mouths that were to remain natural and others where changes in hydrology would be permitted (Brachya 1993).

In spite of these problems, however, nature preservation remains highly valued in Israeli politics. Growing recognition of the economic potential of ecotourism is adding to the forces against encroachment. For example, because of its location at the junction of three continents, Israel is a funnel for tens of millions of birds that migrate south in the fall and north in the spring. Thousands of bird-watchers come to view the storks, pelicans, raptors, and other species. Israeli courts are increasingly open to legal arguments in favour of maintaining existing states of preservation, if not always to those for extending protection to new areas. What still appears to be missing, however, is widespread acceptance of the ecological services of natural areas in protecting the quantity and quality of water outside the reserves.

Some Hopeful Signs

There are exceptions to the generally dismal picture of water quality in Israel. Lake Kinneret has been under a unified management plan that prohibits dumping and restricts uses of water from the lake. As a result, Kinneret has retained its quality (it is the source of half of Israel's drinking water) and its beauty. The power of Mekorot is such that it could impose similar restrictions on other areas of the country, but that would conflict with vested interests. Even Kinneret is not fully protected from agricultural runoff, and one result is that nitrate content in the water, and thus the content of algae, has been rising. New regulations on spraying, however, will greatly reduce the level of pesticides draining into the lake.

Another potential exception involves the Yarkon River, which flows through Tel Aviv, Israel's largest city. Coastal rivers are the most seriously degraded ecosystems in Israel. The Yarkon is typical. Only 27 km long, its flow is greatly reduced because the springs that fed it have been diverted to the National Water Carrier. As a result, industrial wastewater and urban runoff are no longer flushed away. Now the Yarkon will serve as the test case to determine both the physical and economic feasibility of reversing this situation. In late 1988, a special authority was set up to undertake remedial activities and restore the river to a condition that would permit recreational use. So far, efforts have been directed mainly at the cleanup of trash and debris and at restrictions on new dumping.

The program to clean up Israeli rivers has been given additional impetus from an apparent shift in priorities with the appointment of Yossi Sarid as Minister of Environment and from the recognition of their economic potential by the Ministry of Tourism. Tentative plans have been announced for clean-up work to extend to the Kishon, Alexander, Tanninim, and Lachish rivers during 1994.

In addition, in what appears to be a landmark decision, a judge ruled that the financial problems of a factory and nearby kibbutzim discharging wastes into the Na'aman River (south and west of Acco) were not legitimate reasons for failing to meet pollution-control requirements. The case was brought to court by a coalition of community and public-interest groups, which argued that the Water Commissioner and lower level agencies were failing to use their authority to control pollution. In ordering the Water Commission to take action, the judge evidently accepted the coalition's position that public interests had to be placed ahead of private interests.

Israel does have a well-established environmental impact assessment (EIA) process (Brachya 1993). Lodged in the Ministry of Environment, an EIA is highly recommended, and for all practical purposes required, in the construction of new main water carriers, dams and reservoirs, and sewage-treatment plants. There are gaps, however, in the requirements, and by no means all activities that may affect surface or underground watercourses are subject to an EIA. Still, Israel's EIA process is relatively effective, and by now several hundred EIAs have been conducted. EIA processes in Egypt and Jordan are much younger but are slowly becoming institutionalized (Salem 1994). Given that the environment was identified as a sector requiring its own institutions in the Peace Accord between Israel and the Palestine Liberation Organization (see Chapter 9), rapid adaptation of EIA processes to regions under Palestinian control can be expected. In 1994, a Canadian mission was sent to the region to identify the likely needs for EIAs and the local capacity to undertake them, and Canadian-funded training programs to help raise capacities to meet needs are going to follow.

In retrospect, had an EIA process been in place in the early days of Israel's existence, some projects that effectively reshaped the land, and that are now recognized as at least partially in error, might have been avoided. The drainage of Lake Hula and surrounding marshes (1 000 and 6 000 ha, respectively) was accomplished in the 1950s, the young nation's first megaproject. The gain was about 6 000 ha of fertile agricultural land and some 50 Mm^3 of water per year. As well, breeding grounds for malaria-bearing mosquitoes were eliminated. However, a unique ecology was also destroyed (only partially conserved in the Hula Nature Reserve). In addition, the underlying peat was allowed to dry out, resulting in the spreading of slow-burning fires that ignite spontaneously as the peat oxidizes and in the leaching of nitrates that flow to Kinneret. Although these problems were recognized as early as 1970, only in 1988 did the idea to reflood part of the region begin to take shape as both economic and environmental criteria indicated the need for restoration of part of the Hula to a wetland (Avnimelech et al. 1992).

Finally, a modest beginning has been made at introducing organic agriculture to Israel, with a corresponding reduction in runoff. A couple of kibbutzim have found that ready markets and higher prices can be obtained with organically grown vegetables, and it has been suggested that this is an option that might attract Palestinian farmers, once export markets are open to them. Even nonorganic farms are reconsidering their pesticide use. During the 1980s, cotton came under heavy price competition, and the area in Israel devoted to cotton production declined. Faced with a cost–price squeeze, farmers became more efficient: production per hectare climbed, but use of organophosphates (the main pesticide used), and particularly the more toxic organophosphates, declined. Although motivated by profits rather than by ecological considerations, all such reductions in the application of chemicals also reduce farm runoff, with almost immediate improvements in water quality.

Public Support and Public Action

There is growing public demand in Israel for a reduction in water pollution. Israel has always had strong and widely supported nongovernment organizations (NGOs) in the environmental field — most notably, the Society for the Preservation of Nature in Israel (better known simply as SPNI) — and their work has been critical. On occasion, the Israeli environmental movement has been able to bring international pressure to bear on the government and win some significant victories. A notable example involved long-standing joint plans by the United States and Israeli governments to build a powerful Voice of America transmitter in a sensitive area of desert; the struggle lasted more than 5 years until the project was finally canceled in early 1993. Most environmental organizations, however, are underfunded and overburdened, and, just as with the Ministry of Environment, the environmental movement has been more successful at protecting flora and fauna than watercourses.

Growing support for focusing attention on water quality as well as quantity in Israel is reflected in the increasingly vigorous use of the court system to protect environmental values. An environmental NGO — the Israel Union for Environmental Defense — has been formed specifically to use the legal system, much in the manner of the US Environmental Defense Fund. Some of its activities have been cited earlier. As well, the Ministry of Environment has begun to take legal action against polluting firms and even polluting communities, and its hand was strengthened with a 1991 amendment to the 1959 Water Law that applies personal liability and permits individual charges for violations. In 1993, the Ministry of Environment took several communities and a regional council to court to stop water pollution from the Mod'in landfill.

Despite growing awareness and stronger political support, difficult issues remain, including cleaning up older problems and responding to demands to cut corners to mitigate housing problems or create jobs for new immigrants. For example, during the period of rapid immigration of Soviet Jews in 1990 and 1991, the number of communities without sewage-treatment systems actually doubled (*Israel Environment Bulletin*, Winter 1993). Moreover, differences across the Green Line remain stark. The Ministry of Environment did not even have a local environmental unit in the Territories until 1993 (there were 22 in Israel at that time). Although others are scheduled to be established, they come too late to avoid serious problems. Nevertheless, there are grounds to think that Israel may have turned the corner in terms of recognizing that water has a quality as well as a quantity dimension.

CHAPTER 6

DISTRIBUTION OF WATER: THE GEOPOLITICAL CRISIS

More and more we learn (or do we?) that liberties, security and
well-being can only be founded on well used lands, whose
productivity is safeguarded and improved from year to year and
generation to generation. But social justice must also prevail.
For injustices to farmers and peasants have in many times and
places brought about the decay and decline of agriculture and
with them social unrest.

— W.C. Lowdermilk
(introduction to Reifenberg 1955)

WATER HAS BEEN INTEGRAL to local and regional politics in the Middle East for centuries. Water was recognized by the early Zionists to be critical to the success of their dreams. The territorial — and water — claims made by Zionists early in the 20th century were predicated on "the requirements of modern economic life" (Weisgall, as quoted in Zarour and Isaac 1993). These requirements were based, in large part, on the availability of water resources. The World Zionist Organization's submission to the Paris Peace Conference in February 1919 clearly delineated the proposed boundaries of Palestine to include the headwaters of the Jordan River, the lower Litani River in Lebanon, and the lower reaches of the Yarmouk River. These boundaries were initially drawn up by Aaron Aaronsohn, the head of an agricultural experiment station on the Mediterranean coast, and were based on watershed boundaries (see the interesting discussion of this in Wolf 1995). At the conference, Chaim Weizmann, who later became the first president of the State of Israel, stated that it is "of vital importance not only to secure all water resources already feeding the country, but also to be able to conserve and control them at their sources" (Hurewitz 1959, as quoted in Lowi 1992, p. 39; see also Hosh and Isaac 1992, for more recent history). Weizmann later clarified this statement noting that the guiding consideration is economic and "economic" in this con-nection means "water supply" (Wolf 1995). Water was not simply viewed as a valuable natural resource, but as essential to the livelihood of the Jewish people and the viability of a Jewish state.

Until the 1930s, development in Palestine was easily accommo-dated with existing water supplies. By the middle of the decade, how-ever, increasing settlement required the development of new sources. During the next few years, there were various surveys and initiatives developed in the region to assess the availability of water resources and to determine what an "equitable" apportionment might be to present and future residents. The most contentious issues at the time, however, were Jewish immigration and the carrying (or absorptive) capacity of the land.

Two detailed water resource surveys that were undertaken during the 1930s are worthy of note. This first was commissioned by the British government in 1930 to evaluate the potential for irrigation and hydro-electric power in Palestine. The focus was to be on defining this "absorptive capacity" of the land (and hence, the potential for Jewish immigration) without unduly affecting the then-existing Arab popula-tion. The report, prepared by Sir John Hope–Simpson, concluded that there were large tracts of cultivable land in Palestine, but it did not ade-quately assess the hydrology of the region and was, therefore, of little use (Doherty 1965). A second survey of water resources, focusing specif-ically on the Jordan Valley, was undertaken in 1937 by M. Ionides, a British employee of the Trans–Jordanian government. Although the plan proposed a diversion scheme for the Yarmouk River (later adopted in part by the Jordanian government), it also concluded that there were insufficient water resources in the river to sustain a Jewish state (Doherty 1965; Naff and Matson 1984).

While these two surveys were being conducted, supporters of a future Jewish state were also active. In the mid-1930s, the newly estab-lished national water company, Mekorot, developed a plan to supply

water to western Galilee, which then became its first construction project. Toward the end of the decade, Zionists in the United States, possibly alarmed by the Ionides report, convinced the American government
to commission an independent study by W.C. Lowdermilk of the US
Soil Conservation Service. The notion of comprehensive planning for
development of the water resources of Palestine began to take hold and
will be reviewed in more detail in the next chapter.

Although more detailed histories of the development of water
resources and water institutions in Israel are available (see, for example,
Wolf 1995), it requires only this brief overview to illustrate the strategic
significance of water to this region and, specifically, to the State of
Israel. The essential nature of water to the country — due largely to its
ideological ties to agriculture and the importance of immigration — is
as relevant today as it was in the early 1900s, as suggested by an inci-
dent related by Heller and Nusseibah (1991, p. 108):

> So frightening was the spectre of future water diversion that in the mid-
> 1970s a Labour government generally opposed to Jewish settlement in
> the West Bank nevertheless decided to establish a small number of settle-
> ments in Samaria, a few kilometres east of the Green Line, in order to
> forestall the possibility that the initial catchments of the western aquifer
> would be turned over to foreign control

Water Politics from 1948 to 1967

A secure supply of fresh water was an important goal for the early
Zionists. It later became explicit policy for the State of Israel. The reason for this was clear; unencumbered access to fresh water was seen as a
necessary condition for economic growth and security. The pursuit of
this goal — dating back to early civilizations — had raised tensions
between various states and factions in the region. Before the 1967 war,
Israel and the neighbouring Arab states had occasionally feuded over
access to Jordan River waters. Naff and Matson (1984), on the one
hand, document a dozen water-related cease-fire violations in the
Jordan River basin between 1951 and 1967. On the other hand, during
this period, all of the Jordan River riparians more or less accepted the
shares of water defined for them by the Johnston Plan in 1955. Despite
increasing demands for water for agricultural, industrial, and domestic

purposes during the decade before 1967, the status quo seemed tacitly acceptable.

Although we do not subscribe to this view, some analysts have speculated that the need for more water was a major factor in Israel's involvement in the 1967 war. Myers (1993, p. 38), for example, states that "Israel started the 1967 war in part because the Arabs were planning to divert the waters of the Jordan River system." This contention is based on a discussion Myers had with General Moshe Dayan in the mid-1970s. Dayan apparently told him that "Israel unleashed its planes and tanks as soon as it learned that Syria and Jordan were moving to cut off water flows from rivers that originated outside Israel's borders" (Myers 1993, p. 9). This contrasts, with a detailed analysis by Slater (1991, as cited in Wolf 1995) that Dayan was very reluctant to launch an attack on Syria and only after repeated pressure from his advisers and a visit from a delegation from the northern settlements did he take action, three days after the start of the war. Cooley (1984) states that "the constant struggle for waters of the Jordan...was a principal cause of the 1967 Arab–Israeli war...." Naff and Matson (1984) note that "the increase in water-related Arab–Israeli hostility was a major factor leading to the 1967 June War." Bulloch and Darwish (1993) are even more explicit, stating: "the Six Day War was caused largely by competition for waters of the River Jordan."

Studies of the history of water and politics in the region offer mixed support for the contention of a hydrologic imperative on the part of Israel (for example, Naff and Matson 1984; Beaumont 1994; Wolf and Lonergan 1994; Wolf 1995). It is true that throughout 1965 the Israeli army attacked construction attempts to divert the headwaters of the Jordan River in Syria. Skirmishes over Arab attempts to divert water from the Banias River into the Yarmouk River continued in 1966 and 1967 (Wolf 1995). These attacks were the result of tensions between Israel and Arab states over the withdrawal of Jordan River water. In 1964, Israel began operation of its National Water Carrier, withdrawing 320 Mm^3/year from the Upper Jordan. The Arab states responded by planning two diversion schemes involving the headwaters of the Jordan River (although these diversions had been discussed for over a decade). The first proposed diverting approximately 50 Mm^3

annually from the Hasbani River via a tunnel into the Litani; the second involved construction of a canal to divert both the Hasbani and the Banias rivers into the Yarmouk River for irrigation in both Syria and Jordan (Figure 11) (Doherty 1965). What makes the suggestion of a hydraulic imperative on the part of Israel even more confusing is Prime Minister Begin's admission in 1982 that the 1967 conflict was not "a war of necessity, but a war of choice" (quoted in Ball and Ball 1992). Perhaps the most sensible statement appears in Heller and Nusseibah (1991, p. 107): "The development of Israel's National Water Carrier and Syrian attempts to divert headwaters of the Jordan River played a part in the chain of events leading to the Arab Israeli war of 1967."

At the time of the 1967 war, Israel was tapping all of its available freshwater supplies and beginning to take more than its share of Jordan River water. During the war, Israeli planes destroyed a half-completed dam on the Yarmouk River between Syria and Jordan, and also the intake facilities for the East Ghor Canal (now called the King Abdallah Canal) along the Jordanian side of the Jordan River Valley. These structures would reduce (or would have reduced) flow to either the Upper or Lower Jordan Rivers and thus the water available for use in Israel. Whether these attacks were part of a considered plan or targets of opportunity chosen in the midst of a war is, however, unclear.

Water Politics After 1967

Occupation of the West Bank and the Golan Heights by Israel after the 1967 war significantly changed the dimensions of water demand and supply in Israel. (As a water-deficit region, the Gaza Strip was less important in this respect.) First, it increased Israel's fresh water supplies by almost 50%. Second, it gave the country almost total control over the headwaters of the Jordan River and its tributaries, apart from the Yarmouk River, as well as control over the major recharge region for the Mountain Aquifer. Third, although the Banias River, flowing off the Golan Heights, is a relatively minor source for the Jordan River, control of the Heights makes Israel the upper riparian on the river, which has important political and legal implications, and which was likely part of the rationale for its annexation by Israel. In recent months, the new Labour government in Israel has offered to return a large part of the

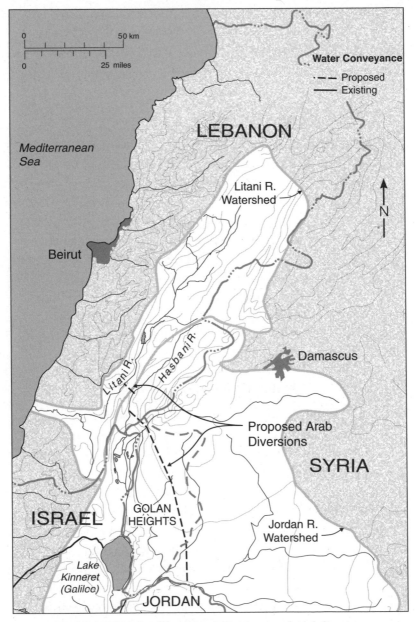

Figure 11. The Litani River watershed and proposed Arab diversions
from the Upper Jordan River.

Golan Heights to Syria. It is not clear, however, to what extent the offer includes the sources of the Jordan River and, hence, to what extent it is strategic for water policy — or for that matter whether Syria is interested in any offer less than a return of the entire territory.

Finally, Israel solidified its position on the Yarmouk River (which forms the boundary between Jordan and Syria and then joins the Lower Jordan River within Israel at a point just below the outlet from Kinneret). Israel was always a downstream riparian on the Yarmouk, but now, as a result of the war, it controls half of the river, compared with 10% previously. This change allowed Israel to increase its use of Yarmouk water, and it now appears to be taking about 100 Mm³/year (this water is diverted to Lake Kinneret), most or all of which Jordan would like to regain to supplement its own very limited sources. More importantly, it made any upstream development of the Yarmouk dependent upon Israeli consent. Although secret negotiations between Israel and Jordan after the war permitted the latter to repair the East Ghor Canal on the Jordanian side of the river (Hosh and Isaac 1992), better use could be made of the Yarmouk if a dam were built to store high winter flows or to divert them to Lake Kinneret for later use in Jordan (Kally 1993). Either plan requires agreement, however, with both Syria and Israel, something that is unlikely, even in the context of a limited peace agreement. Syria has built 25 small dams to capture water draining southward to the Yarmouk and would not want the value of these structures compromised.

More recently, according to Naff (1990), Israel refused to allow Jordan to dredge the entrance to the East Ghor Canal, which has been silting since it was reopened two decades ago. By restricting the water flow out of the Yarmouk, the flow into the Jordan River is increased, which benefits Israel. The evidence for this allegation, however, is indeterminate. The problems with flow from the Yarmouk into the canal — as well as the diversion by Israel into Kinneret, situated downstream from the East Ghor Canal — are only apparent in the summer, during low-flow periods. It is rumoured that the Israelis and Jordanians meet on the banks of the Yarmouk for "picnic table summits" to decide on acceptable diversions for each country. Although these are "technical" discussions, they have not, for obvious reasons, been acknowledged by either country. They do, however, underline the importance of even informal shared agreements when it comes to such a vital resource. Perhaps now with the end of hostilities between Israel and Jordan, informal meetings over a picnic table will be converted to formal meetings around a conference table.

Control of the West Bank and the Golan Heights thus gave Israel access to additional water supplies and better control of existing supplies. As indicated in the foregoing, Israel had for many years been tapping aquifers that rise on the West Bank from within the Green Line. Since the war, the country has become acutely dependent on the aquifers in this region, particularly for drinking water. Almost immediately after the war, Israeli water policies and institutions were extended to the West Bank. As noted in Chapter 3, whenever existing water laws did not allow enough scope, military orders were invoked to ensure total Israeli control over the water resources of the West Bank. The result is — to use a provocative but, nonetheless appropriate term — de facto annexation of West Bank water resources.

In addition to direct use of water from the Mountain Aquifer from wells within Israel, West Bank (and Gaza) water is used to supply new Jewish settlements outside the boundaries of pre-1967 Israel. About 70% of the groundwater on which Israel is dependent, and more than 40% of its sustainable annual fresh water supply, originate in the Occupied Palestinian Territories, mainly in its aquifers. Such figures make it easy to understand (although not accept) the declarations of former Agriculture Minister Rafael Eitan (perhaps the most outspoken politician on the issue) that relinquishing control over water supplies in the Occupied Palestinian Territories would "threaten the Jewish state."

Zarour and Isaac (1991, 1992), together with other analysts, provide figures that allow for rough comparisons of daily water use per capita within Israel proper and by various aggregations in the Occupied Palestinian Territories (Table 9; 100 L/person-day is generally taken as the minimum for adequate health and sanitation). In their view, Palestinians in the Occupied Palestinian Territories are entitled to at least one-quarter of the water resources of the region. They are now getting between one-twelfth and one-sixth.

Table 9. *Selected data on water use in Israel and*
the Occupied Palestinian Territories.

Location	Water for domestic use (L/person-day)	Percentage of cultivated land that is irrigated
Israel (within the Green Line)	125	47
West Bank		5
Villages	40	
Towns	100	
Gaza Strip	85	64
Israeli settlements	250	69

Source: Zarour and Isaac (1991, 1992).

A Potential Surplus on the West Bank

The salient fact about water on the West Bank is that only about 17% (105 Mm^3) of the total underground supply is available to the people who have historically lived there (Benvenisti and Gvirtzman 1993). Israel pumps roughly 450 Mm^3/year for its own needs, with another 40–50 Mm^3 or so being extracted on the West Bank and going directly to Israeli settlements. Arab communities and farmers are said to get about one-third of their total use from wells; but data on withdrawals from wells are unreliable. The remaining two-thirds comes from river water, springs, and cisterns that collect runoff (Heller and Nusseibah 1991; Zarour and Isaac 1991). In short, only a small portion of aquifer water goes to Palestinians living on the West Bank, with the result that consumption in the more than 100 Jewish settlements is one-third that of the entire Palestinian population. These figures appear to be an accurate assessment of current water use on the West Bank. Lowi's (1992) claim that water use in the Israeli settlements is approaching that of the entire Palestinian population seems overstated.

    All water developments in the West Bank are carefully controlled by the Israeli Military Authority, working in collaboration with the Water Commission, which, as was noted, reports to the Minister of

Agriculture. Policies applied to Arab communities and farms on the
West Bank are highly discriminatory (Lowi 1992). For example:

≈ No Palestinian Arab individual or village has received permission
  to drill a new well for agricultural purposes since integration, or
  even to repair one that happens to be close to an Israeli well.
  Some permits are granted to obtain water for domestic use.

≈ Palestinians are only allowed to drill shallow wells, around 70 m
  in depth. In contrast, Mekorot prefers to drill to depths of
  300–400 m to get higher flow rates and better quality water.
  Mekorot wells each yield about 750 000 m³/year, whereas the
  Palestinian wells yield only 13 000 (Heller and Nusseibah 1991).

≈ Water allocations recognize only existing uses of water, which, so
  far as Arab agriculture is concerned, are those of 1968, and allocations are frozen at the 1968 level with only a small margin for
  growth.

≈ West Bank Arabs are not allowed to use water for farming purposes after 4:00 PM, despite the fact that evening is the traditional (and sensible) time to irrigate in arid regions.

≈ Reforestation is prohibited in the recharge areas of the aquifer,
  except on private plots, to promote maximum runoff and thus
  recharging of the aquifer.

These regulations are particularly severe because of the dependence of the West Bank on agriculture, and of agriculture on water.
More than 85% of the water used in the region is for irrigation (Zarour
and Isaac 1991). As noted, it is claimed that the deep wells that
Mekorot tends to drill drain water from the shallower wells of
Palestinian farmers. Pumped wells create a cone of low pressure that
could have the effect of drawing water away from natural springs or
from wells that are higher in the water table. The evidence is contradic-
tory, however. Beschorner (1992) cites a half dozen examples of wells
and springs that have gone dry or that began to flow intermittently after
Israeli wells were drilled nearby. In contrast, Wishart (1989) cites evidence from a military report that in only one case from 1967 to 1980
was there any damage to a Palestinian well, and in that case compensation was offered. Although other effects, such as the prolonged drought,
may also be playing a role, the balance of evidence suggests that in at

least some cases the claimed losses are real. Because Mekorot does not accept responsibility, no compensation has been offered in recent years.

To compound the regulatory discrimination, Jewish settlements receive heavy subsidies for water to promote the extension of agriculture. Naff (1990) calculates that the typical Israeli settler farms 50 ha and irrigates for 250 days a year. The farmer pays $0.10/m^3 for water that costs $0.34, with the total subsidy cumulating to $29 500 (1988 US dollars) per year. In contrast, West Bank Palestinians receive no subsidy at all. Palestinian farmers pay about the same amount for irrigation water that settlers pay for drinking water. Water supplied by local Arab authorities is even more expensive, as high as $1.20/m^3 (Zarour and Isaac 1992). Given that per-capita income on the West Bank is only about one-fifth of that in Israel (and in the Gaza Strip even lower), the inequity is even more pronounced.

Land rights on the West Bank are controlled by the Civil Administration almost as closely as water rights. Land registration by Palestinians has been blocked since 1967, and Palestinians living outside of the Territories can no longer inherit land (Lesch 1992). All land transactions must be approved — and many proposals are rejected. Moreover, through various regulations and military orders, the Israeli government now controls roughly one-half of all land in the West Bank and about one-third of that in Gaza (Lesch 1992). In addition to former Egyptian and Jordanian state land, highways, parks, etc., these lands include large areas reserved for military use and land owned by anyone who was outside the Territories in June 1967.

These (and other) discriminatory practices are enforced through the application of Israeli law to the West Bank. According to Zarour and Isaac (1991): "Although the new legislation conforms to the Israeli water law, it is not consistent with the rights of an occupying power under international law." Clearly, the dispute is in effect over sovereignty, not just over the division of water supplies.

Disturbing as this system is, it is important that it not be exaggerated. The issue is one of economic development, not of thirst. When he was Water Commissioner, Meir Ben Meir stated the issue starkly: "If the demand is for drinking, we must say 'yes'; we do say 'yes'. But we are not going to stop irrigating our orchards so they can plant new ones." This position appears to be consistent with international law. Baskin (1992, p. 6) notes that "international law on belligerent occupation...only demands that the domestic water needs (home use) be accounted for. Industrial and agricultural development are beyond the definitions of the accepted international law." Even domestic water supply, however, has failed to grow with the population; since 1967, water allocations for domestic use have been increased by about 20%, whereas the population of the West Bank has grown by 84% (Baskin 1992). Nevertheless, the principal concern is not that Palestinians will have insufficient water for household use; rather it is that they will have insufficient water to establish a viable economy.

The need for West Bank water in Israel, and therefore its dependency on this resource, is hotly contested. Former Water Commissioner Tsemach Yisahi agrees with Rafael Eitan and claims that Israel must hold onto the West Bank "to make sure that Tel Aviv's taps don't run dry." In October 1993, a panel of experts told the Knesset Committee on Economics that "giving up the water sources in the territories as part of a peace agreement would be disastrous" (*Mideast Mirror*, 19 October 1993). Furthermore, current Water Commissioner Gideon Tsur stated that "Israel could not accept any reduction in either the quantity or the quality of the water available to it" (*Mideast Mirror*, 19 October 1993). Gideon Fishelson of the Hammer Institute (University of Tel Aviv), however, argues that were there more rational policies in Israel, there would be no need for West Bank water. Similarly, Arie Issar (Professor of Water Resources at the Blaustein Institute) says that there is more to be gained in sharing than hoarding water resources (cited in Pearce 1991). Tahal seems to be coming to the same conclusion. In 1991, Tahal, in conjunction with the University of Tel Aviv's Centre for Strategic Studies, prepared a report that indicates how Israel could withdraw from the Occupied Palestinian Territories without jeopardizing its security of water supply. A review of this document, which was classified as secret by Israeli censors until late in 1993, and a broader discussion of Israel's "hydro-strategic" boundaries are provided in Chapter 8.

Some analysts suggest that there could be a surplus of water on the West Bank. Zarour and Isaac (1991) indicate that the "water potential" for conventional sources of water is 850 Mm^3/year, of which 620 Mm^3 is "easily available" — which presumably means at moderate capital costs. This statement conforms closely to a figure from Heller and Nusseibah (1991), who state that aquifers wholly or partly located under the West Bank have a renewable flow of 615 Mm^3/year. As previously indicated, Israeli wells within the Green Line take about half of this amount; Israeli wells that supply settlements account for another 40–50 Mm^3; and Palestinian wells account for another 50–55 Mm^3. Thus, both Zarour and Isaac (1991) and Heller and Nusseibah (1991) have concluded that the West Bank has a water surplus of about 200 Mm^3/year, even excluding the water that is drawn from the nearly 300 springs in the area and by cisterns and tanks that hold rainwater and runoff. The implication of this situation is that there is considerable room for expansion of irrigated agriculture on the West Bank while still providing for industrial and population growth.

Not everyone agrees with the foregoing analysis. Starr and Stoll (1988) state that water in the Occupied Palestinian Territories is currently being exploited to its limit, and Naff (1990) states that the water of the Occupied Palestinian Territories is being overexploited at a rate of 150 Mm^3/year. Both statements presumably include the Gaza Strip, but elsewhere in the same document Naff states that the deficit in Gaza is 70 Mm^3, so that in the West Bank must be 80 Mm^3. These conclusions may have been based on earlier data, before hydrological studies indicated the full extent of West Bank water resources. Shuval (1992), however, who is fully aware of these data, concludes that the entire region is already, or soon will be, short of water, and that the only solution to this problem would be to bring in additional sources of water from outside the region in a "Regional Water-for-Peace Plan." Kally (1993) concurs with this view. Most Israelis attending the First Israeli–Palestinian International Academic Conference on Water held in Zurich in December of 1992 (Isaac and Shuval 1994) seemed to agree with Shuval and Kally. Palestinians were more cautious and argued that, were the distribution of water resources equitable, and were they able to manage these resources themselves, the West Bank could manage without outside water.

For the next few years, the volume of water resources potentially available to the West Bank is probably less important than the capital required for the expansion of water-supply and water-delivery systems. High capital costs are the reason why such systems were not built in the past, when water shortages were perennial. Even today, water shortages persist in some parts of the West Bank. Farmers and communities with inadequate capital must rely mainly on springs and shallow wells (supplemented by river water and storage of runoff in cisterns). A lack of access to capital — or, more accurately, a lack of access to capital at reasonable interest rates — is also the reason that Palestinian farmers have used and continue to use inefficient irrigation methods.

A Deficit in the Gaza Strip

The water balance in the Gaza Strip is much worse than that on the West Bank. The region is mining its groundwater, and there are severe problems as well with water quality. In addition, economic development is well short of what would be necessary to allow for adequate standards of living, and far shorter of what would be necessary to improve the quality of life. According to a Dutch government report, Mekorot is supplying water to much of the area, including the towns, larger villages, and certain refugee camps, through the National Water Carrier (Bruins et al. 1991). Some of the water Mekorot is supplying to the Gaza Strip is simply Gaza water pumped up and into the Carrier; however, some, estimated at 2–3 Mm^3/year, is a net addition to Gaza. The situation is complicated because Palestinians claim that Israeli wells to the east of the Gaza Strip have extracted water that would otherwise have flowed westward through the aquifer underlying the region, a claim that the Israelis deny (Elmusa 1993b). Israel does have about 20 wells located within a kilometre of the Gaza border, but they are, according to Arie Issar (personal communication, 1993), tapping saline water and thus actually improving the quality of water in the Gaza Strip. Palestinian hydrologists in Gaza, however, claim otherwise. As well, some Israeli hydrologists argue that overpumping of the aquifer began before the occupation by the Egyptian administration, and that new regulations have prevented an even worse situation. However, as

Elmusa (personal communication, 1993) points out, the situation has continued to deteriorate, and Israel cannot evade some responsibility.

What is clear is that the water situation in the Gaza Strip is desperate from both quantity and quality perspectives. There is no surface water, except immediately following a rainfall, and the two shallow aquifers that underlie the Strip, one sweet and one saline, are both being overpumped. The portion of the Coastal Aquifer that underlies the Gaza Strip (see Figure 5 on p. 26) is particularly sensitive because of the low rainfall and because it is the only indigenous source of drinking water. Water is pumped from over 2 000 wells, primarily for irrigation purposes, and total withdrawal is estimated at between 84 and 130 Mm^3/year. The wide range of estimates is disturbing, but even the lowest estimate of withdrawal is far above the natural recharge of 25–65 Mm^3/year (UNDP 1993). Indeed, even the total existing quotas for agricultural extraction from existing wells appear to exceed (or at best equal) recharge, and everyone admits there are hundreds of illegal wells and extractions beyond quotas, to say nothing of uncontrolled municipal wells. Israeli officials do not permit the drilling of more wells for irrigation (new wells and higher pumping rates are permitted for drinking water), but the water level in the aquifer continues to fall by 15–20 cm/year.

In addition to the mining of its aquifers, groundwater quality in the Gaza Strip is threatened. The shallow, unconfined nature of the upper, sweet aquifer makes it vulnerable to contamination from all sources. Overpumping has permitted saline intrusion, both from the coast and from depth; heavy fertilizer use is leading to high nitrate concentrations and heavy pesticide use to other residues; and what is probably the poorest sewage control in the region adds to the problems. As a result, the salinity of the main aquifer has doubled over much of the region in the last decade, and a good proportion of the residents of the Gaza Strip are already drinking contaminated or excessively saline water or both (Zarour and Isaac 1991; Shawwa 1992).

Conditions in the Gaza Strip are an example of what happens when several of the four types of water stress identified by Falkenmark et al. (1989) are present. Falkenmark distinguishes among four types of scarcity: too little rainfall (Type A), erratic rainfall resulting in

recurrent droughts (Type B), desiccation of the landscape as a result of
the poor or disturbed permeability of the soil surface (Type C), and
overpumping of aquifers caused by population (or economic) growth
(Type D). In the Gaza Strip, three of these situations exist. Rainfall is
less than 200 mm/year in the southern region and is variable both sea-
sonally and annually (a problem that may be exacerbated by global
warming, as noted earlier). Overexploitation, mainly for agriculture, has
resulted in salt-water intrusion. To this list, we might add a fourth type
of scarcity (different from Falkenmark's) — deteriorating water quality
not simply from overpumping, but from inadequate wastewater disposal
and overfertilization of agricultural lands.

It would seem that any reasonable resolution to the water problem
in the Gaza Strip must include transfers of water from Israel or, as some
propose, from the Nile (Kally 1993). Under these circumstances, it is
hardly surprising that Israeli water policy for Gaza is different from its
policy for the West Bank. Israeli policies and institutions were not
extended to the Gaza Strip, as they were on the West Bank. Rather, old
Jordanian Law No. 40 on soil and water is administered by the military
authorities (Bruins et al. 1991). Just as on the West Bank, however,
Palestinians and Israelis tend to have sharply different prescriptions for
dealing with the problem. Many Israeli analysts argue that the situation
is so severe that immediate construction of new pipelines or desalination plants is appropriate. Palestinians are skeptical of this megaproject
approach, in part for fear that they will get stuck with expensive sources
of supply, and in part because it diverts attention from the inequitable
distribution of existing supplies.

One approach that is conceptually simple would be the construction of a pipeline to transfer what appears to be surplus **treated** wastewater from Israel to the Gaza Strip. The wastewater could replace some
of the irrigation water now being pumped from the aquifers. If it is true,
as commonly stated, that recycled water from Israel is being released to
the sea at Ashqelon, a trunk line only some 25 km long would bring this
water within reach of many farmers in Gaza. Given the opportunity
costs of supplying additional water to the Strip, such a transfer of
treated wastewater is both socially and economically attractive.
Currently, however, there is very little incentive for farmers in the Strip

— most of whom hold permits to pump water — to purchase recycled water from Israel.

Here too the difference in approach also incorporates differing views about sovereignty over land and water resources. It is clear, however, that the Gaza–Jericho Agreement (see Chapter 9) will bring significant investment into Gaza for infrastructure (including water supply and wastewater treatment), which should improve the situation. But it is important that this be undertaken within the context of a detailed water resources management strategy, now lacking for the Gaza Strip.

Pretensions to the Litani River

Although not connected to the Occupied Palestinian Territories, Israel's incursion into Lebanon and the establishment of the "Security Zone" in the early 1980s allows it access to the lower reaches of the Litani River (which flows within 10 km of the Israeli border). These actions, coupled with past unsuccessful attempts by Israel to reach an agreement with Lebanon to share Litani water, have led to great Arab concern that Israel will unilaterally divert the Litani into the Jordan River. Certainly, the value of the Litani was recognized by Zionist planners (Lowi 1992) and, as was noted earlier, the proposal by the World Zionist Organization to the Paris Peace Conference in 1919 included the Litani River within the Jewish state (Figure 12). In a letter to the British Prime Minister, David Lloyd George, Chaim Weizmann noted that Lebanon "is a well watered region...and the Litani River is valueless to the territory north of the proposed frontiers.... It can be used beneficially in the country much further south" (Weisgal 1977, as quoted in Amery and Kubursi 1992). This interest in the Litani continued through the 1950s, when both Prime Minister Ben-Gurion and Moshe Dayan, Israel's Chief of Staff, advocated Israeli occupation of Lebanon up to the Litani River (Amery and Kubursi 1992). The fact that Litani water is very high in quality with a low mineral content only enhances its value — and the perceived threat.

The Litani River rises and flows entirely within the borders of Lebanon (Figure 12), but its possible use by Israel or Jordan or both has increased its international importance. Israel has long claimed that the

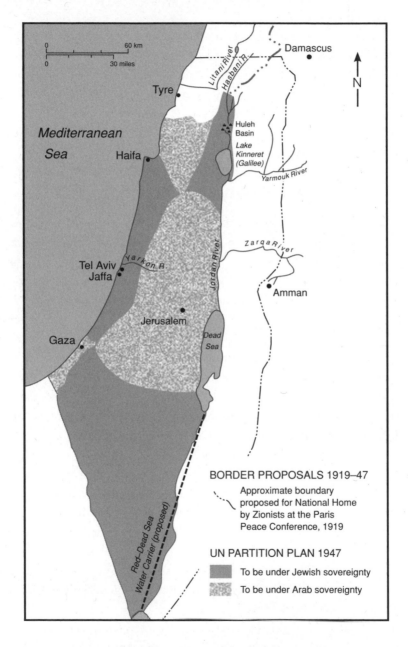

*Figure 12. Border proposals for a Jewish state, 1919–1947
(adapted from Wolf 1995).*

Litani is actually part of the Jordan River watershed, because there is some geological evidence that the lower Litani may provide water for the Hasbani River and the Dan Spring, which form the headwaters of the Jordan (Kolars 1992a). The Litani can be divided into three sections: the upper, lying in the Bekaa valley of eastern Lebanon; the middle, beginning near Qar'oun; and the lower, which flows into the Mediterranean. The natural flow of the river, from springs, runoff, and other inflows, is roughly 920 Mm^3/year (Kolars 1992), of which 500 Mm^3 reaches the Mediterranean. The rest is withdrawn for irrigation, lost to evaporation or seepage, or diverted for hydroelectric power production.

Currently, Israel (or any country other than Lebanon for that matter) has no claim to Litani River waters, and it seems unlikely that Israel would attempt a diversion of the Litani without an explicit agreement with Lebanon. The Government of Lebanon originally placed great priority on developing the river to generate electricity, and more than half of the river's total annual flow is already diverted through the Markaba tunnel below the Qar'oun Dam to the Awali River (also entirely within Lebanon) to increase capacity at generating stations on that river. The Litani is also used for irrigation, primarily in the upper and lower sections, but construction of major irrigation systems has been delayed largely because hydroelectric facilities were more profitable (Naff and Matson 1984).

The issue of water transfers from Lebanon to Israel raises a number of sensitive issues. First, some authors (such as Amery and Kubursi 1992) claim that this water will be needed by Lebanon to service the country's economic growth in the future. Any long-term agreement involving the diversion of water to Israel, therefore, should be avoided. Second, there are political sensitivities involved in selling water to the Israelis. Third, Israel would not be willing to build up a dependency on Lebanese water. Fourth, and last, Lebanon would, in turn, be hesitant to allow Israel an interest in water that might be used as an excuse for military intervention in the future. As a short-term solution to water problems in the region, however, the Litani River could play an important role.

In recent years, there have been unsubstantiated claims that Israel has been withdrawing water from the Litani River. The best evidence indicates that there have been no Israeli withdrawals of water from the Litani River to date, or even construction of infrastructure to facilitate such withdrawal (Kolars 1993; Wolf 1995). If anything, southern Lebanon receives small quantities of water (about 0.6 Mm^3/year) from wells within Israel (Wolf and Lonergan 1994). Occasional articles in the Arab press, and some in the United States, claiming that Israel is withdrawing water from the Litani (see, for example, Naff 1990) appear to be in error.

Nevertheless, uncertainty and tension over this issue remain. The most recent claim that Israel was withdrawing Litani River water was made at the May 1994 ministerial meeting of the United Nations Economic and Social Commission for Western Asia (ESCWA), a regional body consisting of Middle Eastern states from Egypt to the Gulf, but excluding Israel (ESCWA 1994). This report asserted that, since 1978, Israel has been using 215 Mm^3 of water per year from the Litani and Wazzani rivers. The report also claimed that, after its invasion of Lebanon in 1982, Israel drilled an 18-km tunnel linking the Litani River to Israel. A priori, one wonders how such an engineering structure could be hidden so completely from public view. More instructive, the Lebanese reaction was remarkably mild. According to the Mideast Mirror (1 June 1994), Lebanese Foreign Minister Fares Bouez said: "Until now, I can't say that we have evidence that there is a direct theft of water in the South." In response to questions by a journalist about the specific rivers identified, he said "We will study this file carefully and we will have a stand."

The lack of any evidence supporting the claim of an Israeli diversion of Litani River water does not mean that some Israelis do not covet the Litani River. It is the only nearby source of surface water that would allow Israel to maintain its present consumption rates and avoid the difficult choice of whether to reallocate water away from agriculture.

If the political situation in Lebanon continues to stabilize, agricultural, industrial, and population demands will likely place more pressure on water resources. Given current conditions, however, the high quality of Litani water will probably be maintained, and demand will not reach unmanageable levels for some time (Naff and Matson 1984). Still, Lebanon remains dependent on the Litani as a source of water, and if the state is to prosper it must continue to develop and harness the resources of the river. Despite upstream diversions, the Litani gathers more water in its middle and lower sections, and it still carries a volume equal to the flow of the Jordan to the sea. As noted, most Lebanese analysts now believe that the Litani can (and should) be fully utilized for economic development within Lebanon itself. A minority, including apparently Dr Seliom Maksud, who heads the Litani River Administration, do see an interim opportunity to sell Litani River water to Israel and the Palestinians, with Lake Kinneret used as an "international water bank" (Gruen 1994). Maksud immediately goes on to note his worries that, once having established a market, it would be hard to recapture the water 25 years later to meet Lebanon's domestic needs, a position with which Canadians should be very sympathetic. Even if the Maksud option becomes politically feasible, interim solutions will likely be seen as second or even third best by both Israelis and Palestinians, and the Litani is unlikely to play any role in their future water balances.

The Current Negotiations

Officially, little happened to resolve water issues between 1967 and the start of the multilateral negotiations in 1991 (see Chapter 9). Unofficially, Israel and Jordan have been meeting at "picnic table summits" to discuss joint water concerns; for example, Israel has apparently allowed some dredging of the East Ghor Canal. It is unclear, however, what of lasting consequence has been accomplished at these meetings; the Israelis feel that they are a major step toward interbasin cooperation, whereas the Jordanians note that they are of little use and have had no effect on Israeli behaviour relative to water. Clearly, Israel and her neighbours have quite different approaches to negotiations over water.

These differing views are evident in the current multilateral talks over water that are carried on parallel to the higher profile bilateral Middle East peace talks. In these discussions, Israel focuses on "low politics"; that is, they emphasize that, whatever other conditions exist, there is a great deal to be gained by joint management of shared water resources to realize limited but significant gains in efficiency and welfare (Rothman and Lowi 1992; Lowi 1994). The Palestinians and the Jordanians, in contrast, focus on "high politics"; that is, they emphasize the need for overall peace agreements and strategic management of people and economic development before resolution of tactical water issues.

Some analysts see ulterior motives in the "functionalist" Israeli approach. Zarour and Isaac (1991) suggest that Israel uses the water issue to keep talking without really resolving anything. Rothman and Lowi (1992) tend to agree that functionalist low politics are inadequate in the case of intense, protracted, and culture-laden conflicts. Elsewhere, Lowi (1994) has argued that what surfaces as a dispute among riparians takes on the attributes of the greater conflict and that, therefore, the riparian dispute cannot be resolved or even mitigated to a substantial extent in the absence of some sort of ideological consensus, which in this case would have to involve the establishment of an independent Palestinian state.

Water, however, is so essential to life that it can promote cooperation as easily as conflict. Even in the absence of consensus on high political issues, there may be benefits from cooperation on water management and supply. Thus, Rothman and Lowi (1992, p. 69) go on to suggest that, with the parallel bilateral and multilateral tracks of the current peace process, we may at last be witnessing the "iterative process by which progress beginning at the political process — that is, the Arab–Israeli peace process — requires concrete progress at the practical level — for example, sharing water resources — for both consolidation and fruition." Shuval, a hydrologist rather than a political scientist, comes to the same conclusion from a different perspective: "Just because the situation is so desperate, the partners to the dispute may finally realize that only by joining hands in a cooperative effort can they survive" (Shuval 1992, p. 143).

Security of water resources is a major objective of all countries, but hydrology, economics, and politics combine to make it particularly important to those in the Middle East. The options presented in the next chapter must be assessed both in terms of long-term environmental and demographic change occurring in the region and in terms of how they might affect the security of the water supply to Israelis and to Palestinians.

Data Quality and Data Availability

When you look at it through my eyes,
You'll see a different point of view.
Everything changes;
Every fact wears some disguise.
— James Keelaghan, songwriter

Introduction

One of the most important issues faced by analysts and professionals alike, and now being addressed by the multilateral Working Group on Water Resources as part of the Middle East peace process, relates to the availability and quality of data. In the introduction to this book, we elevated problems with data to a fourth "crisis." Because water is considered a security issue by the Israeli government, information on water availability and use (including aspects of hydrology, engineering, economics, and management) is often considered confidential. There has been much discussion in recent years over the unwillingness of the Civil Administration in the Occupied Territories to allow Palestinians access to data on water for strategic reasons. Accurate and reliable data are crucial to development planning, and the inadequacy and lack of data on water resources in the Occupied Palestinian Territories has been a major source of concern for everyone involved.

Concern over data is not limited to the water sector, however. The most recent population census for the Territories was conducted in 1967, just after Israeli occupation. All population estimates are based on these 1967 data, and there are claims made by Palestinians that present Israeli data underestimate the Palestinian population by 10–15%. There exists a disparity even in the reporting of simple, aggregate data, such as the population of Israel. Kolars (1992a) reports the current total population of Israel to be 4.4 million persons, whereas the *Statistical Abstract of Israel* (Israel, Central Bureau of Statistics 1992) reports it to be

5.1 million. This is more than simply a discouraging discrepancy. It brings into question virtually all of the data reported.

Data Quality

Because the quality and availability of data are major issues in the peace negotiations, it is worth examining them in the context of the Middle East. The quality of data, in general, is based on six factors:

≈ **Accuracy**: How closely does the measurement reflect reality?

≈ **Precision**: What is the degree of detail in the data?

≈ **Completeness**: Are there gaps in the data, either spatially or temporally?

≈ **Timing**: When were the data collected?

≈ **Lineage**: How much time elapsed between data collection and data use?

≈ **Control and access**: Who controls the data and how are the data distributed?

Separately, each of these factors presents problems when using data, particularly for the Occupied Palestinian Territories; collectively, they present a huge barrier to future water resource management in the region.

Accuracy — One of the most obvious cases of inaccurate reporting relates to water consumption data. Data on "consumption" are typically measured at the point of dispatch, not at the point of use. This is a particular problem in the Occupied Territories, since water losses are generally 50% or greater (with the exception of the Jerusalem Water Undertaking, which has reported losses on the order of 25–30%). This "unaccounted for water" stems from three causes: water seepage from decayed infrastructure, broken or malfunctioning water meters, and "black water" or unreported withdrawals of water. Water authorities in the Territories have estimated this last category of water "theft" to account for half of the water losses.

Exacerbating this problem is the fact that socioeconomic data in the Occupied Territories are generally based on surveys of the Palestinians by Israelis. Generally, there is an extremely poor response rate on the part of the Palestinians — or a problem of inaccurate responses — which leads to inaccurate reporting. This is a specific aspect of the general concern with measurement error relating to questionnaire design and implementation. There is always a difference between what one wishes to measure and what is actually being measured. Any survey-based data in the region must be considered of dubious quality at best.

There is also a secondary problem of accuracy in reporting data. In many cases, because water data have strategic value, data are "political." Different countries will report different measurements for the same variable. Although this is not unique to the Middle East, it is particularly exasperating when trying to build a suitable database for development planning. In some cases, however, it is not clear that there is a political motivation behind the reporting; the data are just "different." An example is the flow from the Upper Jordan River into Lake Kinneret. On the one hand, Naff and Matson (1984) report this flow to be 790 Mm^3/year, based on additions from springs in the Hula Valley. Inbar and Maos (1984), on the other hand, report this flow to be 500 Mm^3. Kolars (1992a) reports this flow to be 540 Mm^3, an estimate that has been accepted by other authors and that we used in Figure 10 (p. 44).

Precision — The accuracy of reporting data in Israel and the Occupied Territories also reflects on the precision of reporting. Water consumption data are generally reported by aggregate economic sector: industry, commercial establishments, and households. Even these data are sometimes difficult to find, particularly for the Territories. Israel publishes very disaggregate water-use data (for 96 sectors) in its system of national accounts, although these data are in dollars (or NIS) worth of use rather than in physical units. Because there are considerable variations in pricing, estimating water use in physical units is tenuous at best.

Hydrological data in Israel, we suspect, are very detailed; again, problems relate to the availability of such data (for example, recharge rates of aquifers and pumping rates from Israeli settlements in the West Bank) for the Palestinians.

Completeness — Before 1967, water resources in the West Bank were administered by the Jordanian Water Department, a decentralized unit of an agency then called the Natural Resources Authority of Jordan. The Water Department collected data on wells and springs, was responsible for all water-development projects, and licenced water withdrawals of more than 5 m³/h. Landowners had rights to water on and under their own land and could extract it for their own use or offer it for sale provided that doing so did not infringe on the rights of others. Water-supply networks were the responsibility of municipal councils.

The Gaza Strip (then the District of Gaza) was administered by the Egyptian army from 1948 to 1955, and subsequently by an Executive Council appointed by the Egyptian authorities. Water came under the jurisdiction of the Director of Municipal and Rural Affairs. The municipalities of Gaza and Khan Yunis operated their own water-supply systems.

In both regions, hydrological and climatological data were readily available. After 1967, as we have noted previously, the Civil Administration took over control of the Water Department and all data came under the control of the Israeli government. Effectively, this resulted in an absence of publicly available data after 1967 for the Occupied Palestinian Territories. Even today, the various partial time series of data on water in the Territories have yet to be merged into a complete and consistent set. It would be highly valuable to do so.

Timing and Lineage — Despite the limited amount of water data available for the Occupied Territories after 1967, excellent hydrological and climatological data do exist, based on previous studies. Rainfall records for Jerusalem, for example, date back to 1846. The detailed studies that were compiled on water resources in the region before 1955 all include useful data on both surface water and groundwater flows. Although these data are helpful, contemporary information on aquifer recharge, surface water flow, and so on, is available only to the Israelis. This presents an almost insurmountable problem of using 30-year old data to develop contemporary water-management strategies. An even more extreme example of the timing/lineage problem was given earlier regarding the fact that population estimates for the Occupied Territories are based on a 1967 census.

Control of and Access to Data — Central to the issues of data quality and data availability is the control — real and perceived — exercised by the Israelis over all types of data relating to the Occupied Territories. Major disagreements over removal of water from West Bank aquifers, diversion of Yarmouk River water, Israeli extraction of water flowing into Gaza, or simply the size of aquifers are unresolvable without independent corroboration of data. Each party to disputes over water has its own set of figures; there have been reports of misleading data being published, and articles on water issues in the region reflect an unusual lack of consistency over water data. Resolving these data issues is important not only to diffuse the mistrust that exists between the parties, but for effective water-resource planning in the future.

Problems of data accessibility for the Palestinians may change significantly in the next few years. The Joint Aquifer Management Workshop sponsored by the Harry S. Truman Research Institute for the Advancement of Peace (Truman Institute) at the Hebrew University and the Palestine Consultancy Group (held in Jerusalem in June 1994) resulted in commitments from participants to remove barriers to data access for the Palestinians, something that has become feasible now that Israel has declassified much data on water formerly considered security information. Data have already become more accessible, according to Taher Nassereddin, Director of the Water Department of the West Bank. It was also noted, however, that problems of data access are masking a larger problem of insufficient data.

Summary

The "crisis" with data on water in the Middle East has been mentioned by numerous authors, and there have been calls for the establishment of regional data centres or a regional information clearinghouse (Kolars 1992b) to help alleviate this crisis. The problem, however, stems as much from the use of data by parties with their own vested interests as from the lack of data (whether caused by a lack of measurement and monitoring or by Israeli control). In addition, sloppy reporting by analysts, researchers, government agencies, and the media has exacerbated the crisis. In this book, we have tried to present data that are accepted by the majority of professionals working in the field, or at least we have provided detailed citations for the sources of data that may be of questionable quality. It is clear that the poor quality of data and the limited availability of data are issues that will not be eliminated in the near future. But it is also clear that cooperation in the water sector between the Israelis and the Palestinians (and, indeed, other riparian states in the region) will require an agreement on baseline data and a comprehensive plan for sharing data on water availability and use.

That the data are important is clear from the attention directed to it at the multilateral meetings. What is most significant, however, is that this issue is considered a key part of the negotiation process itself.

PART III

TOWARD RESOLUTION

CHAPTER 7

REGIONAL OPTIONS FOR WATER MANAGEMENT

One of the paradoxical qualities of hydro-political problems is that, despite their complexities and stubbornness, they exhibit a tendency in certain circumstances to encourage negotiations where other problems would degenerate into conflict. There is an underlying superordinate interest common to all riparians — water is essential to life — that sometimes can be made to override discords and produce agreements on water issues.

— Naff (1990, p. 158)

THERE ARE NUMEROUS strategies available to deal with a water crisis. Some are complementary; others mutually exclusive; and all are limited by economic, social, and political constraints. Previous chapters have focused mainly on options that are available for Israelis or Palestinians (but mainly the former) to undertake on their own. This chapter focuses on regional options. The first section offers a brief review of relevant international law and of suggestive Canadian experience with interjurisdictional agreements for water. We then briefly review the history of water-management plans in the Jordan River Basin, not only to indicate the extensive set of studies and negotiations that have occurred in the region (mainly before 1955), but also to provide a framework for the discussion on present and future negotiations as well. We then discuss possible ways for Israel and the Territories to augment their water availability through regional transfer of water or importing water over long distances (by tanker or by pipeline). We also discuss militarization (with or without annexation) to acquire additional supplies. Militarization, however, should not be viewed as an "option," but an extremely undesirable result if all other approaches are unsuccessful. The chapter concludes with a discussion on an alternative approach to water planning.

International Law of Shared Water Resources

In 1959, Israel adopted its first comprehensive water legislation, which declared that water resources were public property, subject to control by the state, and to be used by residents of the state for the purpose of development of the country (Teclaff 1967). This legislation included all water resources, both surface and subsurface, as well as drainage and sewage water. Although no individual or group could own water (or have exclusive right to its use), the legislation guaranteed that everyone had the right to receive water. Domestic use, agriculture, industry, handicraft and commerce, and public services were explicitly recognized as legitimate uses. All licencing of water use was done by the Water Commissioner, and all water management was to be administered by the Ministry of Agriculture and the Water Commissioner.

This legislation was adopted in the context of ongoing discussions of international law dealing with transboundary waters. International law in this area, however, has been largely ineffective. Any legal obligation has been based only on general principles (see Appendix 2), and, as Caponera (1985) notes, the real difficulties in water-resource management concern the political willingness of states to enter into formal cooperative arrangements regarding water resources.

Surface Water

Historically, conflict over the use of water resources has stemmed from the adoption of one of two principles of sovereignty over water by riparian states. In general, upstream states have preferred the principle of absolute territorial sovereignty, whereby a state has the exclusive right to use and dispose of international waters that flow through its territory. Alternatively, absolute territorial integrity, the preferred principle for downstream riparians, implies that downstream users are to be provided with a water supply that is unaltered in terms of volume and quality. The rule of law, however, dealing with the nonnavigable use of water resources has most recently been based on general principles and recommendations arising out of United Nations rulings or on past principles used by states within water basins or systems. Although no general rule of international law exists, two principles are commonly accepted:

- ≈ Common water resources are to be shared equitably among the states entitled to use them, with related principles of: limited sovereignty, duty to cooperate in development, and protection of common resources.
- ≈ States are responsible for substantial transboundary injury originating in their respective territories (Teclaff 1967; Caponera 1985).

Historically, international relations on the use and development of water resources were based on navigation. Significant consumption for multiple uses in the last half century has resulted in numerous conflicts over international river basins and has stimulated a need for laws that adequately cover transboundary water use. Gleick (1992) has noted that in almost 50 countries the percentage of land that falls in international river basins is greater than 75%. In addition, 13 major rivers have five or more riparian states. This has resulted in major recent conflicts not just on the Jordan but also on the Danube, Indus, Ganges, Euphrates, Plata, and Nile Rivers.

In 1966, the International Law Association adopted the "Helsinki Rules," which provided general guidelines for water resource use on the basis of watershed boundaries. More recent United Nations documents (see, for example, United Nations 1983) have adopted the use of a watercourse system to describe the water resources shared by many states not simply as a physical unit, but as a system that connects to other components and resources.

The key article of the Helsinki Rules of 1966 is Article IV, which states that "Each basin state is entitled within its territory to a reasonable and equitable share in the beneficial uses of the waters of an international drainage basin." This principle was further described in an International Law Commission (ILC) report (ILC 1983):

> An international watercourse system and its waters shall be developed, used, and shared by system States in a reasonable and equitable manner on the basis of good faith and good neighbourly relations with a view to attaining optimum utilization thereof consistent with adequate protection and control of the watercourse system and its components.

Determining what is "reasonable and equitable," quite obviously, is the relevant question. What is reasonable depends on the natural features of a given watercourse, whereas equity depends on the social, economic, and political context. The Helsinki Rules of 1966 and the ILC report of 1983 detail the list of factors that should be considered in determining what is "reasonable and equitable" (Table 10). Although reasonableness and equity cannot, as Caponera (1985) notes, be considered rules of law, they do amount to a rejection of both historic principles: absolute territorial sovereignty and absolute territorial integrity.

The implication of these rules is that states bordering an international watercourse have the duty to cooperate to ensure the long-term future of these water resources. This duty includes protecting both the quantity as well as the quality of the water for other riparians. States must also account for any activities that adversely affect the interests or rights of other states. This duty was stated explicitly in a 1974 resolution of the United Nations General Assembly on the Charter of Economic Rights and Duties of States. It states:

> In the exploitation of natural resources shared by two or more countries, each State must cooperate on the basis of a system of information and prior consultation in order to achieve optimum use of such resources without causing damage to the legitimate interest of others...all States have the responsibility to ensure that activities within their jurisdiction or control do not cause damage to the environment of other States or of areas beyond the limits of national jurisdiction.

Underground Water

The distribution of fresh water on the Earth readily justifies the emphasis on groundwater concerns internationally; 77.2% of fresh water is found in ice, 22.4% in groundwater, 0.36% in surface water, and 0.04% in gas in the atmosphere. International law related to groundwater, however, is both more and less developed than that related to surface water. It is less developed in the sense that it came to be an issue much later in the history of international law for shared natural resources, but it is more developed in the sense that, partly because of that lag, there has been systematic thinking about a technically and legally adequate regime for international groundwater resources. Only since the Helsinki Rules of 1966, however, has groundwater been formally included within

Table 10. Principles of reasonableness and equity, according to the Helsinki Rules of 1966 and the International Law Commission (1983).

According to the Helsinki Rules:

(1) What is reasonable and equitable share...is to be determined in the light of all the relevant factors in each particular case.

(2) Relevant factors which are to be considered include, but are not limited to:

    (a) the geography of the basin, including in particular the extent of the drainage area in the territory of each basin State;

    (b) the hydrology of the basin, including in particular the contribution of water by each basin State;

    (c) the climate affecting the basin;

    (d) the past utilization of the waters of the basin, including in particular existing utilization;

    (e) the economic and social needs of each basin State;

    (f) the population dependent on the waters of the basin in each basin State;

    (g) the comparative costs of alternative means of satisfying the social and economic needs of each basin State;

    (h) the availability of other resources;

    (i) the avoidance of unnecessary waste in the use of waters;

    (j) the practicability of compensation as a means of adjusting conflicts among users; and

    (k) the degree to which the needs of a basin State may be satisfied, without causing substantial injury to a co-basin State.

The ILC report of 1983:

1. In determining whether the use by a system State of a watercourse system or its waters is exercised in a reasonable and equitable manner in accordance with article 7, all relevant factors shall be taken into account whether they are of a general nature or specific for the watercourse system concerned. Among such factors are:

    (a) the geographic, hydrographic, hydrological and climatic factors together with other relevant circumstances pertaining to the watercourse system concerned;

    (b) the special needs of the system State concerned for the use or uses in question in comparison with the needs of other system States including the stage of economic development of all system States concerned;

    (c) the contribution by the system State concerned of waters to the system in comparison with that of other system States;

    (d) development and conservation by the system States concerned with the watercourse system and its waters;

    (e) the other uses of a watercourse system and its waters by the State concerned in comparison with the uses by other system States, including the efficiency of such uses;

    (f) cooperation with other system States in projects or programmes to attain optimum utilization, protection and control of the watercourse system and its waters;

    (g) the pollution by the system State in question of the watercourse system in general and as a consequence of the particular use, if any;

    (h) other interference with or adverse effects, if any, of such use for the uses or interests of other States including but not restricted to, the adverse effects upon existing uses by such States of the watercourse system or its waters and the impact upon protection and control measures of other system States; and

    (i) availability to the State concerned and to other system States of alternative water resources.

Source: Adapted from Caponera (1985).

the scope of legal discussions about international drainage basins (Hayton and Utton 1989).

In one way, it is strange that the development of international law for groundwater has lagged so badly. More than 60 times as much fresh water occurs underground as occurs in lakes and rivers (Pearse et al. 1985), and many industrial countries depend heavily upon groundwater — three-fourths of all the water used in Denmark and the Netherlands, and nine-tenths of that used in Belgium, is groundwater (Hayton and Utton 1989).

Like surface sources, groundwater rarely stays within a political boundary. The Disi Aquifer, for example, underlies Jordan and Saudi Arabia and contains an enormous quantity of nonrenewable fossil water. It is heavily pumped (1 600 Mm^3/year, with most going to Saudi Arabia), with the water currently being used for irrigation as the aquifer is not located near populated areas. Despite huge capital costs and high pumping costs, however, the water may eventually be piped to Amman, some 300 km from and 1 000 m above the wells. The Northeast African Aquifer underlies parts of Chad, Sudan, Libya, and Egypt, and is being affected by Libyan initiatives to build a 1 600-km canal from an oasis in the southern part of the country to the coast. In short, only the specific political aspects make the conflict over shared aquifers of Israel and the West Bank unique.

The general principles of management for states sharing groundwater resources are similar to those related to surface water. As expressed by Barberis (1991, p. 167), they are "the obligation not to cause appreciable harm to shared resources, the duty of equitable and reasonable use, the obligation of prior notification, and the duty to negotiate."

Barberis also points out that, even in the absence of accepted law for groundwater, there is more than a 100-year history of the successful application of these principles. Optimum management, however, can become highly complex when it is not just a question of transboundary groundwater but also of interactions between groundwater and surface water or of political boundaries between the location of the aquifer outflow and its recharge area, which is exactly the case for the Mountain Aquifer in Israel and the West Bank.

The most significant new development in the international law of aquifers is a draft treaty developed over a period of 8 years by an international group of specialists (Hayton and Utton 1989). The Bellagio Draft Treaty focuses on mutual agreement among those entities that share the aquifer, and it is remarkably comprehensive. Besides the obvious areas of withdrawal and recharge, it also includes articles dealing with contamination, depletion, and transboundary transfers. Special provisions are made for drought conditions, including equitable sharing of any hardships; for public participation; and for a series of dispute-resolution techniques up to and including formal arbitration or submission to the International Court of Justice.

Might such a treaty work for Israelis and Palestinians? Certainly they each have more to gain (Palestinians in the near term; Israelis in the long) by coming to an agreement than by taking unilateral action. Moreover, the treaty is designed expressly to minimize interference with national actions. It is worth quoting at length from Hayton and Utton's description of the approach taken in the Bellagio Draft Treaty (Hayton and Utton 1989, pp. 664–665):

> In order to minimize the intrusion into the sovereign sensitivities of independent countries, three concepts are used:
> 1. rather than comprehensive administration along the entire border, control is to be asserted only in zones considered to be critical because withdrawals are exceeding recharge or contamination is threatening groundwater quality;
> 2. actual enforcement would be left to the internal administrative agencies of each country with oversight and facilitating responsibility lodged in an international agency; and
> 3. the "black letter" provisions delegate only a limited amount of substantive discretion to the joint agency, but, above all, they instruct the Commission to take the initiative, subject to Governments' approval, in preparing for and confronting the full range of problems involving the Parties' transboundary groundwaters.

This approach seems reasonably likely to satisfy those who will sooner or later be faced with negotiating an agreement on sharing the aquifers that underlie Israel and the Occupied Palestinian Territories.

Relevant International and Canadian Experiences

There have been numerous experiences internationally with the application of water law and the development of institutional frameworks and formal cooperative arrangements regarding transboundary water resources. Four of these are discussed below, primarily to provide an overview of the range of agreements that have been implemented. Two of these involve Canada, and one is solely within the country (the Prairie Provinces Water Board). Because the Canadian provinces have ownership over resources within their boundaries, the interjurisdic-tional water issue in Canada is much like that of an international river basin. These examples represent the types of institutional arrangements that may be appropriate in the Middle East.

International Joint Commission (IJC) — The International Joint Commission is a permanent, impartial tribunal consisting of six mem-bers, three from the United States and three from Canada. It was estab-lished as an institutional mechanism under the 1909 Boundary Waters Treaty between the two countries, which set out to bring about rational water management of the transboundary waters. The IJC has three basic functions. First, it sits as a regulatory body that manages the levels and flows of boundary and transboundary waters. Second, it is a commission of inquiry to monitor, investigate, and report on problems along the common frontier between the United States and Canada. Third, it serves as a court of arbitration, providing principles for the equitable use of boundary waters. The role of the IJC is similar to the UN Security Council and GATT (General Agreement on Tariffs and Trade) in that it arbitrates disputes between the two countries and has the power to prescribe conditions and provide protection from indemnity for injuries arising from the action of one of the two parties on the other. The Commission, however, has no policing powers and hence cannot actively enforce its decisions and must draw on other institutional means for enforcement.

The Prairie Provinces Water Board (PPWB) — The Prairie Provinces Water Board is the administering agency for a cooperative surface water apportionment agreement among three provinces (Alberta, Manitoba, and Saskatchewan) and the federal government in Canada. This agree-ment represents the only interjurisdictional apportionment agreement in Canada, and it serves as a useful model of the type of agreement that could be signed in the Jordan River Basin. The agreement specifies the "reasonable and equitable" apportionment of river waters by allotting provinces 50% of the natural flow arising in or flowing through an upstream province, thereby balancing the concepts of territorial sovereignty and territorial integrity. All water diversions and consumptive uses come under the agreement. Prior notification of changes to the water regime is required, and a dispute resolution mechanism is defined. The weaknesses of the agreement are twofold: it allows provinces to unilaterally pass legislation that would exempt that province, and actions are only taken with the agreement of all parties. Its strength, however, is that it establishes a regional authority composed of senior managers from each jurisdiction with the ability to resolve interjurisdictional disputes, but that leaves provinces free to manage their own water.

The Mekong Committee — The Mekong Committee was established in 1957 under the auspices of the United Nations Economic Committee for the Far East and Asia as an independent body to formulate a comprehensive plan for the development of the Lower Mekong. The Committee is made up of the four riparian countries (Cambodia, Laos, Vietnam, and Thailand), and it is assisted by 21 other nations and 12 international agencies. The primary goal of the Committee is to promote the "comprehensive development of water resources and related resources of the lower Mekong basin." Despite the difficult political situation in the region over the last two decades, the Committee has acted to develop an integrated planning approach to the Mekong, and recently has concentrated on hydroelectric development. The effectiveness of the Committee has been largely undermined by political problems and distrust, and it has been criticized for not responding to democratic and environmental criticism. Nevertheless, it appears that the Committee will play an important role in river basin planning over the next few decades.

The Joint Rivers Commission (JRC) — After Bangladesh's independence in 1972, a 25-year "friendship treaty" was signed with India. One of the articles in the treaty incorporated water issues, such as river basin development, flood control, and hydroelectric power generation. Soon after, a Joint Rivers Commission was established to promote development of the Ganges/Brahmaputra basin. The mandate of the JRC was limited to project development and excluded the question of water sharing or policy development. Although it represented the first formal forum in which bilateral technical discussions over water were held, the political nature of the Commission, disagreement over shared information, and the dispute over water sharing have limited the utility of the JRC in resolving transboundary water conflicts in the region.

Management Plans in the Jordan River Basin: An Historical Perspective

It is clear from the previous discussion that the politics of water practiced today in the Jordan River Basin has its roots in negotiations dating back to the early 1900s (if not before). Although some of the early attempts at assessing the availability of water (and the number of people that could be supported by this water) are mentioned briefly in an earlier chapter, the purpose of this section is to provide an historical perspective on the development of management plans and attempts to reach agreements over water resources in the Jordan Basin. The discussion begins with the Palestine Mandate of 1922, which established Palestine as a distinct political unit (the original Mandate of 1920 had included Transjordan, but the two were separated in 1922 despite strong Zionist objections; Khouri 1985). This historical perspective also provides context for many of the contemporary proposals for water allocation and joint water management that have been — and are being — discussed in the multilateral talks.

The 1920s

The British–Palestine Mandate of 1922 was significant in that it marked the official international recognition of the historical connection of the Jewish people with the land of Palestine. The cornerstone for the Mandate between Britain and the League of Nations had been laid 5 years previously, in a letter from British Foreign Secretary Arthur Balfour to a private British subject (later known as the "Balfour Declaration"). Indeed, the groundwork had been laid long before this, because there had been ongoing pressure on Britain for a Jewish homeland since the first meeting of the World Zionist Organization in 1897. The letter referred to a national home for the Jewish people to be established in Palestine (Khouri 1985). The British Mandate incorporated the Balfour Declaration in its entirety. It also spawned the development of a Jewish agency to assist with the administration of Palestine and, in the minds of many Zionists, implicitly provided for an independent Jewish state (although this was not part of the Mandate). Soon after, a number of national development agencies and projects were created, including the Jewish-owned Palestine Electricity Corporation, which was founded by Pinhas Rutenberg. In 1926, the Corporation was granted a 70-year concession to the waters of the Jordan and Yarmouk rivers for the purpose of generating electricity, and subsequently a dam was built at the confluence of the two rivers. It was through this concession, which was formalized by the British High Commissioner, that Arab farmers were denied the right to use the waters upstream of the junction of the two rivers for any purpose without the express permission of the Electricity Corporation. This permission was never granted (Doherty 1965; Hosh and Isaac 1992). Although the dam was destroyed in the 1948 war, Wolf (1995) notes that Israel continually used the "Rutenberg" concession in later years to argue for a greater share of Yarmouk River waters.

The 1930s

Questions about the absorptive capacity of Palestine arose during the 1930s as Jewish immigration and settlement in the region and, concurrently, Arab opposition, increased. As noted in Chapter 6, the British government responded to this growth and opposition by assigning Sir John Hope-Simpson to assess the potential of the land to accommodate an increased population in Palestine. He concluded that, given reasonable growth in Arab agriculture, the remaining lands were "insufficient to maintain a decent standard of life for the country's Arab rural population" (Esco Foundation 1947, as quoted in Wolf 1995). This report was followed by a formal policy document known as the Passfield White Paper, which agreed with Hope-Simpson that there was little land available for Jewish immigrants. These documents were severely criticized by the Zionist community, primarily because they failed to take into account the regional hydrology or the potential for intra-regional transfer of water. Hence, the issue of the true absorptive capacity of Palestine was not adequately addressed. In 1931, in response to the criticisms of the Zionists and, in particular, Chaim Weizmann (who claimed that "we shall be able to put at least 50,000 additional families on the land, without the least injustice to its present occupants" (as quoted in Wolf 1995)), British Prime Minister MacDonald reiterated the British Mandate's obligation to encourage Jewish immigration and settlement on the land of Palestine. In effect, this amounted to a dismissal of the conclusions and recommendations of both the Hope-Simpson Report and the Passfield White Paper.

The first regional water supply project in Palestine was implemented in 1935–36 by Mekorot,[9] the newly established national water company under the guidance of S. Blass. The plan involved supplying water from three sources, Kfar Chasidim, Ousa, and the falls of the Carmel near Yagur, to provide 4 Mm^3 of water to the western Galilee (Fishelson 1989). This project was followed by the assignment of M. Ionides by the British to be Director of Development for the East Jordan Government for the express purpose of assessing the water resource and irrigation potentials of the Jordan River Basin (Hosh and Isaac 1992). The Ionides Plan contained three primary recommendations (Doherty 1965; Naff and Matson 1984; Hosh and Isaac 1992):

- ≈ That Yarmouk River floodwaters be diverted along the East Bank of the Jordan River and stored in Lake Tiberias (Kinneret);
- ≈ That these stored waters, along with a small quantity of Yarmouk River water, be diverted through a new canal (the East Ghor Canal) to provide irrigation for lands east of the Jordan River; and
- ≈ That irrigation water of the Jordan River be used primarily within the Jordan River Basin.

Consistent with the Hope–Simpson Plan, the assessment by Ionides also concluded that there would be insufficient water to sustain a Jewish state. Although the Ionides Plan was never implemented in its entirety (because the Palestine Electricity Corporation still had authority over the waters of the Jordan and the Yarmouk), it did serve as a

---

[9] "Mekorot" comes from the Hebrew word for sources or springs.

basis for Jordan's future water development planning, and provided important input to the UN Partition Plan of Palestine (Doherty 1965; Hosh and Isaac 1992).

The 1940s

The issue of the absorptive capacity of Palestine and, accordingly, of Jewish immigration, had still not been adequately resolved by 1940. Although it is not clear precisely why, a director of the US Soil Conservation Service, Walter Clay Lowdermilk, was sent to the region in 1938 to examine the issue of land conservation. On the one hand, Fishelson (1989) notes that the Americans commissioned Lowdermilk to undertake a detailed study of the region because they thought this research would aid US efforts with respect to land conservation, but this seems a dubious justification. Wolf (1995), on the other hand, implies that the British sought US help after both Arabs and Jews expressed increasing opposition to the resolution of this issue by the British. Others have suggested that Zionists, unhappy with previous plans, pressured the United States directly to commission a separate study.

Regardless of the reason, it is clear that Lowdermilk felt that, with appropriate water management, the water available in the Jordan River basin could sustain a much larger population than existed at that time. Included in his initial idea was the formation of a regional water authority based on the Tennessee Valley Authority (TVA) in the United States. In 1944, he published his comprehensive plan for the region, entitled *Palestine: Land of Promise*. The plan proposed that, by exploiting unused water resources adjacent to Palestine, particularly the Litani and Yarmouk rivers, water could be diverted for irrigation throughout the Jordan Valley and south to the Negev. In his own words (Lowdermilk 1944, p. 122):

> Further study of the possibilities of what I shall call the Jordan Valley Authority or JVA has convinced me that the full utilization of the Jordan Valley...will in time provide farms, industry and security for at least four million Jewish refugees from Europe, in addition to the 1,800,000 Arabs and Jews already in Palestine.

At this time, S. Blass and Mekorot also prepared a comprehensive plan for resolving the water resource problems of Palestine (Mekorot

1944). The plan developed a "national" water resource project that focused on irrigation and hydroelectric development, and incorporated both surface water (from the Yarmouk, the Yarkon, and the Jordan, as well as springs and floodwaters) and groundwater (Fishelson 1989). Blass estimated that a population of 8 million could be served by this plan, which included major water diversions from the Jordan and Yarmouk rivers, and a canal from the Mediterranean Sea to the Dead Sea, which would prevent the drying up of the Dead Sea and, in addition, allow for hydroelectric power generation (Blass seems to have been the first person to propose a Med–Dead Canal). Also included in this plan was a recommendation that the Mandate border be redrawn to include the headwaters of the Hasbani, Dan, and Banias rivers, eastward to include territory for a conduit along the shores of Lake Hula, and upstream on the Yarmouk to allow for a set of impoundments along the river (Mekorot 1944; also noted in Fishelson 1989 and Wolf 1995). Although the report also recommended the diversion of Litani River waters into the Jordan River, Wolf (1995) notes that Lebanese territory was not included in the recommended adjustments to the Mandate borders, and it was assumed that agreement would be reached with the Lebanese before undertaking any such diversion.

There was strong Zionist support for both the Lowdermilk and Mekorot plans, and the World Zionist Organization then asked James B. Hays, an engineer who had worked on the Tennessee Valley Authority in the United States, to draw up development plans based on Lowdermilk's ideas. Hays agreed with Lowdermilk's estimates of the absorptive capacity of Palestine (Khouri 1985) and published his plan in a book entitled *T.V.A. on the Jordan* (Hays 1948). The development plan contained seven elements:

- ≈ Development of groundwater resources;
- ≈ Development of the Upper Jordan River's summer flow for irrigation of nearby lands (including diversion of the Hasbani River for irrigation, and assumed Lebanese agreement);
- ≈ Diversion of Yarmouk River waters into the Sea of Galilee and their storage there;
- ≈ The Mediterranean Sea–Dead Sea Canal that had been proposed by Blass;

≈ Recovery of the Jordan River's winter flow for irrigation of the coastal plain;

≈ Reclamation of the Hula swamps. The Hula Valley was a marshy area that was flooded by winter flow from the Jordan River; the plan was to construct a series of drainage canals to control both floodwaters and groundwater levels and convert the marsh into fertile irrigation land; and

≈ The use of floodwaters for irrigation in the Negev.

Although disagreement remained as to the number of people the region could absorb and the types of water projects needed to provide for population growth from natural increases and from immigration, the UN Partition Plan of 1947, the animosities that had developed between the Arabs and Jews, and the subsequent 1948 Palestine War set the stage for inevitable conflicts over water for the next few decades. In hindsight, it appears that the 1948 borders could have been drawn by an evil water-god, intent on provoking conflict among riparians. The Jordan River and its tributaries — so crucial to the economic development of three states and a population of now dispossessed Palestinians — formed the border between, flowed adjacent to (the Syrian border was only 10 m from Lake Kinneret), or wound in and out of four riparian states. It is of little surprise that, with the exception of intense negotiations in the early 1950s conducted in the context of armed conflict in the region, the development of water resources in the Jordan Valley after 1948 was unilateral, and largely dictated by the new State of Israel, with its growing military and political power, and its superior access to both capital and technology.

The 1950s

The first formal plan for water management from Jordan in the post-independence period was the MacDonald Report in 1951 (Wishart 1990). The MacDonald Report outlined the conflicts between Jordan and Israel, particularly with regard to interbasin transfers of water, and proposed that all developed water remain in the Jordan Valley. The proposal also included the Hays component of diverting the Yarmouk into Lake Kinneret. As Hosh and Isaac (1992) note, however, the

Arabs were concerned over sharing a reservoir with Israel, even though
it was a much cheaper alternative (Kally 1993), and favoured a plan
proposed by M. Bunger, an American engineer working in Amman,
which involved the construction of a high dam on the Yarmouk River
that would provide water storage and hydroelectric capacity. The dam
was to be built at Maqarin, and be a joint project between Jordan and
Syria. Although it did not involve the joint storage of water in Lake
Kinneret, which the alternative storage site on the Yarmouk made
unnecessary, it did provide for irrigation water for the eastern Jordan
Valley and parts of Syria, which would help increase productivity and
release the pressure placed on Jordan by Palestinian refugees. The dam
would also use the winter flow from the Yarmouk to generate electricity
for both Syria and Jordan (with 75% going to Syria) (Doherty 1965;
Wishart 1990). Despite Israel's objections that the original Rutenberg
Concession gave it exclusive rights to the Yarmouk River (Hosh and
Isaac 1992), construction of the dam began in 1953. Because it would
allow for the permanent resettlement of Palestinian refugees, the proposed project was supported by the United Nations Relief and Works
Agency (UNRWA). Israel, however, raised strong objections to the
unilateral development of the Yarmouk, and pressured the United
States to withdraw funding for the plan (which, according to Hosh and
Isaac (1992), "surprised" the Jordanian government).

Accepting that a unified plan might diffuse some of the developing conflicts between riparians on the Jordan, UNRWA asked the
Tennessee Valley Authority (TVA) to develop such a plan. In 1952,
the TVA requested Charles T. Main, Inc. to produce a "unified plan,"
which would combine all the work previously conducted by the parties
into one combined plan. In his letter of transmittal of the plan to
UNRWA, the Chair of the Board of TVA stated that the Main Plan
"does not consider political factors or attempt to set this system into the
national boundaries now prevailing" and that "the present location of
national boundaries suggests that the optimum development and utilization of the water resources of the Jordan–Yarmouk watershed could only
be achieved by cooperation among the states concerned" (as quoted in
Doherty 1965). The Main Plan was based on irrigation by restricted-
gravity flow within the watershed only, borrowing the basic principle

from the earlier Ionides and MacDonald proposals (Doherty 1965). Similar to other plans, the Main Plan included the drainage of the Hula marshes, storage of Yarmouk River water in Lake Kinneret, a Med–Dead Canal proposal, and dams on the Hasbani and Yarmouk rivers for irrigation and power (Doherty 1965). The Main Plan would form the basis for the proposals later submitted to Israel and the Arab states by an envoy of US President Eisenhower.

Despite the evident need for a regional water plan, Israel was proceeding with unilateral development of the Jordan in 1953, beginning construction on its National Water Carrier at a site in the demilitarized zone north of Lake Kinneret. Syria responded by sending troops to the border (Davis et al. 1980) and, according to Cooley (1984), Syrian artillery units opened fire on the construction site. Syria also protested to the United Nations, resulting in a Security Council order that work in the demilitarized zone be halted. The intake site for the National Water Carrier was subsequently moved to the shores of Lake Kinneret, which, as Wolf (1995) notes, was a "doubly costly" move, for Israel. First, the salinity of Lake Kinneret was much higher than the Upper Jordan; this forced Israel to divert saline springs away from Lake Kinneret and into the Lower Jordan, which has caused other problems. Second, the water now had to be pumped up 250 m from the intake location before heading southward. Clearly, on the one hand, "The Jordan waters question had now become a serious threat to peace in the Middle East" (Smith 1966). On the other hand, Israel chose to accept the high technological costs of locating the intake site for the National Water Carrier at Lake Kinneret and avoid a conflict. (Included in these additional "costs" was the cost of electricity for pumping, which, at the time, meant more imported oil.) This is an excellent example of a situation in which, in the face of the disproportionate costs of a war, an alternative solution to a conflict over water was found.

Although tensions had been temporarily diffused by the Israeli decision to move the intake site for the National Water Carrier, the pressing need for a regional solution to problems involving Jordan River waters and increasing pressures from Congress to resolve the issue of Palestinian refugees resulted, in late 1953, in the appointment by President Eisenhower of Eric Johnston as a special ambassador to lead a mission focusing on unified water development of the Jordan River Basin.

Johnston presented the technical features of the Main Plan (later called the "Johnston" or "Unified" Plan) to Israel and the Arab states as a set of proposals that would set the stage for future discussions of unified development of the Jordan. There were five key issues at stake in the subsequent negotiations:

≈ Mutually favourable water quotas;

≈ Use of Lake Kinneret as a storage facility;

≈ Use of Jordan River waters in other watersheds, mainly the Negev;

≈ Inclusion of the Litani River as part of the Jordan system; and

≈ The nature of international supervision of any unified project.

The Johnston Plan contained three major components: storage, distribution, and allocation. Water storage included components from both earlier proposals for diverting Yarmouk River water and consisted of the construction of two primary facilities: a dam near Maqarin for irrigation and power generation, and a diversion structure and canal to store Yarmouk River floodwater in Lake Kinneret (also approximately 300 Mm^3/year). The distribution system focused primarily on providing water to Jordan's East Ghor Canal, which would then supply most of the surface water to the country. Water allocations were based on the principle that Arab states should receive enough water to meet their irrigation needs with the remaining water divided between Jordan (the Yarmouk) and Israel (the Jordan).

Not surprisingly, the Main/Johnston Plan was not acceptable to either Israel or to the Arab states. Israel argued that a unified regional plan should include all water sources of the region, including the Litani, and considered the allocations it was to receive under the plan insufficient. The Arab states remained concerned about the storage of Yarmouk River water in Lake Kinneret as well as the high allocation given to Israel. Accordingly, both groups prepared alternative proposals (Doherty 1965). The Israeli proposal, known as the Cotton Plan, was prepared by an American engineer, Joseph Cotton. Included in the plan was a provision for 50% of the water of the Litani River to be used for power production, and an allocation to Israel of 55% of Litani and

Jordan waters (compared with 33% under the Main Plan). The Cotton Plan also allowed for the use of Jordan River water outside the watershed (for irrigation in the Negev).

The Arab proposal (by the Arab Technical Committee under the guidance of Mohammed Ahmad Salim) was consistent with the Main Plan in that it required that all waters be used within the watershed, but it reduced Israel's share to 20% (and did not include the Litani River). It is important to note that all of the parties recognized the need for regional cooperation for efficient utilization of water resources; the primary disagreements were on water allocations and the transfer of water outside the watershed (Table 11).

Using the two counterproposals, along with a recently completed hydrographic survey commissioned by the Jordanian government, Eric Johnston submitted a revised set of proposals to the riparians in 1955. The "Unified" Plan allowed for interbasin transfer within the context of the allocations to each country and incorporated many of the engineering features of the Main Plan. Disagreements remained, however, over allocations and international supervision. (The Arabs were in favour of direct supervision by an international body, whereas Israel preferred supervision by a small body of engineers from the region.) In late 1955, Johnston reported that "they [the riparians] have made it clear...that the technical and engineering aspects of the plan...are now satisfactory to

Table 11. Allocations of the Jordan River under the Johnston Plan (and counterproposals by the Arabs and Israelis).

Country or region	Johnston 1953		Arab Tech. 1954		Cotton 1954	
	Water (Mm^3/year)	Area ('000 km^2)	Water (Mm^3/year)	Area ('000 km^2)	Water (Mm^3/year)	Area ('000 km^2)
Jordan–Palestine	774	49	861	49	575	43
Syria	45	3	132	12	30	3
Lebanon	—	—	35	4	450	35
Arab states (total)	819	52	1 028	65	1 055	81
Israel	394	42	200	23	1 290	179
Total	1 213	94	1 228	88	2 345	260

Source: Isaac and Hosh (1992).

them" and that the negotiations had reached the "one inch line" (as cited in Garbell 1965). The Plan, however, was never implemented, largely because of Arab distrust of Israel, but also partially because of Israel's opposition to UN involvement (as an infringement on the country's sovereignty; Khouri 1985).

Wishart (1990) presents a detailed explanation of the Johnston negotiations and the eventual breakdown, and concludes that the Arab states had little to lose by not entering into the agreement; indeed, many of the projects outlined in the Johnston Plan were subsequently undertaken unilaterally by the riparian states. As well, formal acceptance of the plan by all of the riparians would have amounted to implicit recognition of the sovereignty of Israel, something the Arab states were unwilling to grant at the time. Nevertheless, all of the riparians unofficially accepted the Johnston Plan, with the exception of Syria, which did not reject it, but simply failed to accept it. It is also worth noting that there was no explicit allocation in the Johnston Plan for the Palestinians; their water was included in the Jordanian share. It is doubtful whether either Israel or Syria would now accept the Johnston Plan because both have installed and operate their own water infrastructure, which gives each more water than the allotments under the Johnston Plan.

Recent Years

Since 1955, there has been little discussion about shared water agreements. Countries in the region have continued to develop their water resources, commonly at the expense of other countries. In addition, groundwater, which was not covered in the Johnston negotiations, has now become an important issue, particularly for Israel and the Occupied Palestinian Territories. Subsequent to the dissolution of the Johnston Plan, Israel constructed the National Water Carrier, and Jordan further developed the East Ghor Canal off the Yarmouk River for irrigation. Plans for the major, multipurpose (irrigation, drinking water, hydropower) Unity Dam on the Yarmouk River were revived by Jordan and Syria in the early 1970s. Israel's territorial gains from the 1967 War had provided it with a stronger riparian position on the Yarmouk and, because impoundment of Yarmouk flows would affect downstream availability of water, Israel now had to be consulted and agree to the proposal. Before agreement between Israel and Jordan could be reached, problems arose between Syria and Jordan, resulting in the postponement of the Unity Dam project at Maqarin in 1980.

Allocation by Calculation

Allocation of Water by Formula

The issue of water allocations and water "rights" still plays a central role in both the arguments/discussions surrounding regional cooperation over water and in the perceptions of the riparians and the Palestinians. As a result, there has been much written in recent years about the application of surface water and groundwater law in international river basins in the region, as well as the development of different allocation schemes based on the interpretation of these "laws" or using other criteria. Some of these schemes involve the use of mathematical formulae.

Zarour and Isaac (1992), for example, have recently proposed a "pragmatic, applicable and dispassionate formula" for the allocation of water rights. Beginning from the principles of limited territorial sovereignty in water use, and of the drainage basin, including both surface and underground water, as the relevant unit of analysis (based on the Helsinki Rules of 1966), they develop an equation that grants rights on the basis of equal weighting of contributions to supply and the sum of human withdrawals and natural losses. The allocation scheme is presented in the following equation:

$$S_{(i)} = 50 * \left[\frac{B_{(i)}}{B_{(T)}} + \frac{I_{(i)} - L_{(i)}}{I_{(T)} - L_{(T)}} \right]$$

where $S_{(i)}$ is the size of the right/obligation of state i (percent); $B_{(i)}$ is the area of the basin/storage volume within or under the territory of state i; $B_{(T)}$ is the total area/storage volume of the basin; $I_{(i)}$ is the natural input to the basin originating within the territories of state i; $I_{(T)}$ is the total input to basin T; $L_{(i)}$ is the natural loss from the basin's waters occurring within the territories of state i; and $L_{(T)}$ is the total natural loss of water occurring throughout the basin.

Although the lack of available data hindered the authors' applica-tion of the allocation scheme to the Jordan Basin, it is obvious that the model focuses mainly on the natural boundaries of surface and subsur-face basins and ignores the social and economic aspects included in the Helsinki Rules.

In a different approach to setting allocations by formula, Moore (1992) starts from the perspective that both the surface water and the aquifers shared by Israelis and Palestinians are common property resources, and that, therefore, it is futile to search for an ideal allocation that is inherently "equitable and reasonable." Instead, he offers four pos-sible perspectives on equity, adopted from the Helsinki Rules: existing water utilization, recharge area, natural flow, and population. He then suggests that the "optimal allocation regime" (elsewhere termed the "least worst regime") can be determined mathematically by minimizing the summation of the "error distances" from a notional line connecting points of 100% allocation to Palestinians and 100% allocation to Israelis.

Moore (1993) later extended the approach to allow for six possi-ble definitions of equity and, in the case of surface water, for Syrian, Jordanian, and Lebanese as well as Israeli and Palestinian allocations. In the case of aquifers, storage capacity was added and population was replaced by projections of agricultural, industrial, and domestic needs. In the case of surface water, catchment area replaces recharge area and average annual discharge replaces storage area; otherwise, the two for-mulae are identical. Results for aquifers ranged, depending on weight-ing, from a 60–40 to an 80–20 split in favour of the Israelis. Results for the combined Jordan–Yarmouk rivers were very different, with Israel getting about 30% (about what it would have received under the Johnston Plan), Jordan 22%, and the Palestinians little more than 2% (but more than twice what they are getting now).

Although intriguing, such formulae seem too rigid to satisfy the many concerns other than geography and economic power (some might say "greed"). As well, what Elmusa (1993a) calls their "neatness and simplification of the web of factors" can go too far in just that direction. Apart from the physical characteristics of the basin or aquifer, none of the variables is truly objective. The emphasis on "need" in Moore's formulae is particularly questionable. The very fact that results differ so sharply between the Zarour–Isaac and the Moore formulae suggests that objectivity may be in the eye of the modeler.

The approaches suggested in the foregoing show that the definition of equity is anything but obvious, but they do show that methods exist that can provide negotiators with suggestive schemes for sharing available, common property water. Moreover, if they are taken as indicative rather than definitive approaches, the mathematical methods might have additional value. For example, various formulae could be applied with a range of weights and the derived results compared to see whether they might be acceptable to the relevant parties. If a resolution with some degree of convergence is identified, the formula could be investigated further. In effect, our suggestion is to go from result to formula rather than from formula to result.

Commercial Transactions for the Sale of Water

A number of authors have suggested that the evident surplus of water on the West Bank could, after independence is achieved, become not only a resource for internal development but also one that could be sold for hard currency. Heller and Nusseibah (1991, p. 112) recognize this potential but are cautious in their suggestions:

> It is conceivable that the primary benefits that [the new Palestinian] state will derive from the river waters will be indirect, for example, through an agreement with Israel to make use of its National Water Carrier or to purchase at reduced rates certain water-intensive agricultural produce from Israel.

Somewhat in contrast, Zarour and Isaac (1992, p. 23) suggest full acceptance of water as a market commodity, with potentially significant benefits for a future Palestine:

> An international open water market in the Middle East would be a good promoter of international cooperation in the area. Countries with water surpluses would be willing to trade water with shortfall countries, in an arrangement fairly valuing water like any other commodity.... One potential application of this would be that the anticipated Palestinian entity could trade water rights with rights to access and use Israeli costs.

Canadians may have some reservations about the final sentence, given the way Americans have sometimes cast longing glances at water

to the north, but the same perspective should give them grounds for recognizing why Palestinians at all levels feel that water is such a critical
resource for their future. Just as with Canadians, the issue for
Palestinians is not whether there will be enough water for drinking and
sanitation but whether water will be available in large enough quantities and at low enough costs and in appropriate locations to allow for
sustainable economic development.

Zarour and Isaac (1991) suggested a variation on the proposal for
an open market for water. They proposed using the water surplus found
in the West Bank to supply the Gaza Strip, which has a water deficit.
No mention is made of financial aspects, but it would surely be cheaper
and technically more efficient to work out a trade under which the
West Bank would supply Israel and Israel, in turn, would supply Gaza.
This is exactly the sort of approach that Zeitouni and her colleagues
had in mind. Using a mathematical analysis, they simulated the results
of two alternatives for auctioning rights to water futures, both of which
use market mechanisms to achieve welfare-maximizing results (Zeitouni
et al. 1991, p. 2):

> The two proposed economic incentive mechanisms are: (a) a market for
> percentage rights, where potential water consumers bid for a share of an
> uncertain quantity of water, and (b) a market for priority rights in
> which potential consumers bid for a slot in a queue, and once assured a
> position, are in a position to use as much water as they need and is left
> by bidders further up the line.

The method is as applicable among consumers within a nation as
it is between national entities. Although the authors find that either
method improves the welfare (in an economic sense) of all parties, better results are achieved with the percentage-rights method. They note,
however, that the market for priority rights might be favoured, particularly in an international situation, as more wealth is transferred to the
sellers of water, which is likely to be the Palestinians.

A type of futures market for water is apparently operating success-
fully in Australia, where capacity in a common storage reservoir can be
privatized (Dudley and Musgrave 1993). Assuming there is confidence
in the managing authority, capacity sharing both minimizes the inter-
dependence of different users (allowing each to follow its own optimizing behaviour) and reduces their costs to achieve any given level of

certainty and risk avoidance. The system is not without problems (for example, upstream participants are not allowed to reduce inflows from the catchment area, at least not without compensation to downstream participants), but it is worthy of consideration if any of the various options for using Lake Kinneret for joint storage of either Litani or Yarmouk water become feasible. A similar scheme was advocated by Salim Maksud, Director of the Litani River Administration, when he suggested selling water from the Litani to Israelis and Palestinians (see Gruen 1994). It would also be appropriate for optimizing a design to capture and use high winter flows in the Yarmouk River.

Calculating the Social Value of Water

Economic valuation as a way of improving the social allocation of water, and of approaching the issue of water rights, is at the heart of a water model for the region developed at the Institute for Social and Economic Policy in the Middle East, which is located at the Kennedy School of Government, Harvard University. The Institute created the Harvard Middle East Water Project to investigate and propose "a rational economic method for analyzing water issues that may help the parties to perceive the conflict and approaches to its resolution in a new way" (Fisher 1994a). Although only a first-generation model is available, and no formal reports have been published, the work has been under way at Harvard and Massachusetts Institute of Technology (MIT) in collaboration with research teams of Israelis, Jordanians, and Palestinians for nearly 2 years. (The existing model includes three "countries": Israel, Jordan, and Palestine; Syria and Lebanon could be included in a later version.) Everyone agrees that further work is needed on the model, but the current version and initial results are attracting the attention of both researchers and policymakers (if, indeed, in this region there is any distinction between the two). The timing for this approach appears right and, if so, the hopes expressed in Fisher's quotation may, in fact, be realized.

The approach that underlies the Harvard water model is summarized in the accompanying text box. Everything begins from the unquestioned fact that water is scarce, which, to an economist, implies that the water has a monetary value. More formally, economists say that the

The Harvard Middle East Water Project

1. Water is a scarce resource. Scarce resources have value. In the case of water, however, that value is not merely the price that water would obtain in a free market. National aims, including agricultural, employment, and social policy, are involved in the value of water.

2. The Project seeks to calculate the current value of water in the region and for each of several years in the future. It first examines the costs of supplying water at different points and of transporting it. Next, it estimates private demand curves for water — demand from households, industry, and agriculture. Finally, it incorporates national water policy expressed as additional demand for water at different prices. Equilibrium prices for water are calculated — prices that equate supply and demand.

3. With the full value of water calculated, the value of the property rights at issue can be assessed. Because water cannot be worth more than the cost of replacing it, an upper bound for that value can easily be obtained. **It appears that the value involved in different suggested solutions to the property rights dispute between Israel and the Palestinians is less than roughly $200 million per year — and probably considerably less.** This means that the property rights dispute is one over a sum sufficiently small that nations can negotiate about it. By monetizing the dispute, the Project expects to lead to its solution.

4. Suppose that water is priced at its value (including its social value, incorporating national aims as well as private demands). Owners of water who use the water themselves do not, in fact, get the water at no cost. Such owners give up the money that they could make by selling the water to others. Hence, such owners (like anyone who uses the water) are really buying the water.

5. The right of ownership, therefore, is a property right entitling the owner to the monetary value of the water. That is true regardless of who uses the water.

6. As a result, the question of property rights — of who owns the water — and the question of how the water should be optimally managed and used are analytically separate questions. Both questions are of great importance and both must be answered in any agreement, but one can think about them separately.

7. The Project envisages a water authority jointly operated by Israel, Jordan, and Palestine. That authority will transfer water from one country to another at prices reflecting the full social value of water as determined by each side.

8. It is important to realize that when a country determines for itself how much water it demands at a particular price — including the demand coming from considerations of national policy — then it should be willing to sell additional water to a neighbour at that price or any higher price. If it does so, it can use the money obtained for greater social benefit than **(according to its own policies)** would be obtained from the water itself. In effect, the selling country has already said what additional water is worth to it. At that price, it must be indifferent between using and selling such additional water. If it wishes not to sell, then it has placed too low a value on the water, and the price should be adjusted upward.

Source: Fisher (1994a); emphasis as in original.

water has an opportunity cost (which is based on the next-best use of the water). Individuals who own some water can sell it and realize a return, or they can use it themselves (or just leave it in place), in which case they forego the amount they could have earned by selling it. In the latter case, they are, in effect, buying the water from themselves even though no financial transaction takes place. Exactly the same is true for a country; it can sell the water, use the water, or just leave it in place — but no matter which option it chooses, either it receives a return (the first option) or it accepts an opportunity cost for not selling (the latter two options). This sort of approach stems from a general proposition in economics that the question of ownership (in this case, of water) is *analytically* distinct from the question of optimal (water) use. Neither can be neglected, but, as indicated in the box, for purposes of analysis, the determination of efficient patterns of extraction and use can be defined independently of how ownership shares are divided.

In the simplest free-market approach, the definition of private costs and private returns would be the end of the matter. Almost no one argues, however, for pure markets for water in the Middle East (or any-where else, for that matter). For one thing, many people believe that everyone is inherently entitled to some volume of potable water; how-ever, the total volumes implied by such entitlements are small. More importantly, national policies with various goals (such as to promote agriculture or to protect employment or even to deny surplus water to another nation) must also be considered, and they typically involve large volumes. So too are the unpriced (and often unrecognized) ecological services provided by water in place — as wetland for animals or for purification of effluents or for stabilization of river flows — as well as some partially priced services, as for recreation and fishing. The current version of the Harvard water model makes explicit provision for what it calls national policy demands for water as well as for individual demands, but, in its current version at least, it does not incorporate ecological demands (which means that, to some extent, the water is undervalued).

More specifically, the Harvard water model calculates the **social** value of water based on real costs (extraction, transport, and disposal) and on the sum of private demands (households, industry, and agriculture) in the region plus national water policy (expressed as demands for additional water at various prices). The resulting figure is the social value of water at the border and, given this value, water can be transferred from one country to another at that price or a higher price. Almost by definition, both parties gain: the buying country gets water at a price that it sees as worthwhile, and the selling country has already defined that, above that price, it would rather have the money than retain the water. Each would be better off after the transaction than before, which is the object of the exercise. Better yet, the system tends toward equilibrium, which is to say that the market clears at prices that bring supply and demand together. Of course, some form of water office operated jointly by Israeli, Jordanian, and Palestinian officials would be needed to administer the transfers, but no policy decisions would be involved.

Although the Harvard water model is admittedly an abstract view of likely markets for water in the region, it does show that water sales across borders would improve economic prospects for all three peoples. In a sentence, what the model does is convert property rights to monetary claims and, at the same time, it provides the information needed to evaluate the profitability of alternative investments in new water-supply systems, imports, or even conservation. Abstract though it may be, the potential for moving toward more rational use of water has a lot of appeal within the region. Not only are the results reasonable, but this approach demands perhaps the minimum of changes in internal water policies (although markets for water between countries are created, nothing requires that internal markets be free), requires the fewest policy decisions, and fits most easily with proposals for joint management of shared waters. Perhaps most importantly, the model seems broadly acceptable to all three of the national groups most concerned.

The Harvard water model may also provide information of direct use in the negotiations. The very fact that property rights can be redefined as monetary claims tends to make discussion more objective. (Admittedly, no price is truly objective as each reflects social and cultural as well as purely economic forces. Prices are, however, better than slogans and appeals to history.) More importantly, the somewhat counterintuitive result of the approach is that the total value of those monetary claims is not particularly large. As argued by Fisher (1994b), the total value of the water cannot be worth more than the cost of replacing it by desalination. Given that there is some 600 Mm^3 of water in dispute, replacement costs are roughly $600 million per year. This creates a stream of annual values that, at typical interest rates, yields a present value throughout time of $5–10 billion. This figure, however, is certainly too high, for it assumes that desalination is the cheapest alternative source, that the equilibrium prices for water are as high as desalination costs, and that one side or the other gets all of the disputed water. Relaxation of these assumptions yields annual costs closer to $200 million (Fisher 1994a) and a present value of $2–4 billion. Those are not enormous sums in international negotiations. Water may be critical to life, but, for most of its uses, it is simply false to consider it "priceless," and recognizing that fact makes negotiation feasible; recognizing further that the price, hence the total value, is relatively low, should make it desirable.

In summary, it appears that some form of controlled rather than fully open market for water could play a role both in balancing water supply and demand across borders and in supporting the economy of an underdeveloped Palestinian entity. Given the limited availability and high cost of reservoirs in the region, the possibility of a market for storage capacity is particularly appealing. Certainly, inadequate water storage rather than absolute water scarcity is the key issue for most of the region north of Gaza and the Negev. As well, the availability of a market and the trading of water supplies or even water futures would open up a potential source of income for what might otherwise be a constrained Palestinian economy.

International Transfers of Water

Importation of Water by Sea

Importation of water is under active consideration in the Middle East. Apart from short-term and small-scale deliveries by tanker trucks, the two options most relevant to Israel involve transportation by pipeline from Turkey or Egypt, and by ship or barge from one of a number of countries (but most likely Turkey). This section will review the prospects for importing water by sea as a long-term option. The next section will review the prospects for international pipelines.

Had the long drought continued into 1992, Israel was planning to import water from Turkey using converted oil tankers to meet its short-term needs for domestic and municipal water. Turkey is the one country in the region with an unqualified surplus of fresh water, and rivers such as the Manavgat (which flows at an average rate of 140 m^3/s, or about 4 000 Mm^3/year) appear to be large enough to supply, and deep enough offshore to provide anchorage for, ocean-going vessels. Some analysts have also suggested Lebanon as a source of water for export, but any surplus there will soon be absorbed by a growing population and economic development (Amery and Kubursi 1992). Loading facilities are not negligible in either scale or cost, but neither is there anything unique about the design (mainly tunnels and piping) that, assuming a Manavgat source, would link a dam 12 km upstream on the river to an offshore loading terminal.

Two main options have been considered: converting oil tankers to carry water or loading the water into large bags that would be towed by tugboats. The latter go by the name of "medusa bags" (not in reference to the character of Greek mythology, but because they move in the water like jellyfish of the same name, allowing waves to pass through them rather than being tossed about).

Estimates of the cost of operating a tanker delivery system range by a factor of about three: from \$0.35 to \$1.10/m^3. Per cubic metre of water delivered, supertankers can operate for much less than smaller tankers, but conversion costs and the cost of loading facilities (mainly because of their deep draft) are much higher. At the lowest end of the cost estimates, which most analysts question, the tanker option would be of marginal interest.

Potentially more feasible are medusa bags, which were developed using Canadian technology (Cran 1992). The bags, each of which carries about 1.5 Mm^3, are made of thick nylon coated with vinyl and reinforced with nylon straps. According to a study by Tahal Consulting Engineers Ltd. (1989), costs for a complete system (bags, tugs, and loading and unloading facilities, and even a 5% royalty) with a capacity of 250 Mm^3/year would be \$0.17–0.23/m^3, depending mainly upon interest rates and the capacity factor (the proportion of time each bag is carrying water as opposed to waiting at the terminal or undergoing maintenance). Initial capital was estimated at about \$280 million for a six-bag/six-tug system. If these figures prove to be correct, Tahal concluded that medusa bags would be competitive with some conventional sources of fresh water and very much so with most alternative sources. Tahal warns, however, that its initial cost estimates are subject to technical uncertainties that require large-scale or prototype tests for resolution. Final costs could be significantly higher.

Much the same conclusion of optimistic prospects, but significant uncertainties for bag technology, has apparently been reached by the state of Alaska, which is exploring possible exports of water to southern California and Mexico. The state is sufficiently convinced by the figures to begin "encouraging investment groups actively pursuing water imports from Alaska to develop a full-size bag and begin trials immediately" (quoted in Savage 1994).

Neither the Tahal study nor the review of the Alaskan study mentions environmental impacts. Apart from the storage dam at the source, however, and impacts that might occur during the construction phase, they should be minor. The draft required by bags large enough to move sizable quantities of water means that they will need deep-water ports or remain well offshore. In summary, of all the alternatives for importing

water, medusa bags seem to be the most deserving of funding for prototype design and operation.

Even assuming that importation of water in medusa bags is economically attractive for Israel or other coastal nations in the region,
transportation of water by sea, regardless of the means of conveyance,
faces serious political barriers in the Middle East. Turkey was apparently
so embarrassed by a 1990 article in the *Wall Street Journal* discussing
possible water sales to Israel that it broke off negotiations. Adverse
Arab reactions could be reduced if the imports to Israel were balanced
with a release by Israel of equal volumes of, for example, Jordan River
water for use in the Occupied Palestinian Territories or in Jordan. In
this way, the imports would become part of a regional solution.

Water tankers, barges, and bags are extremely vulnerable from a
military point of view. Two options have been suggested to reduce the
risk of hostile action. First, if the imports are explicitly coupled with
releases of water to Arab states, as suggested earlier, an agreement could
be signed such that any shortfalls resulting from hostile action would be
shared among all the parties. Second, instead of using the water to feed
directly into distribution systems, it could be used to recharge the
Coastal Aquifer. In effect, the imported water would be treated as "capital" for future consumption rather than as "income" for immediate consumption. To this extent, it would mimic the Gur pipeline proposal and
also eliminate the fear that any city would go thirsty because a ship had
been lost. Indeed, use of imported water for recharge should reduce costs
because it would eliminate the need for storage facilities.

Importation of Water by Pipeline

Importation of water by pipeline as a long-term solution to Israel's water
problems is also under consideration. Egypt and Turkey have both been
mentioned as possible input sources for the pipeline. Despite some initial enthusiasm in Israel and Egypt for a pipeline to transfer Nile River
water to Israel, Gaza, and the West Bank, interest has cooled considerably. Egypt predicts less of a surplus in the Nile than originally thought,
and diversions of this scale would require agreement among all nine of
the nations that share the Nile River basin. Quite in contrast to its
reserve about water exports, Egypt has declared its openness to a natural

gas pipeline to Israel, which indicates that the issue is the nature of the resource, not Middle East politics (*Mideast Mirror*, 11 February 1994). Still, there remains lingering interest in the Nile option to supply the Gaza Strip, partly because a pipeline already exists in the northern Sinai as far as El-Arish, little more than 50 km from the border with Gaza, and partly because costs seem likely to be lower than desalination. Indeed, Kally (1993) argues that it is by far the best option for supplying water to the Gaza Strip, and not a bad option for the Negev. Although the politics of the two destinations differ enormously, Kally argues that they should still be considered (they are not alternatives). His calculations show that, because the costs of providing Egyptian water to the Gaza Strip and the Negev are so much below those of pumping through the National Water Carrier, a trade-off could be worked out by which the water Israel would have supplied to those regions would instead be directed to the West Bank.

Active interest in pipelines has more recently come from Turkey, which would like to play a major role in the future as water broker for the region. Approximately 98% of the Euphrates River has its source in Turkey (Kolars 1990). The river flows from central Turkey through Syria and then Iraq before emptying into the Persian Gulf, and it probably holds the greatest potential for supplying water to those parts of the region suffering from a water deficit. All depends, however, upon Turkey's "water plan," which is based on its Southeast Anatolia Project and includes a number of major dams, some already built and some under construction or still in the planning stage.

For Israel, the relevant part of the plan is a Turkish proposal to build two pipelines (generally referred to in the singular as the "Peace Pipeline") to take water from two rivers, the Seyhan and the Ceyhan, both of which empty into the Mediterranean Sea, southward to the Arab states and maybe Israel (Figure 13). Kolars (1990) states that these two rivers do not have enough water but that the Goksu River does and only requires that the pipeline be 80 km longer. In the Turkish plan, the western line would extend 2 800 km and pump 3.5 Mm^3 of water per day (1 300 Mm^3/year) to Syria, Jordan, and western Saudi Arabia; this line could include an extension into Israel. The eastern line would cover 4 000 km en route to the Persian Gulf through Kuwait, eastern

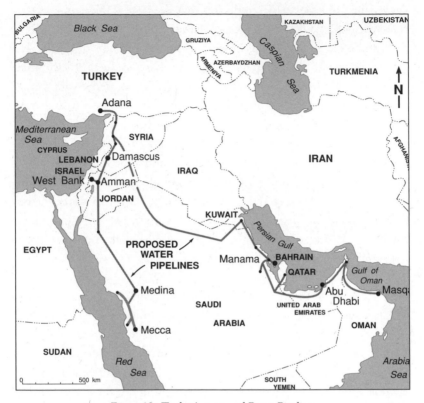

Figure 13. Turkey's proposed Peace Pipeline.

Saudi Arabia, Bahrain, Qatar, the United Arab Emirates, and Oman. The two pipelines together would cost $21 billion. A more modest "minipipeline" has also been proposed (though not by Turkish officials) to supply water to Syria, Jordan, and the West Bank. It would have a capacity of about 2 Mm^3/day (730 Mm^3/year) and cost perhaps $5 billion.

The success of any of these projects is dependent, first, on resolving the present dispute over Turkey's control of the Euphrates River, which has often had negative impacts downstream (Kolars 1990). For example, during the filling of the reservoir behind the Ataturk Dam in 1990, Turkey cut off the Euphrates River for 30 days, which forced Syria and Iraq to ration water and limit the use of electricity. The pipeline projects are also dependent on strong political support within Turkey. Finally, even if political problems could be resolved, the projects would still require financing. In any of its versions, the Peace Pipeline would be a megaproject, and no country or international bank has indicated much interest in providing the funds. Plans for the Peace Pipeline, therefore, are currently on hold.

Despite the current lack of interest, pipeline proposals continue to surface (Gruen 1994). Recently, Alaska looked at the pipeline option to export water, but concluded that it was not feasible (Savage 1994). Although costs are high, they may, nevertheless, be acceptable under some circumstances and in comparison with other alternative sources, particularly for landlocked countries. Cost figures in the Middle East generally range upward from about $0.40/m^3$, not much above present costs, exclusive of any payment for the water itself.

Security of supply is an important issue among countries that have seldom known peace. The possibility that Israel, or any country, would relinquish part of its sovereignty to Turkey, which would control the flow of water in the pipeline (as would, to a reduced extent, every nation higher on the pipeline) is remote, at least without the establishment of an international authority to operate and monitor the pipeline. Options to reduce the vulnerability associated with importing water by pipeline are similar to those associated with importing water by sea.

Finally, the environmental impacts of interbasin water transfers in the Middle East remain to be determined. Likely minor in the case of tankers or medusa bags, they could be sizable at both ends of a pipeline. Little of the considerable discussion on the potential for pipeline projects has addressed the issue of environmental effects.

A Final Note on Interbasin Megaprojects

This section reviews the range of possible regional megaprojects that, apart from desalination projects (reviewed in Chapter 3), represent the only alternatives for significantly increasing the supplies of water to the region. Although we remain somewhat skeptical of all of them, except possibly medusa bags, none can be dismissed as either technically infeasible or so expensive as to be economically irrelevant.

During the next few years, all of the interbasin megaprojects face two overriding limitations. First, they are only second-best choices. Each of the regional parties has technically proven and cost-effective options that remain to be fully exploited. Chief among these are greater efficiency and conservation on the demand side plus low-tech methods such as rainwater harvesting on the supply side. Not far behind are full recycling of wastewater and greater use of saline water for irrigation. Second, all of the projects have significant economies of scale, and the lower cost estimates all depend upon supplying large volumes of water. The only end-use that could absorb such large volumes is irrigation, but few irrigated crops anywhere in the region have a marginal value that makes it worth paying the cost of conventional sources, much less those of an even more expensive pipeline or port facilities.

The foregoing considerations can be turned to advantage, however. Each of the megaproject options deserves consideration, but a decision on adoption need not be made in the near future. Time, therefore, is available for a careful assessment and comparison among the options on a range of criteria: technical, economic, social, environmental, and political. It is also unlikely that more than one of these options can be built at any given time. Several groups, including the World Bank and Freedom House (an economic thinktank in New York City), have reached the same conclusion. What remains is to find the collection of people with the appropriate balance of disciplines, temperaments, and national origins needed to analyze them, and a donor with enough money and enough patience to wait for results. Indeed, results could be so complex and so disparate among criteria as to require still another organization with strong negotiating and mediating skills to create the process for producing the final report.

Militarization and Annexation as a Solution

In the absence of any concerted effort and action on one or more of the foregoing alternatives, there remains the slim possibility that Israel would use military force to supplement its existing water supplies. As discussed previously, water has been a military issue in the past, and it can readily be argued that this may also be the case in the future. Thus,

King Hussein of Jordan has been quoted as saying that he could con-ceive of few reasons to go to war with Israel, but water is one of them (Naff 1990). Over the years, many people have argued, mainly from a journalistic perspective, that a war over water in the region is more or less likely. Recently, an entire book was devoted to the history of con-flict over water and the potential for water wars in the Middle East (Bulloch and Darwish 1993).

Not everyone agrees that war is inevitable in the absence of inter-national agreement. Water scarcity is certainly a constraint on develop-ment, but this does not lead logically or inevitably to war as a way of removing the constraint. Those who anticipate a war neglect the wide range of options ordinary people have devised to overcome or get around water scarcity. Wishart (1989) reviews many of the earlier arti-cles imputing a "hydraulic imperative" to Israel and finds the arguments either economically or politically dubious. Among other things, he points to the transfer or adaptation of more efficient technologies, such as drip irrigation, as a much better alternative and one that, in his words, has low "transaction costs" compared with either war or multi-lateral negotiations.

Although water is likely to remain a source of conflict in the region, we share the view that water wars are unlikely. As we have argued in the foregoing, relatively minor reallocations of water away from agriculture can relieve the pressure so much more cheaply and with so much less risk. Such reallocation not only allows for some water to revert to the Palestinians but also shifts water to sectors that can be expected to pay their own way and that do not have the same emotive appeal as "making the desert bloom." Using a different approach, this is exactly the conclusion that researchers in the Harvard Middle East Water Project have reached. To repeat, according to their calculations, the total value of water in dispute between Israelis and Palestinians probably lies close to $200 million per year and cannot in any case exceed $600 million. As they say, "These are sums over which nations can negotiate" (Fisher 1994b, p. 8). Indeed, the **annual** cost for loss of water is well under the **daily** cost of modern warfare.

If water wars in the Jordan Valley are unlikely, one wonders whether they will occur anywhere. Despite the provocative title of their book, *Water Wars*, Bulloch and Darwish (1993) make a good case for water as a continuing source of conflict in the Middle East but not such a good case for the conflict escalating to open warfare. Beaumont (1994) reviews the potential for water wars in a number of hot spots around the world, and concludes that they are unlikely. Everywhere he finds that, just as in the Jordan Valley, there are simply better alternatives available to national governments. This is not to argue that those other alternatives are politically easy or free of conflict. In a study of environmental change and acute conflict, Homer-Dixon et al. (1993, p. 45) best summarized what appears to be the consensus: "Water shortages will aggravate tensions and unrest within societies in the Jordan River Basin," but warfare among riparians is unlikely. They go on to quote Thomas Naff in suggesting that "internal civil disorder, changes in regimes, political radicalization and instability" are the more likely consequences of water shortages.

In summary, fighting over water simply does not make sense. As Tamir (1988; as cited in Wolf 1995) noted: "Why go to war over water? For the price of a week's fighting, you could build five desalination plants. No loss of life, no international pressure, and a reliable supply you don't have to defend in hostile territory." Despite this simple economic logic, water security remains a very important issue throughout the region. Accordingly, it is one component of the larger issue of "livelihood security" for Israelis and residents of the Territories, and is often difficult to isolate from other elements of "security." Therefore, although the use of force to acquire additional water supplies makes no "economic sense," one cannot completely rule out this possibility.

Planning for a Different Future

There are many analogies between the post-1973 experience with energy and what is now occurring with water: both water and energy have been priced below true costs. In both cases, environmental damages occur at the production and end-use stages; both are governed by institutions geared to augment supply rather than to manage demand; and both are so widely used that many people doubt that conservation can be an effective option.

The conventional approach to supply–demand problems with either energy or water focuses on ensuring that adequate supplies exist to meet present and future energy (water) "requirements," typically expressed graphically as curves of consumption that rise with time. This perspective (with its roots in the old dogma of the insatiability of human wants — now questioned by both ecologists and economists) leads to a supply orientation in which demand is treated as virtually exogenous to policy, a "given" that must be satisfied by ever-greater development of new sources of supply. Conservation may be considered but, generally, as a way to buy the time necessary to bring new supplies on line.

The alternative approach to the analysis of energy, dubbed the "soft energy path," challenges conventional wisdom at each of these points (Lovins 1977). Space does not permit even a cursory review of soft energy analysis, but at its core are three principles: focus on demand and, more specifically, on the services provided by energy, not on the commodity itself; emphasis on the quality of energy as well as on the quantity; and attention to the future rather than the present. Each has its analogy with water.

Demand First

The most distinctive policy implication of soft-path analysis is its emphasis on correcting apparent supply demand imbalances from the demand side, quite the opposite of traditional energy or water policy. This approach is based on recognition that energy (water) use is only a means to an end, not the end in itself, and that the purpose of energy (water) consumption is to satisfy particular end-uses or services, such as growing a certain amount of protein or cooling a certain amount of material. The question then becomes how each end-use or service can be most efficiently satisfied.

The soft path stands the conventional approach on its head. Analysis always starts with end-uses, not sources of supply, and this reversal forces a bottom-up rather than top-down view. From this perspective, conservation and efficiency are not merely interim necessities, but the primary component of rational resource planning, the first place on which to focus attention. Each end-use is broken down (in as much detail as data permit) so that more and more efficient approaches to satisfying the service can be identified. As Lovins (1977) remarks: "In the soft path, how much energy we use to accomplish our social goals is considered a measure not of our success but of our failure." Once beyond the 40 or so litres of water per person-day needed for drinking, cooking, and sanitation, exactly the same is, or should be, true of water.

The analogy, however, between energy and water is not perfect. Among other things, water lacks the direct linkage to thermodynamics that permits energy efficiency to be defined precisely; except for hydropower, energy supply does not vary from year to year; direct use of water is more important than indirect use (unless irrigation water is ascribed to food); and water use is more highly concentrated by sector than energy. Whereas the common energy sources appear in an enormous variety of natural forms (among them coal, oil, wood, and sunlight), water is available in but a single form with three phases (liquid, ice, and vapour). Piped water is even less analogous to oil, mainly because of the difference in unit value; well under a dollar per cubic metre for pure water and well over \$100 for crude oil, which explains why it is economically feasible to transport oil, but not water, over great distances. Nevertheless, the analyses already done and referred to in Chapter 4 suggest enormous opportunities to maintain standards of living, and very possibly raise the quality of life, while lowering the consumption of water. For both water and energy, the amounts actually needed to support life, indeed to support a high quality of life, represent but a small fraction of total consumption. Beaumont (1994) points out that it would take less than 700 Mm^3/year to provide every Israeli with as much water as urban dwellers in the West consume even without increases in efficiency. The lesson for both Israel and the Occupied Palestinian Territories is that the largest, safest, and cheapest "source of supply" for water is likely to be found through conservation and reallocation of existing uses.

Quality is as Important as Quantity

The second distinctive characteristic of soft-path analysis is its emphasis on quality as well as quantity: in the case of energy, on the usefulness of each unit of energy as well as the amount of energy, as measured by litres or tonnes or kilowatt-hours (or joules); in the case of water, on the usefulness of each unit of water as well as the amount of water, as measured by litres or cubic metres.

In the most precise sense, the meaning of quality is clearer in the case of energy than of water. The quality of energy defines the ability to do work, which can be expressed in thermodynamic units. In this sense, there is no direct analogy to water, unless one defines water quality in terms of the amount of energy needed to restore it to a higher quality. We can, for example, increase the quality of water, no matter how degraded, by distillation, but only by expending both dollars and energy. Measuring the former would give an economic indication of the loss of quality, whereas measuring the latter would yield a thermodynamic one. This concept has yet to be tested extensively to see whether it has either heuristic or practical value. Other characteristics, however, of the various forms of energy, such as compactness and cleanliness in use, are also of importance to us and are worth paying for. For example, oil and coal are valued differently depending upon the amount and nature of impurities they contain; the camper or someone with a fireplace is well aware that some forms of wood burn longer or hotter than others. In this sense, there is a clear analogy between energy and water. Water too is valued differently depending upon the nature and characteristics of impurities, such as salts, bacteria, and heavy metals.[10]

Quality considerations may be less obvious with water than with energy, but their relevance is the same. The higher the quality of the water or the energy, the more end-uses it can satisfy, and for many purposes it is more important to preserve the quality of energy (water) than to preserve its quantity. High-temperature heat can be used to boil water to turn a generator and produce electricity or it can be used to warm a room, but low-temperature heat can be used only for heating the room; high-quality water can be used for drinking or it can be used to irrigate fields, but low-quality water can be used only to irrigate fields. For certain industries (food processing, for example), one needs

---

[10] The value of water also varies depending upon its temperature, but this is essentially a question of adding energy to the water, and is not really a quality of the water itself.

high-quality water with strict limitations on the content of impurities; for industrial cooling and for irrigation, one can accept much lower quality water. In a very real sense, the first law of conservation of matter assures us that the quantity of any resource, water included, will remain the same over time, but the second law assures us that, as we use any resource, its quality will inevitably diminish. Our task is to ensure that the loss of quality is as slow as possible and that we do as much with the resources as possible while their quality is diminishing. In practical terms, this has two implications:

≈ One should use water of a quality appropriate to the end-use being served.

≈ One should use water over and over again as it degrades in quality by "cascading" from higher quality to lower quality uses.

The notion of quality as a characteristic of energy was never widely recognized outside physics classes before the energy crisis, and it is still not widely used. For many reasons, but mainly because water quality is directly linked to human health, quality considerations have been implicitly recognized for centuries and, at least on an ad hoc basis, cascading has been practiced. Water of different qualities is already used for different purposes and, as we have seen, water is recycled widely in some areas of the world and notably in the Middle East. What is now needed is an extension of the concept so that the need to conserve water quality becomes more explicitly recognized in planning and so that cascading is designed into watershed management as a specific objective rather than as happenstance.

Backcasting Instead of Forecasting

Water is so closely connected with life itself, and with our common history in agriculture, that one tends to forget that it also has economic and ecological dimensions. Thus, we should be suspicious of projections that show increasing deficits between water use and water flows — deficits that cannot possibly be sustained. It would be more useful to recast the analysis in terms of scenarios and experiment with "backcasting" to determine where the system can give and the feasibility and impacts of alternative policies and reactions (Robinson 1988, 1990).

This too is part of the experience from soft-energy analysis and a part whose virtues have been demonstrated. Traditional forecasting always showed the need for greater supplies, whereas backcasting indicated the option to maintain or cut consumption. Actual energy-use patterns have turned out to be much closer to those suggested by the soft path than by traditional analysis.

There are at least three other ways in which backcasting of soft-water paths could work to reduce conflict in the Middle East. First, because it is concerned not with what futures are likely to happen but with how desirable futures can be obtained, backcasting is an explicitly normative exercise. It has none of the pretensions to objectivity some-times alleged by forecasting. This makes it an ideal partner for political science in a search for regional cooperation and accommodation. All sides see close linkages between water availability and national political and economic security. It is, therefore, only through the exploration of alternative futures, not simply a projection of the present into the future, that ways will be found to minimize the potential for continuing conflict.

Second, apparent conflicts between economics and environment that arise so commonly when viewed from the supply side are typically attenuated, if not totally eliminated, when viewed from the demand side. With only scattered exceptions, the same policies that promote more efficient use and greater conservation also support environmental protection. For example, efficient irrigation systems reduce the risk of soil salinization, and low-flow household appliances cut wastewater flows into sewers. As environmental values become more and more important, along with concerns about the quality of water, backcasts will show degrees of flexibility in policy that are typically obscured by forecasts.

Third, backcasting can test the resilience of alternative scenarios to the extreme weather patterns that are typical of climatic patterns in the Middle East. The impacts of weather patterns on water supply are much greater than on energy supply (where they affect mainly the volume of hydroelectricity that can be generated). Backcasting water end-use scenarios can, with relative ease, incorporate loops to show the impacts of sharply different levels of water availability on the economy.

The potential of a "soft-water path" has never been evaluated for the Middle East. This is hardly surprising. Only a few communities around the world, and no nations of which we are aware, have given the alternative approach serious consideration. Perhaps, for just the reasons cited by Naff in the quotation that began this chapter, Israelis or Palestinians will be the first to do so.

CHAPTER 8

WATER AND SECURITY IN ISRAEL

Environmental degradation imperils nations' most fundamental aspect of security by undermining the natural support systems on which all of human activity depends. Because environmental degradation and pollution respect no human-drawn borders, they jeopardize not only the security of the country in which they occur, but also that of others, near and far.

— Renner (1989)

IN A PREVIOUS CHAPTER, we indicated that, even though Israel may not pursue a "hydraulic imperative" or engage in "hydronationalism" (maintaining control of the West Bank and the Golan Heights strictly for water reasons), there are strong advocates of both of these positions within government as well as within the academic community. What must be accepted, however, is that water is a strategic resource to Israel and other nations in the Middle East and, as such, it must be considered an important aspect of Israel's international security relations. The purpose of this chapter is to explore in more detail the linkage between the environment/resources and security, and to illustrate the importance of water as an element of security to Israel. Activities that affect the availability of fresh water (of suitable quality) must be viewed in the broader context of the security of the nation. This is no less true today than it was in 1919 when Chaim Weizmann noted that "economic means water."

Unconventional Threats to Security

Although the reasons for conflict between nation-states defy simple explanations, the role of "unconventional threats to security" has been increasingly acknowledged as important in recent years.

Unconventional threats arise from the nonmilitary activities of individuals or groups in society, or from changes in the stocks or flows of resources available to groups or nation-states. These types of threats are often cumulative, and usually are not perceived as threats to security, at least not initially. Examples include: religious fundamentalism, human rights abuses, and resources and the environment (the depletion/deterioration of which has caused widespread alarm). Many researchers perceive these unconventional threats as important contributors to, if not causes of, violent conflict throughout the world (Bedeski 1992). Ullman (1983) notes that the root of most of the violent conflicts in history has been competition for territory and resources. Such conflicts are likely to intensify as resources become scarce and the quality of the environment degrades. Thus, widespread environmental degradation has the potential to aggravate international relations, behaviour, and security (Gleick 1989). The World Commission on Environment and Development (WCED 1987) recently emphasized that environmental stress could be a cause, as well as a result, of conflict, and the US National Academy of Science (1991) has recognized that even global environmental issues, such as climatic change, may well be an important contributor to political instability in the future — most significantly in regions where social and economic changes are already posing security threats.

The concepts of food security, energy security, and access to resources have been widely discussed over the past two decades, but the realization that these issues also pose powerful driving forces toward conflict is of more recent concern. Westing (1989) has noted that comprehensive security has two intertwined components: **political security**, with its military, economic, and humanitarian subcomponents; and **environmental security**, including the protection and utilization of resources and the environment. Each of these aspects must be satisfied to ensure the sustainability of the other. Indeed, the relationship between environment and security is increasingly being acknowledged, and articles on all facets of the issue have appeared recently (for example, Myers 1986; Westing 1986; Gleick 1989; Homer-Dixon 1991; Lonergan and Kavanagh 1991; Homer-Dixon et al. 1993).

Acceptance of the link between security and the environment, however, is by no means universal. Although acknowledging the destructive effects of war on the natural environment, Deudney (1991) notes that most environmental degradation is not caused by war or even by nation-states preparing for war. Similarly, he believes that promoting environmental deterioration as a threat to security is largely rhetorical; an "old horse" (security) attached to a "new wagon" (the environment). Although the linkage between environment and security is not so "clear" as some authors, such as Gleick (1992; in his response to Deudney), perceive, neither is it so obscure as Deudney contends. One of the difficulties in assessing the nature of the linkage is caused by the ambiguity surrounding the term "security." Researchers working in the area of environment and security come from a variety of backgrounds and disciplines, and each interprets the term "security" in a different way, ranging from a strict definition of safety from armed conflict to a more general interpretation of "human security," or "human livelihood security," which includes social, environmental, and other broader aspects. The purpose of this chapter is not to argue for the most appropriate definition of security, but simply to provide an overview of how issues surrounding water quantity and quality in Israel and the Occupied Palestinian Territories are related to security. The focus, therefore, is on exploring the nature of the environment/security linkage, given that there are different interpretations of what is meant by "security."

Resources, Environment, and Conflict

Many types of environmental changes may have the capacity to produce conflict. Certainly, constraints on resources are a crucial factor (Choucri 1991). Rapid industrialization and population growth together have resulted in an increased demand for both renewable and nonrenewable natural resources and, as Ullman (1983) and others have noted, competition for resources has historically been a major cause of conflict. The availability of water in a number of regions (including the Middle East), depletion of fish stocks off the east coast of Canada, and deforestation in Brazil, Thailand, and elsewhere — all of these have been the source of (or have the potential to be the source of) conflict. Atmospheric change, both global warming and ozone depletion, also has the potential to cause significant societal disruption (particularly when it may affect the availability of strategic resources, as noted previously). Land degradation, or land-use change in general, may directly affect society's ability to provide food resources for a growing population, or may indirectly affect other changes, such as global warming.

That control of water in the Middle East is considered an issue of security is unquestionable and, as noted in previous chapters, there have been numerous incidents of conflict over water resources involving Israel and its neighbours over the past 45 years. This relationship can be exhibited on a number of levels. Israel's application of restrictions on Palestinian development and use of water not only improves its access to West Bank water, but also extends its control in the Occupied Palestinian Territories. This situation increases resentment and adds to the potential for conflict in the area. Arabs in the West Bank have protested for years to Israeli authorities that their agriculture and economy are being negatively affected or even ruined by unfair water policies and that the wells supplying the Jewish settlements have drastically depleted the villages' water resources. The Palestinians have been frustrated in their efforts to change their circumstances and, given no power, they can only watch while fresh water is diverted to Israel or Israeli settlements. Although some of the Palestinian charges are disputed (see Chapter 6 and Appendix 1), the issue is a highly emotional one, and a number of authors have used the metaphor that the water situation in the Occupied Palestinian Territories is a "time bomb waiting to explode."

Types of Conflict

Similarly, many types of conflicts may result from environmental change or resource depletion or both. The type of environmental change — whether catastrophic, cumulative, or otherwise — dictates the type of conflict that may occur. Homer-Dixon (1991) lists three types of conflicts resulting from environmental change: simple scarcity conflict, group-identity conflict, and relative-deprivation conflict. For the purposes of this book, we are interested only in the first — conflict resulting from resource scarcity. Gleick (1992), provides a more detailed breakdown of this linkage by identifying different types of simple scarcity conflicts. He classifies resource and environmental threats to security in five categories:

≈ **Resources as strategic goals** — An obvious example would be territorial conflicts over energy resources. With the advent of greatly expanded international trade and world spot markets for resources, this link between resources and international conflict may be weaker now than in the past. This is not the case, however, with water in the Middle East. Gleick also notes a potentially more important source of conflict related to the inequitable distribution of resources (see below).

≈ **Resources as strategic targets** — Modification of resources and the environment for military purposes is a long-standing issue. In 146 BC, the Romans plowed salt into the farm fields around Carthage, destroying the city's economic base; before this, in about 2400 BC, Sumerians dug a canal to divert water from the Tigris to the Euphrates to gain independence from Umma (Roots 1992). Energy production and transmission facilities and water-supply projects are often primary targets of military activity. A present-day example is the destruction of Kuwaiti desalination plants by the Iraqis during the Gulf War.

≈ **Resources as strategic tools** — The most obvious example in this category is the threat by Turkey to restrict the flow of the Euphrates to Syria and Iraq to pressure Syria to discontinue its support of Kurdish separatists in Turkey. Despite assurances to the contrary by then Turkish President Ozal that the country would never hold downstream riparians hostage by restricting the flow of the Euphrates, it is obvious from the specific threat to Syria that Turkey would be more than willing to use water as a strategic tool.

≈ **Resource inequities as roots to conflict** — Growing disparities between resource-rich and resource-poor regions or groups, in terms of access to resources, has created a constant tension in some areas and open rebellion in others.

≈ **Environmental services and conditions as roots to conflict** — Disruptions of the waste assimilative capacities of ecosystems or the deliberate manipulation of the flow of environmental services can lead to conflicts. This issue is currently being addressed by the

United Nations General Assembly in its proposed revisions to the *Convention on the Prohibition of Military or Other Hostile Use of Environmental Modification Techniques* (popularly called the ENMOD Convention). The Convention was originally signed in May 1977, and focused more on weather modification and modification of Earth processes, such as earthquakes and tsunamis for strategic use. Proposed revisions will expand the Convention to include a broad array of environmental processes, such as forest fires and the massive release of airborne pollutants (for a complete discussion of the ENMOD Convention, see Roots 1992).

Gleick's categories, although not mutually exclusive, are useful in characterizing the different uses of resources and the environment for strategic purposes. Even though it is important to note that resources have historically been at the root of many violent conflicts, as Ullman (1983) suggested in the foregoing, there must also be a recognition that the potential for extensive modification of the environment for strategic purposes is far greater now than it has been in the past. Additionally, the vulnerability of society to modifications in the environment may be greater now than in the past.

Water resources in Israel are undoubtedly an important component of the country's security. As described in Chapter 7, Israel and its neighbouring Arab states have, on numerous occasions, feuded over access to Jordan River water. Although we do not subscribe to this view, many analysts consider the water issue a major factor in the tensions leading to the 1967 war (some authors have even claimed that water was the major reason for the war). Regardless of whether Israel was exercising an hydraulic imperative, control of water resources in the West Bank and the Golan Heights is now seen by many as essential to Israel's future. Currently, Israel draws more than 40% of its freshwater supplies from the West Bank alone, and the country would face immediate water shortages and a significant curtailment of its agricultural and industrial development if it lost control of these supplies. This sentiment has been echoed by numerous analysts, although, as we suggest throughout this book, there are many strategies that, if adopted, could reduce Israel's dependency on water. At present, the strength of the link between water and security in Israel is clearly evident in that examples of all five elements in Gleick's classification scheme are present in Israel's present approach to dealing with water resources.

It is clear from the preceding chapter that Israel at least thinks in terms of water as a strategic goal. It would actually be surprising if water were not considered a strategic goal. Water has the highest marginal value of any input to the Israeli economy; it is crucial to the establishment of new settlements; it is essential to an ideology centred on agricultural development; and it is "life itself." Thinking about water as a strategic goal and acting on those thoughts are, however, two very different things. Initial proposals to establish the boundaries of a Jewish state explicitly considered water as a strategic resource. In addition, evidence suggests that there has also been discussion among Israeli government officials for many decades on the possibility of acquiring Litani River water from Lebanon.

The acquisition of territory to augment water supply is not the only basis for viewing water as a strategic goal. As noted in Chapter 6, much of the conflict over water between the Palestinians and the Israelis relates to the blatant discrimination in water pricing, allocation, and delivery systems. Water is priced 3 to 7 times higher to Palestinians in the Territories than it is to Jewish settlers. And, to no one's surprise, per-capita water consumption of the settlers is many times that of Palestinians. Water is available to Palestinian villagers only one or two days a week (and is otherwise stored in water tanks on the roofs of houses), whereas it is made available daily to Israeli settlements. These discriminatory practices are enforced through the application of Israeli military orders to the West Bank and Gaza and, although this may be a more subtle use of water as a strategic goal, it certainly is an example of using available water for Israeli interests at the expense of the Palestinian population. These examples also illustrate the third water/security link, that of resource inequities.

Water has been a strategic target both for and against Israel over the past four decades. In 1953, when Israel began construction on its National Water Carrier, the intake site was in the demilitarized zone north of Lake Kinneret. Syrian troops were then moved into the area and they opened fire on the construction site (Cooley 1984). This skirmish, in conjunction with an official protest lodged by the Syrians at the United Nations, resulted in Israel accepting the costly alternative of moving the intake point to the northwest shore of the lake.

Israel has also been the initiator of armed conflict following Arab construction on diversion projects in the Jordan River's headwaters. Financed by Egypt and Saudi Arabia, the plans for this project involved diverting the Hasbani River into the Litani and the Banias River into the Yarmouk, and it would have cut by 35% the installed capacity of Israel's new National Water Carrier and would have increased the salinity in Lake Kinneret (Wolf 1995). On three occasions in 1965 and 1966, the Israeli army attacked the site (Cooley 1984), and it is these attacks that have led analysts to conclude that water was a primary factor in the 1967 war.

The evidence for the overt use of water by the Israelis as a strategic tool is quite speculative, but two situations are worthy of mention. Wolf (1995) notes that during an interview an Israeli officer told him that "plans were investigated, but never used, to cut water to Beirut to enforce a siege" during the 1982 war with Lebanon. More recently, in 1989, the Israelis apparently cut the power supply to the Jalazun refugee camp near Ramallah to reinforce a curfew during the *intifada* (it has been rumoured by some authors that the water supply was also cut, but this was not the case). Pearce (1991) notes that villagers in Jiftlik complained in the summer of 1990 that their water supplies were cut off in retaliation for stone-throwing incidents (but this is unverified). Admittedly, this is weak evidence to prove that Israel uses water as a strategic tool. One must also recognize, however, that the total control of water in the Occupied Territories by the Israeli Military Authority (officially, the Water Department of the Civil Administration) is a subtle, but powerful, example of using this vital resource as a strategic tool. Although the Palestinians are not denied access to water for drinking, they are denied access to water for almost all other uses. In addition, there are more than 175 villages (each with more than 150 persons) that do not have running water. Although Mekorot has offered to supply water to many of these villages (at the cost of 1.8 NIS/m^3), very few of the villages have accepted, defying the attempt by the Civil Administration to control their services.

There have also been disruptions in the flow of environmental services to the Palestinian population (and to Jordan as well). Two examples should suffice. The first situation involves the Israeli diversion of the saline springs at the lower end of Lake Kinneret away from the lake and into the Lower Jordan River. Along with domestic and industrial waste, and agricultural runoff, this saline water has caused significant deterioration of the Jordan River below the lake — enough to render it useless even for agricultural purposes. Second, the deep Israeli wells in the Territories (often 500–600 m), built to obtain higher flow rates and better quality water, are believed to have drained water from shallower Palestinian wells. In both of these cases, the issue was less a purposeful alteration of the environment (or environmental services) than an insensitivity to the broader social and environmental costs of resource extraction and use.

Israel's Hydrostrategic Boundaries

The Mandate and Israel, 1948

The absence of a clearly delineated "hydraulic imperative" on the part of Israel does not diminish at least the perception on the part of many Israelis that the country must retain all water resources currently under its control (including those within the Green Line, in the Occupied Territories, and in the Golan Heights) to ensure its economic survival. It is sometimes difficult, therefore, to separate issues pertaining to the acquisition of land, whether through negotiation, occupation, or annexation, from those relating to the acquisition of water. It has been apparent to Zionist planners since the early 1900s that water was crucial to the economic vitality of Palestine. For example, Chaim Weizmann pleaded with the British and others to have the Litani River included within the boundaries of Palestine, because he understood the vital nature of this resource to the future of any Jewish state (see Chapter 6 and Figure 11, p. 126). As noted earlier, he was unsuccessful and later complained bitterly that his position was totally undermined by the British (Hof 1985). The eventual establishment of Israel's northern border with Lebanon (and the exclusion of the Litani from Palestine) was the result of lengthy negotiations between the French and British from

1916 to 1923. Despite Zionist appeals, the boundary was a compromise between French interests to retain the Litani completely within their territory and a British intent, based on "Biblical diplomacy," to have Palestine extend from "Dan to Beersheba" (Hof 1985). The final agreement did place much of the Upper Jordan watershed within Israel, although the reason for the border turning north toward Lebanon and then south after it crossed the Hasbani seemed to have as much to do with including the northernmost Jewish settlement at the time (Metulla) as it did with ensuring that as much of the Upper Jordan watershed was included as possible. The resulting boundaries were a disappointment for the Zionists, because Weizmann had already noted that if Palestine were ever cut off from the Litani, the Upper Jordan, or the Yarmouk, it could never be economically independent (Hof 1985). It was also at this time that the League of Nations discussed the issue of the French/Syrian Mandate and the British Mandate, giving the Golan Heights to the Syrian Mandate, again over the objections of the Zionists. This effectively gave Syria sovereignty over the Golan, which included the upper reaches of the Banias River, part of the Upper Jordan.

The western border of Palestine was set in 1919, as the delegates at the Paris Peace Conference decided that the Jordan River just south of Lake Kinneret would make a "convenient administrative division" between the two new mandates of Palestine and Trans-Jordan (Smith 1966). Although the northern border with Lebanon eventually formed the border of the State of Israel, the western border of Israel was redrawn as part of the UN Partition Plan of 1947. The failure of the Zionists to obtain the Litani, all of the Jordan headwaters, and the Yarmouk (except for a small section) seriously limited Israel's water resources and, as noted previously, by 1967 the country was using almost all of its available water supplies. Control of the West Bank and the Golan Heights after 1967 provided Israel access to much needed additional supplies of water. This water is now seen by many as essential to the country's economy.

One reason that the present discussions over borders in the Middle East Peace Talks are so important is that these borders, present and future, will define not only the land of Israel but the water of Israel as well. Access to the Upper Jordan River, the Yarmouk River, and the Mountain Aquifer are all a function of international agreement over Israel's borders. This situation is one of the reasons that water and security, not only in Israel but throughout the Middle East, are inextricably linked.

The Tahal–Jaffee Report

Water and security were highlighted less than a month after the signing of the Peace Accord, when on the 8th of October 1994, the daily *Ha'aretz* (sometimes called "*The New York Times* of Israel") published excerpts from a study conducted by Tahal, in conjunction with the Jaffee Centre for Strategic Research Studies at the University of Tel Aviv. The principal authors of the report were Joshua Schwarz and Aaron Zohar from the Jaffee Centre. The report concludes that "without solving the water problem, there can be no security arrangements. Israel must do all it can to safeguard its existing water assets in the territories" (*Ha'aretz* 1993; see Schiff 1993). Although completed in 1991, this report was classified for security reasons by then Agriculture Minister Rafael Eitan because it contained maps outlining possible withdrawal lines on the Golan Heights and the West Bank that would still safeguard water sources currently used by Israel (Schiff 1993). These "hydrostrategic" maps were "leaked" to the press in late 1993, and are included as Figures 14 and 15. (The general feeling is that the Labour government allowed the report to be leaked, essentially removing it from classified status.) It is worth looking at what appears to be the Tahal–Jaffee report in more detail.

The Golan Heights — Schwarz and Zohar (as cited in *Ha'aretz* 1993; see Schiff 1993) conclude that, without appropriate cooperative arrangements, if Israel withdraws to its 1967 borders with Syria, there will be a "renewed threat of diversion of sources of the Jordan" (recall the Arab diversion attempts of the early 1950s). Such a withdrawal would cede almost 40 Mm^3/year to Syria. In addition, there would remain the threat of contamination of Lake Kinneret and, accordingly,

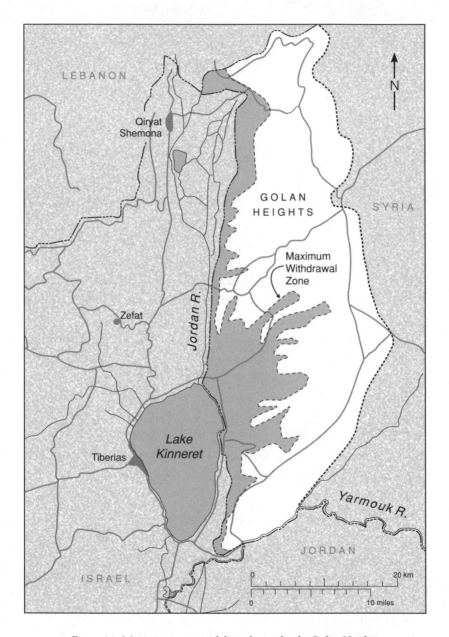

Figure 14. Maximum water withdrawal zone for the Golan Heights
(Ha'aretz; *see Schiff 1993*).

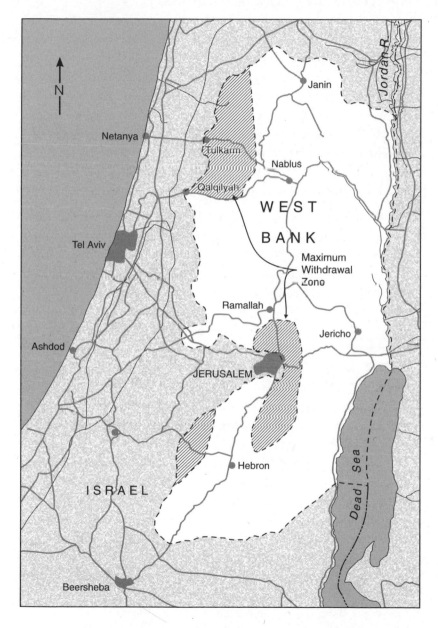

Figure 15. Maximum water withdrawal zone for the West Bank
(Ha'aretz; *see Schiff 1993*).

Israel's major water supply source. This is considered by many to be too high a price to pay for relinquishing the Golan.

The report proposes two withdrawal lines for Israel in the Golan. The first is what Schwarz and Zohar consider as the "reasonable withdrawal line," which follows the watershed line (see Figure 1 on p. 6). This would involve only a minimal transfer of land in the Golan to Syria. The second is the line of maximum withdrawal, which delineates the maximum amount of land Israel could relinquish while minimizing the possible damage to its water supplies (Figure 14). The report also notes that unless there is substantial cooperation between Israel and Syria, which explicitly addresses control over water supplies, Israel would not be able to withdraw beyond this latter line.

The West Bank — Roughly 500 Mm^3 of water is taken annually from the Mountain Aquifer by Israel, with most of the wells inside the Green Line. The Tahal–Jaffee report concludes that Israeli separation from the West Bank without a prior Palestinian commitment for joint water management would be the worst possible outcome (Schiff 1993). The major concern relative to water is that much of the Mountain Aquifer underlies the West Bank (see Figure 6 on p. 32). In addition, 90% of the recharge area is within the West Bank (Benvenisti and Gvirtzman 1993). This makes both recharge and depletion of the aquifer subject to potential Palestinian control. Equally important, the quality of the water in the aquifer is primarily a function of Palestinian land use in the recharge area. Increased pumping by the Palestinians would disrupt water supply from Israeli wells and contamination (primarily from salt) would be unavoidable, and the "drinking water of primary population centres in Israel will be harmed" (as cited in *Ha'aretz* 1993; see Schiff 1993). Although most Jewish settlements in the West Bank are supplied with piped water from Mekorot, there are settlements in the Jordan Valley that will likely be affected by disruptions in water supply as a result of Palestinian control of the aquifers. Ninety-three percent of the annual recharge to the Mountain Aquifer is now exploited by Israel, and any increase in Palestinian use would, in turn, impact Israeli use. The report also proposes a maximum withdrawal line for the West Bank (Figure 15). This line is based on the presumption that outside the marked territory, it would not be economical to pump the aquifer for the sole reason of disrupting Israeli supplies, and that full cooperation over drilling and groundwater output between the Israelis and Palestinians would allow withdrawal to this line.

In addition to presenting "maximum withdrawal lines" for possible Israeli withdrawal from the West Bank and the Golan Heights, the Tahal-Jaffee report deals with other elements of water security for Israel. On the issue of possible Israeli involvement in regional water initiatives, the report is categorical. As reported in *Ha'aretz* (8 October 1993), it concludes that "Israel must not rely on the transfer of water from neighbouring states even given cooperation with Arab neighbours." In the view of the authors of the report, projects such as the "Peace Pipeline" from Turkey would be subject to disruption by Arab states and would require relinquishing a portion of national sovereignty. The Tahal–Jaffee report also looks at the Gaza Strip, where hydrostrategic boundaries are of less concern given the geology and what appears to be a net positive flow of water from Israel to Gaza. The report proposes that water for Gaza be supplied either by desalination or by transfer from Egypt rather than from Israel.

Given the social, economic, environmental, and political importance of water to Israel, and the crucial relationship between water supplies and international borders, it is apparent why there is such strong resistance from certain groups and individuals within Israel to a complete withdrawal from the Golan Heights and the West Bank. Although the ideas in the Tahal–Jaffee report are not entirely unique — Wolf (1995) independently proposes similar water withdrawal lines — they do present a compromise solution. More importantly, they legitimize the position held by many of the more liberal politicians that Israel could relinquish its control over much of the Golan Heights and the West Bank (and of course of Gaza) without significantly jeopardizing its water security. At the same time, the report allows political conservatives to point to those hydrostrategic borders on a map and then say, in effect, "this far and no further!"

CHAPTER 9

THE PEACE ACCORD AND ITS AFTERMATH

The Government of the State of Israel and the Palestinian team representing the Palestinian people agree that it is time to put an end to decades of confrontation and conflict, recognize their mutual legitimate and political rights, and strive to live in peaceful coexistence and mutual dignity and security to achieve a just, lasting and comprehensive peace settlement and historical reconciliation through the agreed political process.
— Preamble to the Israel–PLO Peace Accord

MANY IMPORTANT EVENTS occurred in rapid succession in the late summer of 1993. Representatives of Israel and the Palestine Liberation Organization (PLO) initialed "a draft agreement on Palestinian self-rule" (20 August), the document generally called "the Peace Accord." The agreement was then approved by both the Israeli Cabinet and the Council of the PLO. The entire process was consummated by a handshake between Prime Minister Yitzhak Rabin and PLO Chairman Yassar Arafat on the lawn of the White House in Washington, DC, on 13 September 1993. That handshake was the culmination of a partially open and partially secret, partially formal and partially informal process that had been under way since the beginning of peace negotiations in Madrid in October 1991, and that had accelerated after the Labor Party was elected to power in Israel in June 1992. It was also the start of a less secret but more protracted and difficult process to add substance to the outline in the draft agreement.

This chapter will review the bilateral and multilateral tracks of the peace process, which were the formal parts of the peace process; the Peace Accord, which resulted from a largely informal process (see Elon

1993); and subsequent actions and reactions. Except for general background, we have no intention of analyzing the process itself; rather, our discussion will focus on specific references to, and implications for, water.

Bilateral and Multilateral Talks

Under the joint sponsorship of the United States and the former Soviet Union, a new form of Middle East peace process was initiated in Madrid at the end of October 1991. Although always referred to as the Middle East peace process, more accurately it was an Arab–Israeli peace process with a focus on (but not exclusively about) Palestinian–Israeli peace. The Madrid meeting brought together Israel and three Arab delegations (one from Syria, one from Lebanon, and a joint delegation representing Jordan and the Palestinians) for the first face-to-face negotiations in many years. The intention, since realized in numerous rounds of well-publicized negotiations, was to conduct sequential bilateral talks between each of the Arab delegations and the Israeli delegation on the outstanding political issues that were blocking achievement of regional peace.

Recognizing that the bilateral talks would include difficult problems and that they might stall for periods of time, the United States and the Soviet Union also proposed a second and parallel track for the peace process. This track would differ from the bilateral track in at least three ways. First, discussions would be multilateral; not only would all of the Arab parties and Israel be at one table, but so too would about 30 other nations. Second, the talks would be divided into separate working groups on five specific subjects: arms control and regional security, refugees, regional economic development, environment, and water resources. Third, discussions would to the greatest extent possible focus on technical rather than political issues. Canada was invited to participate in the multilateral track, and has subsequently played an active role in all of the working groups, including the one on water. Canada plays a special role in the Working Group on Refugees where it "holds the gavel" — a diplomatic term that connotes general guidance of the meeting but something less than acting as the chair. (The United States holds the gavel for the Working Group on Water Resources, and Japan for the Working Group on Environment.) As a matter of principle, Syria (and, therefore, Lebanon) refused to participate in the multilateral talks; they argue that such talks imply a normalization of relationships with Israel and are inappropriate until significant progress is made at the political, bilateral level.

Multilateral Working Group on Water Resources

The multilateral track of the Middle East peace process was initiated with an organizational meeting in Moscow in January 1992 and, since then, there have been six rounds of meetings of the five working groups. Through 1994, the Working Group on Water Resources met in Vienna (May 1992), Washington, DC (September 1992); Geneva (April 1993), Beijing (October 1993), Muskat, Oman (April 1994), and Athens (November 1994). For the last three rounds, the Palestinians were represented by their own delegations, as opposed to a joint Jordanian–Palestinian delegation.

Meetings of the Working Group on Water Resources, as with all the other working groups, are held behind closed doors. Some of the other working groups issue brief press releases or summary statements at the end of each meeting, but this has not been the practice for the one on water. Little can be said, therefore, beyond what can be inferred from the limited information released by other working groups and from intersessional activities (that is, workshops, training sessions, or missions developed in response to requests from the regional parties and undertaken by one of the other participating nations). Clearly, the high-politics approach of the Palestinians (as described in Chapter 6) is going to clash with the low-politics approach of the Israelis. Yet, progress is apparently being made — witness the statement from Munther Haddadin, head of the Jordanian delegation and former Director of the Jordan Valley Authority, who is quoted in the journal MEED (28 January 1994) and who is not known for overstatement: "There has been substantial progress — so much so that we may have to slow down so that others can catch up."

The Israel Environment Bulletin reports from time to time on what is under way in the Working Group on Environment, and it would appear that there is agreement that it will deal with water quality issues, particularly sewage and waste management, so that the water group can deal with quantity. The range of intersessional activities suggests that data availability and management are a major concern of the Working Group on Water Resources, as are alternative sources of supply. Data are no doubt an area on which substantial agreement is possible, even if more sensitive issues remain unresolved.

Canada has contributed to a number of the intersessional activities, including the preparation of a machine-accessible database on alternative supply technologies (IWEC 1993) and the design of a pilot program of rooftop rainwater-catchment systems for the Gaza Strip. As well, under the auspices of the Working Group on Environment, Canada sent a mission to the region to assess its need for, and its capability to undertake, environmental-impact assessments — something that, if it takes hold in the region, will have a major (and largely limiting) impact on future water supply or diversion options.

The Technical Committees

One other set of actors must be mentioned specifically with reference to the negotiations on water. In contrast to all of the other parties, the Palestinians had no government structure and bureaucracy to which they could turn for support of their activities in the multilateral talks. Technical committees were organized, therefore, with an explicit mandate from the PLO (something that Israeli authorities conveniently ignored before the Peace Accord) and from the local Palestinian leadership to provide advice and support to the negotiating teams. The committee's structure was coordinated by Dr Sari Nusseibah from offices in Orient House in East Jerusalem, and one such committee, chaired by Prof. Marwan Haddad of An-Najah University in Nablus, focused on water. In addition, because of the sharp differences in hydrology between the West Bank and the Gaza Strip, a subcommittee focusing on the latter was formed and chaired by Prof. Riyad El-Khoudary, President of Al-Azhar University in Gaza.[11] Originally formed specifically to aid the negotiating process, the technical committees,

---

[11] Professor El-Khoudary later became head of the Palestinian delegation to the Working Group on Water Resources.

including the one on water, were later given the broader mandate of proposing appropriate institutional structures, which was an implicit indication that some form of peace accord was anticipated.

A Third Track

As the bilateral and multilateral tracks of the Middle East peace process continued with steady but frustratingly slow progress toward a resolution of major issues, some Israelis and Palestinians suggested that academics might achieve what politicians could not. In a region as small and as highly charged as Israel and the Occupied Territories, the separation between academic and political tracks is somewhat artificial. Not only does each academic statement carry political content, but often an academic will later be on a delegation representing her or his government. Nevertheless, the atmosphere at an academic discussion is (or at least can be) different, and the stakes are (or at least seem to be) lower.

None of these "third track" or "academic" statements is official, and none of the recommendations binding. With the exception, however, of the Economic Development Working Group, which also found the third track to be productive, Israelis and Palestinians interested in water issues took more advantage of the third, academic track than did members of the other working groups. They have met in several arenas to discuss their common water problems; the most notable arena was a conference convened in Zurich in November 1992 under the joint sponsorship of the Harry S. Truman Research Institute for the Advancement of Peace (Truman Institute) at the Hebrew University and the Jerusalem Centre for Strategic Studies (generally known by its Arabic acronym, MAQDES).

The First Israeli–Palestinian International Academic Conference on Water (a cumbersome title but one in which every word was loaded with meaning) was a success — in part simply because it happened; in part because key issues were discussed from technical, social, and economic perspectives; and in part because of the personal interaction it facilitated. The conference was not without occasional flare-ups, but Peter Gleick, a specialist in water conflict from the United States, commented in a summary statement that he had heard more anger in discussions between coal strip miners and environmentalists in the

United States than between Israelis and Palestinians during this conference. Although it proved to be impossible to produce a statement supported by all conference participants, a strong resolution was obtained
to the effect that water data for Israel and the Occupied Territories
(much of which had been declassified in the last year or two) should be
made available to all researchers on an equal basis, and that studies on
the possibilities for creating a jointly managed, regional database should
be initiated.

The papers presented at the Zurich conference suggested the limitations of the current debate about water issues. First, although almost
all of the participants assumed that fresh water would have to be shifted
out of agriculture, almost no one discussed government policy to
encourage the shift or reduce the cost of transition. Second, except for
recycling of water and one paper on recharging aquifers (Assaf 1994),
smaller scale supply options received little attention compared with that
given to megaprojects for importing or desalinating water. Third, apart
from some mention of sewage disposal, water-quality problems were
almost totally neglected in favour of water quantity.

The Zurich conference was held despite strong opposition from
senior government officials from both sides. Both the date and the location were changed several times, and it was not clear whether key Israeli
or Palestinian analysts would participate until a week before the conference actually took place. Ironically, the conference was held in a brief
window of détente, after one of the multilateral sessions and barely a
week before the Israeli government exiled for a year 417 alleged leaders
of the militant Palestinian group, Hamas. Had it been scheduled for the
week after those expulsions, the meeting could not have taken place.

The third track continued to operate, albeit more quietly, after
the expulsions. Roundtable discussions, sponsored by the
Israel–Palestine Centre for Research and Information (IPCRI), both
preceded and followed the Zurich conference. IPCRI is a group that has
strived for years to bring Israelis and Palestinians together to discuss the
issues that separate them. Its office, close to the Damascus Gate in
Jerusalem, practically straddles the Green Line. The roundtables have
offered a venue where issues as contentious as the future of Jerusalem
could be discussed over the course of a year or longer in a neutral

setting. IPCRI has produced one collection of papers (Baskin 1992) and numerous shorter notes and statements on water. There have also been joint proposals to Canada's IDRC from the Truman Institute and MAQDES (later the Palestine Consultancy Group) for studies on alternative management options for the Mountain Aquifer. The Palestinian component of this study was funded by IDRC, and the Israeli component by the CRB Foundation, the Israeli arm of the Bronfman Foundation, and the study began in early 1994. Discussions have also taken place between Israeli and Palestinian hydrologists and statisticians to share water data and to work toward common terminology and units.

Use of the third track by other working groups can also be seen in the regional work on environmental and developmental problems in the Gulf of Aqaba, whose waters are shared by four nations: Egypt, Israel, Jordan, and Saudi Arabia. Although not an issue that affects Palestinians directly, interest in the gulf was stimulated by the Japanese delegation's emphasis on alternatives for protection and development. The Gulf of Aqaba is vital as an industrial, commercial, and recreational centre, but it also represents a unique ecology, including some of the few coral reefs in the region. An attempt in the late 1980s by the International Federation of Institutes of Advanced Studies to stimulate parallel studies on the gulf was not successful, but subsequently the (US) Environmental Law Institute coordinated work by environmental organizations in Egypt, Israel, and Jordan to come together in a year-long process to review and report on options for cooperative regional management of the gulf's resources (Sandler et al. 1993). Although the key issues in the gulf involve salt water, the success of this effort is further evidence that alternatives to formal meetings can result in significant advances.

The Draft Agreement

The Peace Accord is in many ways a remarkable document. Observers of international negotiations under conflict have described it as "mature," "balanced," and "far reaching." Even the preamble, cited at the beginning of this chapter, suggests that the two parties are striving for more than just an end to hostilities. By no means was everything resolved with the Accord, however. Issues that were too difficult or too politically sensitive were left for permanent status negotiations, to begin not later than 3 years and conclude not later than 5 years after an Israeli withdrawal from Jericho and Gaza. Such issues include, among other things, Jerusalem, refugees, settlements, security arrangements, and borders. Moreover, as with any such accord, the details remain to be worked out, and in that process there can be shifts in the balance of power. In addition, the full meaning of "mutual legitimate and political rights" — hence, the question of whether the Jericho–Gaza territorial compromise and the 5-year transition period were just a test (as the Israelis maintain) or the core of a new state (as the Palestinians maintain) — remains to be determined. Mutual recognition by the PLO and Israel has been achieved, however, and after more than 45 years of bitter conflict, this alone was a major accomplishment.

Water in the Peace Accord

Water is mentioned explicitly at several points in the Peace Accord and its many annexes, but the references to water also typcially involve far-reaching implications and sketchy detail. For example, the long-standing issue of Palestinians "rights" to water seems to have been resolved in principle — evidently it is now accepted that Palestinians do have such rights — but not the specific ways in which those rights will be exercised nor the quantities of water to which they may be entitled.[12] The explicit references to water and to the environment are as follows:

Article VII: Interim Agreement
   4. In order to enable the Council[13] to promote economic growth, upon its inauguration, the Council will establish, among other

---

[12] The concept of rights is also vague, but we believe that it was meant broadly to include both actual ownership and apportionment of water and all of the means for managing, making policy decisions, and resolving conflicts about water resources.

[13] Article I makes provision for the establishment of "a Palestinian Interim Self-Government Authority, the elected Council (the 'Council') for the Palestinian people in the West Bank and the Gaza Strip, for a transitional period not exceeding five years, leading to a permanent settlement based on Security Council Resolutions 242 and 338."

things, a Palestinian Electricity Authority,...a Palestinian Environmental Authority, a Palestinian Land Authority and a Palestinian Water Administration Authority,...in accordance with the Interim Agreement that will specify their powers and responsibilities.

Annex III: Protocol on Israeli–Palestinian Cooperation in Economic and Development Programs

The two sides agree to establish an Israeli–Palestinian Continuing Committee for Economic Cooperation, focusing, among other things, on the following:

1. Cooperation in the field of water, including a Water Development Program prepared by experts from both sides, which will also specify the mode of cooperation for the management of water resources in the West Bank and Gaza Strip, and will include proposals for studies and plans on water rights of each party, as well as on the equitable utilization of joint water resources for implementation in and beyond the interim period.
10. An Environmental Protection Plan, providing for joint and/or coordinated measures in this sphere.

Annex IV: Protocol on Israeli–Palestinian Cooperation Concerning Regional Development Programs

2B. The Regional Economic Development Program may consist of the following elements:
2. The development of a joint Israeli–Palestinian–Jordanian Plan for coordinated exploitation of the Dead Sea area.
3. The Mediterranean Sea (Gaza)–Dead Sea Canal.
4. Regional desalinization and other water development projects.

Given the number of years during which the two sides barely recognized the existence of each other, the number of points at which cooperation is anticipated is truly remarkable. It is, therefore, hard to disagree with those who believe that a major step has been taken toward self-government if not full independence for the Palestinians.

Although none of the new institutions is yet fully staffed, we do want to call attention to one anomaly in the titles assigned to the new Palestinian institutions. In Clause VII.4, provision is made for a

Palestinian Water **Administration** Authority. It is not clear what, if anything, to make of the insertion of the word **Administration** into what might simply have been called the Palestinian Water Authority. One could surmise that those persons who drafted the document intended to imply a more limited role than for the Palestinian Land, Environmental, and Electricity Authorities, all of which are mentioned in the same clause. It is equally possible, however, that the title is simply a drafting error. The latter theory gains credibility in that today almost everyone refers to the new institution as the Palestinian Water Authority (PWA) rather than by its assigned title. Accordingly, we have used the shorter (and more appropriate) title throughout the text.

Implicit References to Water

Many other provisions, not included in the foregoing list, deal implicitly with water. For example, the questions of settlements and of refugees, both among the issues to be resolved during subsequent "permanent status negotiations," are inseparable from concerns about water use in the Occupied Palestinian Territories and, by implication, in Israel. More immediately and included within the initial transfer of power, Palestinian authorities will assume control of certain sectors, including health and tourism (Article VI; S2), which are both significantly dependent upon adequate quantities of water of good quality. In addition, an Israeli–Palestinian Continuing Committee for Economic Cooperation is to be established (Article IX) that will cooperate, among other things, in electricity development and in the exploitation of oil and gas resources, including a possible petrochemical complex in the Gaza Strip (see Annex III of the Accord).

Two further provisions have equally significant implications for the water sector. First, Article XV, on Resolution of Disputes, provides for continuing negotiations by a Joint Israeli–Palestinian Liaison Committee and, for disputes that cannot be settled by negotiation, processes of conciliation and even formal arbitration. One can assume that many direct and indirect water issues will be presented to this committee for resolution. The allocation of rights to specific quantities and qualities of water is often determined by comparable tribunals in other countries and, given the recent history of this part of the world, even greater recourse to administrative tribunals should not only be expected but encouraged. Some years in the future, the same tribunals could hear cases for adjudication of water issues brought by individuals or by public interest groups.

Second, Annex IV refers twice to the multilateral peace efforts, and Section 2C states that "The two sides will encourage the multilateral working groups, and will coordinate towards its [sic] success. The two parties will encourage intersessional activities, as well as prefeasibility and feasibility studies, within the various multilateral working groups." As indicated earlier in this chapter, one of the working groups focuses on water, another on environment, and a third on economic development. These groups will all have a great deal to explore in coping with the explicit and implicit references to water in the Peace Accord.

Israel–Jordan Track

Within a day of signing the Peace Accord on the lawn of the White House, the Jordanian government released a document that had clearly been in preparation for some time called "Israel–Jordan Track Common Agenda." Although formally linked to the bilateral negotiations, the timing of the announcement obviously was delayed until there was some evidence of progress in the Israeli–Palestinian negotiations. Just as with the Peace Accord, the Common Agenda has a very broad goal: "The achievement of just, lasting and comprehensive peace between the Arab states, the Palestinians and Israel as per the Madrid invitation."

Water is mentioned at two points in the Common Agenda. Clause 3 is entitled "Water" and includes provisions for "securing the rightful water shares of the two sides" and "searching for ways to alleviate water shortage." Clause 6 refers to future bilateral cooperation and, under subsection "a" on natural resources, lists "Water, energy and environment" and "Rift Valley development." Vague as these items are, they are encouraging; as with the Peace Accord, they assume that rights to water exist, and they imply that there are grounds for a resolution of the common problems that would be acceptable and even advantageous to both parties.

The Israel–Jordan track burst back into the headlines with the meeting between Israeli Prime Minister Yitzhak Rabin and Jordan's King Hussein in Washington, DC, on 25 July 1994. The document they signed ended 46 years in a state of war (but stops just short of a formal peace treaty) between the two nations. The meeting was capped by the symbolic handshake, which some journalists see as even more important than the famous handshake some 10 months earlier; whereas the Rabin–Arafat handshake implied mutual recognition between two peoples, the Rabin–Hussein handshake reflects wider Arab and possibly Islamic acceptance of Israel as a part of the Middle East (*Mideast Mirror*, 25 July 1994).

Although it was an open secret that very senior representatives of the Israeli and Jordanian governments had been meeting for some time and that, as indicated in Chapter 6, water officials had been working together for years at "picnic table summits" to determine withdrawals from the Yarmouk River and discuss management issues concerning the Jordan River, the meeting of the two leaders initiated an open process of face-to-face meetings of officials in a tent literally on the border of Israel and Jordan. The binational peace process had advanced to the stage where joint projects and formal agreements could be considered.

The first agreements (signed in Washington) focused largely on transportation and communications linkages between Israel and Jordan. (One also provided for linking their electrical grids, which is critical for pumping water). Water remains high on the agenda of the continuing talks. Indeed, Israeli negotiators had been admitted to Jordan for the first time about a week earlier before the meeting in Washington, DC, and part of the ensuing discussion related to water. Details remain vague, but Jordan can be assumed to have argued both that Israel is taking more than its share of Jordan and Yarmouk water (based on the allocations proposed in the Johnston Agreement) and that the design and operation of the Israeli water system is adversely affecting the Lower Jordan and the Dead Sea. As indicated by the subsequent Peace Treaty (see Afterword), discussion also included provisions for dams on the Yarmouk River, which Israel had been blocking by rejecting World Bank loans for construction, as well as on use of groundwater in the Arava Valley, water that is now pumped exclusively by Israel.

Although the first meetings did not produce any agreement on appropriate shares of water, Israel did accept unambiguously and for the first time that Jordan does have "rights to an equitable allocation" of water from the Jordan and the Yarmouk rivers (*Mideast Mirror*, 10 August 1994, p. 15); the statement was made at a joint Israeli–Jordanian press conference, itself a remarkable event). Understandably (and sensibly), these first direct talks seem to be focusing on the water that is already available to Israel and Jordan. The final agreement will likely also encourage further study (as opposed to immediate construction) of the Red–Dead Canal.

Public and Political Reactions in Israel

The signing of the Peace Accord stimulated an intense round of formal negotiation and informal comment. Given the need for immediate attention to issues of security and policing, it is not surprising that other issues, water among them, received scant attention. In Israel, at least, water was not completely ignored. The issue of water came up in discussions about any deal involving the exchange of land for peace, and Israeli politicians were not loathe to use water as a way either to support or attack the Rabin government.

The Israeli–Syrian discussions (both sides hesitate to call them peace negotiations), which have been under way since early 1993, probably drew the greatest attention to water issues. Syria has always insisted on complete Israeli withdrawal from the Golan Heights, which Israel has occupied since the 1967 war. Hence, any discussions with the Syrians stimulated concern about what Israel would have to give up in its withdrawal from the Golan to achieve a peace agreement with Syria (as well as what the Syrians would be giving in any such peace agreement). The January 1994 meeting between President Clinton of the United States and President Assad of Syria heightened concerns and expectations. Most of the media attention at this meeting, however, focused on the strategic importance of the Golan from military and counterterrorist perspectives. Despite its importance in terms of both physical and legal control of water supplies in Israel, water was decidedly (if incorrectly) secondary in the public's mind.

A brief flurry of attention to water came nearly a month after the signing of the Peace Accord, when parts of the Tahal–Jaffee report were leaked to Ha'aretz. As discussed in Chapter 8, this report clearly identifies a number of withdrawal options by which Israel could pass political control of the Golan to Syria, and of the West Bank to the Palestinians, without giving up the major levers needed to ensure a secure water supply (Schiff 1993). Those options do not involve complete withdrawal, but they do suggest that, with relatively minor border adjustments, Israel could surrender most of the occupied land without surrendering control of the water sources.

The unexpected, partial release of the Tahal–Jaffee report just after the announcement of the Peace Accord probably explains the special session on water held by the Economic Committee of the Israeli Knesset on 18 October 1993. In a very one-sided debate, speaker after speaker emphasized that it would be disastrous for Israel to give up control of water sources in the Territories. Although the speakers did admit that the amount of water Palestinians were demanding for household and domestic uses could be spared, there was not, they argued, sufficient high-quality water for widespread irrigated agriculture on both sides of the Green Line. Soon after, Water Commissioner Gideon Tsur argued that, although joint management of the Territories' water was possible, "Israel could not accept any diminution in either the quantity or the quality of water available to it" (Mideast Mirror, 19 October 1993). Given that condition, it is hard to know what incentive "the Arabs" would have to engage in joint management. If one takes the Water Commissioner's position literally, there is little reason to discuss, let alone negotiate, issues of water supply and demand in the Occupied Territories and Gaza–Jericho. It is arguable, however, that much, if not all, of this highly vocal opposition (at least that in the Knesset) was simply posturing and intended mainly for Arab ears, as if to emphasize the strength of the opposition to any compromise on water.

Despite the Tahal–Jaffee report, it was several months before specific implications of the Peace Accord for water began to be discussed. In one of the few comments that did appear, Yedidya Atlas, a free-lance journalist writing in the increasingly hawkish Jerusalem Post (24 February 1993), summed up what is probably a common, if not majority, view when she wrote: "The political and strategic significance is clear. Withdrawing from Judea and Samaria would create a situation whereby the fate of the country's water supply would be determined by whatever autonomous Palestinian Arab entity controls the administered territories and the Syrians." Growing water shortages in Damascus, Syria's unresolved dispute with Turkey over the Euphrates, and its just-resolved dispute with Lebanon over the Orontes only added to the concerns. Hence, it was hardly surprising that polls in January of 1994 showed that a solid majority of Israelis favoured partial withdrawal from the Golan, but an almost equal majority rejected total withdrawal (*Mideast Mirror*, 21 January 1994). Not long after, in a parliamentary manoeuvre, Likud members of the Economic Committee of the Israeli Knesset waited until the Labour-dominated coalition was short of members and hurriedly passed a resolution calling for exclusive Israeli control of the water sources in the "Golan Heights, Judea, and Samaria" (*Mideast Mirror*, 18 January 1994).

In summary, with periodic exceptions (mainly related to the Golan Heights), relatively little attention has been given to water in the aftermath of the Peace Accord. Indeed, in the Middle Eastern press, more was written about the conflict between Syria and Turkey (and, with the role of Syria reversed, between Iraq and Syria) over the water of the Euphrates River than about the conflict between Israelis and Palestinians over their shared rivers and aquifers. Ironically, at the same time as it remains Israel's most implacable enemy, Syria shares some political positions with Israel in terms of both water rights and its pre-emptive actions to retain water that would otherwise flow to the Yarmouk.

One indication of how water will be handled by the Israeli government in the interim period is demonstrated by its reaction to the discovery of a shallow brackish water aquifer with an annual flow of 60–80 Mm^3/year and a salt content of around 5 000 ppm. Located near Ein Fash'ha, about 15 km south of Jericho, the aquifer is likely outside the Palestinian self-rule zone, but within the West Bank. Two immediate uses of this water are evident: it could be desalinated for domestic use or it could become the basis for a tourist industry (the water is too salty for irrigation but not for swimming). When settlers in the area proposed these alternatives to the Government of Israel, however, they were told that no new investments would be contemplated before negotiations with the Palestinians. Indeed, Marwan Haddad of An-Najah University and head of the Palestinian technical committee dealing with water immediately expressed interest in the economic potential of the water. It would appear that cooperation may occur in individual cases while designs of the Peace Accord are being completed and while the Palestinian administrative and policy structures are being established.

CHAPTER 10

PALESTINIAN WATER MANAGEMENT IN A TRANSITIONAL PERIOD

If the sea were ink, the reeds pens, the skies parchment, and all people scribes, they would not suffice to describe the complexity of government.

— Talmud: Shabbath 11a

PERHAPS ANTICIPATING that Israeli–Palestinian affairs were reaching a point at which some normalization would have to occur, three major reports appeared on the future development of the Occupied Palestinian Territories within a period of about 18 months between 1992 and 1993. The first, organized by Villanova University (Lesch et al. 1992), addressed issues of institutional design as well as economic development; the latter two, one by Harvard University (Hausman and Karasik 1993)[14] and one by the World Bank (1993a), focused mainly on economics and investment. In addition to these three broadly based reports, some sectoral reports on water supply and demand also appeared in the same time frame, and an astounding number of conferences were held on water problems in the region.

All three reports are collective efforts with many contributors, including analysts from countries in the Middle East. Despite being independent, the reports share many conclusions. For example, all three emphasize the importance of the transition period; the linkages among the Israeli, Jordanian, and Palestinian economies; the importance of training and capacity building; and the need for carefully managed financial flows, including bilateral and multilateral aid, on the one

---

[14] To avoid confusion with the Harvard Middle East Water Project described earlier, we refer to this report as the "Harvard economics report."

hand, and direct private investment, on the other. The reports differ in the extent to which they advise reliance on market forces and advocate a regional free-trade zone, as well as on the balance they would recommend between governmental and private sources of funding. Reflecting their original objectives, the report from Villanova University emphasizes institutional design as opposed to economic investment, whereas the report from the World Bank has the opposite emphasis. The economics report from Harvard University falls somewhere between the others, but devotes less attention to natural resources in favour of financial and fiscal issues. The report from Villanova is unique among the three studies in devoting attention to the importance of public involvement and participation in decision-making. This emphasis is particularly important in regard to issues, such as water, that affect daily life (as opposed to issues such as international finance, with which the average person has little direct contact).

With one exception, we make no attempt to review or comment on the great number of recommendations in these three reports. Instead, we focus only on those parts of the reports that emphasize investment in water, institutions for managing water in any of its many aspects, and public involvement in decision-making about water. Table 5 (see Chapter 4, p. 75) provides general economic and social information about the region. Because the institutional framework and the pattern of investments are well established in Israel but are only now being developed in the Occupied Palestinian Territories, this chapter focuses mainly on the latter.

Before proceeding, let us raise the exception to our reluctance to comment on the more general issues. It is impossible for Canadians to ignore the growing debate over free trade between Israel and the future Palestinian entity, or possibly regional free trade. Even after recognizing the differences in "starting circumstances," open economies are unabashedly advocated by the Harvard economics report (Hausman and Karasik 1993, p. 48): "our basic proposal is for Israel, Jordan and the West Bank and Gaza to pursue coordinated policies in the transitional stage that are consistent with eventually achieving a free trade area in goods, services, capital, technology and in due course, labour." Free movement of the factors of production, however, has been challenged strongly by commentators as being bad for the Palestinians and possibly for Israelis as well (Avineri 1994). The debate mirrors that over the Canada–US and, more recently, the North American (Canada–Mexico–US) free-trade agreements. The position one takes will have a lot to do with one's views on the gains to be expected from market economics and on the appropriate role of the state in managing the economy and protecting culture.

Investment in Water Systems

While Israelis and Palestinians disagree, and disagree often passionately, on many issues concerning the future of the OT [Occupied Territories], they agree on one issue: the urgent need for stimulating economic development in the OT.

— World Bank (1993a, p. 1)

Economic Growth in the Occupied Territories

At the risk of oversimplification, it is possible to summarize the record of economic growth in Israel as one of strong growth in the first decade after 1967, and much slower growth thereafter. The same general pattern was exhibited in the Occupied Palestinian Territories, but with less well balanced growth (World Bank 1993a; Avineri 1994). Imbalances were reflected in the heavy dependence on external employment (in Israel and in other countries of the region), limited industrialization and infrastructure, and trade dominated by linkages to Israel. Partly because of these imbalances and partly because of problems related to the *intifada* (and partly, no doubt, for other reasons), the Territories experienced more economic volatility, with stronger growth in the earlier years of occupation and greater stagnation in the latter. Both Israel and the Occupied Territories depend significantly on outside financial flows — direct remittances, bilateral and multilateral aid, plus direct foreign investment, and, in the case of Israel, bond sales to Jews around the world — that together account for as much as one-sixth of Israeli gross national product (GNP) and an unknown but large share in the Territories.

Past Investment in Water

The adverse effects of slower and even less balanced growth in the 1980s were magnified in the Occupied Territories because "In contrast to impressive gains in private incomes and consumption, the provision of public services and physical infrastructure in the [Occupied Territories] is highly inadequate" (World Bank 1993a, p. 10). Water is no exception. Although the proportion of households in the Occupied Palestinian Territories with access to safe water climbed from 15% in 1970 to 90% in 1991 (World Bank 1993a, box 2.3),[15] the amounts available per day are limited in some areas and safe wastewater collection systems have lagged behind delivery of water supply. As mentioned previously, although Mekorot has offered to connect Palestinian villages to the Israeli water system, and some 250 have accepted (Vesilind 1993), many others still refuse the offer, either on a point of principle (not wishing to condone the Israeli occupation) or because they find the price Mekorot charges for the water to be too high.

Financial limitations in part explain the poor state of water and sanitation systems in the Occupied Territories, particularly in the Gaza Strip. The Civil Administration and municipalities operate these systems strictly on a cash basis. Expenditures are limited to revenues from taxes, fees, and utility tariffs. Other than funds available from international aid and United Nations channels (and, before 1988, from Jordanian sources), money for investments in the construction of new systems and in the maintenance of existing systems must come from these sources, as opposed to the conventional source of money — borrowing in advance of needs.

Investment Needs in Water

The World Bank (1993a) has estimated the total investment requirements in the Occupied Palestinian Territories; "high priority investment needs" for public sector "physical and social infrastructure" in the

---

[15] The numbers seem remarkably high given the condition of refugee camps in the Gaza Strip and the large number of small villages in the West Bank. The word "access" does not, however, necessarily imply house-by-house connections. The original source for the data is the *Statistical Abstract of Israel* (Israel, Central Bureau of Statistics 1992), but this is supplemented by estimates by World Bank missions.

first 10 years (assumed to be 1994–2003) after a peace settlement would cumulate to $3 billion. This sum includes roads, electrical facilities, solid-waste systems, schools, and hospitals, as well as water-supply and sewage projects. Water projects alone represent just under half a billion dollars, about one-sixth of the total, with most work required during the first 5-year period. In addition, the World Bank estimates that $18 million of technical assistance will be required for the water and wastewater sectors, most of it for "project feasibility studies and project preparation work." The lack of need for general technical assistance in water probably reflects the competence of Palestinian agencies (see section on existing institutions). The World Bank also suggests that private capital of about $2.5 billion would be required in addition to the $3 billion in bilateral and multilateral aid.

The World Bank appropriately cautions that all of its estimates of public sector investment needs are preliminary. Among other things, they assume no major return of the Palestinian diaspora. In the case of water, they also depend upon specific elements of the final peace settlement. Palestinian estimates of the additional investment that will be required are two to three times higher than the World Bank estimate, but they probably include private as well as public investment.

Understandably, but regrettably, starting from the specific options mentioned in the Peace Accord for joint water investment, the focus continues to be on supply augmentation — and for the most part on a megaproject approach to augmentation. National governments, donor agencies, and multilateral banks in the region have all traditionally focused efforts on expanding supply to accommodate greater numbers of Jewish and, in some cases, Palestinian refugees and to stimulate export-led economic growth. Almost nothing has been said about investments to reduce use, either by improving the efficiency of existing water use or by converting the economies (notably in Israel) to less water-intensive products (mainly crops). The only exception to the general neglect of demand management is some attention to price systems for water, particularly to increasing the price of water for irrigation. The Harvard economics report, which for the most part leaves water to a separate project (see Chapter 7), emphasizes that progress in mitigating conflicts in agriculture "will demand, among other things, that the water

authorities in each of the areas begin pricing that commodity in a closer
relationship to its real market value" (Hausman and Karasik 1993,
p. 51). (As indicated in Chapter 4, the Government of Israel has
moved, in its fiscal 1995 budget, to increase water prices for farmers.)
Reflecting the general thrust of the report, it goes on to suggest that
"movement toward a free trade regime in agriculture must be accompanied by a rationalization of water use."

Water Investment in the Settlements

The ultimate disposition of Israeli settlements in the Occupied
Palestinian Territories must be raised as an issue, although we have no
idea as to how it may ultimately be resolved. There has already been a
major investment in water and, in some cases, wastewater systems for
the settlements. On the one hand, should a final Peace Accord include
provisions for many (if not all) of the settlements to come under
Palestinian jurisdiction, a significant water infrastructure will become
available, although not necessarily at zero cost. We cannot conceive of
an Israeli pullout that would allow the physical destruction of these
communities, as occurred when Israel withdrew from settlements in the
Sinai after its peace treaty with Egypt in 1982. On the other hand,
under the reasonable assumption that the settlers would expect to be
compensated for leaving, the estimated cost of the peace settlement
would increase by $4–5 billion (and this excludes the settlements
immediately around Jerusalem) (Rabushka 1993).

It is difficult to say without further analysis directed specifically at
the issue whether the transfer of most settlements to Palestinian control
would or would not be a net investment cost. Although the immediate
impact would be evident in the compensation payments, there would be
some offsetting savings in investment required by the Palestinian community. Because the settlements are, with very few exceptions, a sizable
net drain on the Israeli economy, there would be additional annual savings as well.[16] Even with a partial transfer, Palestinian water institutions

---

[16] The high cost of the settlements has been abundantly documented in a
series of reports by the "Settlements Watch Team" of Peace Now, one of the leading
parts of the Israeli/Zionist peace movement.

would need to be capable, within 5 years, of absorbing and operating the infrastructure, perhaps jointly with the Israelis.

In summary, huge investments will be required in the region, primarily in the Occupied Territories. These investments, coupled with the economic stability that will accompany a peace settlement, may stimulate an economic boom for the region. Some argue that integration of the three economies (Israeli, Jordanian, and Palestinian) in a common market will stimulate growth; others disagree strongly. At this point, all we are willing to say is that the added investments that are anticipated in water and wastewater systems are overdue, and they can only improve the standards of living and the quality of life for the Palestinian people. So far as integration is concerned, there is no choice with water; the nature of the resource is such that joint management by Israelis, Jordanians, and Palestinians will be essential to minimize costs or maximize benefits, singly and collectively.

Institutions

Article VII of the Peace Accord made provisions for a Palestinian Water (Administration) Authority (PWA), along with other authorities for electricity, land, and the environment. The Peace Accord left to a future interim agreement, specification of the Authority's "powers and responsibilities." A broad interpretation of those powers and responsibilities is implied by Annex III of the Peace Accord, which envisages active economic cooperation in the field of water under the auspices of an Israeli–Palestinian Continuing Committee for Economic Cooperation. In this case, somewhat more detail was given, including reference in the first clause to studies and plans on water rights and equitable utilization of water. Clause 10 does not refer to water, but it does refer to "joint and/or coordinated measures" for environmental protection. Finally, Annex IV is something of a "megaproject wish list," which includes a number of proposed water megaprojects. None of the items listed in these annexes will be very meaningful unless the PWA has strong policy-making, as well as administrative, "powers and responsibilities."

Whatever the final definition of powers and responsibilities, what is most important now is the transfer of authority from Israelis to Palestinians. This transfer is as important symbolically as it is practically, and not just in the water sector. As stated in the Harvard economics report (Hausman and Karasik 1993, p. 77):

> Indeed, if significant control is not extended to a self-governing authority with regard to natural resources such as water and land and with respect to trade, taxation, and finance, then the political purposes of autonomy — recognition of a distinct people, their separation from others, and ownership rights — cannot be achieved.

The next section will discuss the timing of the transfer of powers and responsibilities to the PWA, and the following sections will consider human resources within the Occupied Palestinian Territories that can support the PWA.

Interim Responsibility for Water Management

The Harvard and Villanova reports emphasize the need for Palestinian authorities to take over, as rapidly and fully as possible, existing institutions (including water utilities) that are currently managed by the Israeli Civil Administration. Given that Article VII grants water rights to Palestinians, it should be a simple matter (given that elusive "good will") to identify the areas in which authority for water management needs to be transferred to Palestinians. In a work that in many ways presaged the terms of the Peace Accord, Lesch and her colleagues suggest that an interim government (comparable to "the Council" in the Peace Accord) could establish a Water Department that would "regulate domestic, agricultural and industrial water use; issue permits for drilling wells; provide technical assistance to construct reservoirs, dams and water networks" (Lesch 1992). Final policy-making and financial authority should remain with the Council, but either responsibility could be delegated to departments. Such authority "would include the ability to set and revise policy and programs in each department, control the budget, set and collect taxes and fees, and prepare medium and long range plans for programs and personnel," and the Council would "also have the power to hire, promote, fire and set standards for personnel in each department" (Lesch 1992, p. 43).

The question remains as to how these powers might be made effective in the context of water, yet not threaten Israeli security in its water supply beyond a point that is tolerable for the Israeli government. The resolution to this question will be determined both in high-level negotiations concerning, for example, the determination of final borders, and in low-level negotiations over, for example, local water diversions and water allocations. The model for the former process is the bilateral negotiations and the model for the latter process is the "picnic table summits," both discussed in previous chapters.

The Harvard economics report implies a similar approach, but emphasizes that, to cope with immediate economic problems, the Palestinians could accommodate their institution-building most easily if the new governing body simply takes over existing institutions from the Civil Administration. We support this approach, but caution that, in the case of water, those institutions are administratively linked to Israeli institutions, and the water works are in some cases physically connected to Israeli works. The recommendation that the Palestinians avoid building "a shadow set of alternative institutions" to operate after a transfer of authority is no doubt wise. Some shadow policies, however, and some shadow institutions will be necessary if the two water systems are to be operated not as a fully integrated (which is to say Israeli-dominated) system.

The report from the World Bank mission seems to advocate an organization of the water and sanitation sector that is somewhat at odds with that suggested by Lesch et al. (1992). This report states (World Bank 1993a, p. 23):

> To provide a sound basis for autonomy, accountability and efficiency, it is recommended that commercially oriented utility companies be established. Municipal governments should disengage from the direct role of provider of water and electricity, to the indirect role of owner.

This is not a prescription for privatization (although neither does it exclude that policy option; indeed, the World Bank seems to suggest that it is desirable), but rather for a more technically, less politically, oriented administration. Given that water planning and policy are also likely to fall within the mandate of the Palestinian Water Authority, it is a naive recommendation. The critical role of water in both economic development and quality of life means that even such "technical" issues

as pricing and regulation are inherently political, as they shift the benefits and costs of water supply from one sector to another.

As a result of concerns for both overall system coordination and
the political implications of water management, we must also question
the longer term institutional plan envisaged by the World Bank mission. The report recommends that: "(a) the roles of policy-making,
ownership and regulation be separated among different institutions; and
(b) the ownership (shareholdings) be spread as widely as possible among
different municipalities, pension funds and other public or private agencies" (World Bank 1993a, p. 23). Given the need for regional
approaches to water, we find this recommendation even less acceptable
than the others; a narrowly focused and diversely (possibly privately)
owned corporation would be no match for the sophisticated water agencies in Israel and in Jordan.

In our view, a more appropriate approach to the sharing of management responsibilities in each country in the region, and one that is
fully compatible with the approach suggested by Lesch, is advocated in
a study of environmental health problems in the Gaza Strip that states
(Fuller et al. 1993, p. ix):

> The goals for development of the environmental health sector can be met
> only if institutional support and development match the planning and
> execution of technical improvements. In the long run, this will require
> formation of centralized, semi-autonomous institutions for (1) water,
> sewage, and solid waste management responsibilities and (2) environ-
> mental planning, monitoring, and control.

Although this recommendation is intended for a single sector and just
one part of one country, it could be applied much more widely.

In summary, responsibility for water policy within the Palestinian
entity will ultimately devolve from the highest political body, but the
question remains as to how that devolution will be made effective. It is
the absence of such devolution in Israel, where water policies come
from the Minister of Agriculture, that has led to such imbalanced policies there. There is no need to replicate this imbalance in the new institutions that will be needed in whatever political structure evolves in the
Occupied Territories. What will be needed over the next year, and
indeed throughout the transition period, is enough capacity in the

PWA so that it can analyze options and then develop and present a coordinated and comprehensive position in negotiations.

Existing Institutions

Palestinian responsibility for management of water resources, limited as it has been during the Israeli occupation, has not been entirely eliminated. A remarkably high level of capacity for analysis and management of water resources has been maintained. There are at least four sources of existing personnel and expertise on which the work of the PWA can be built. First, remnants of the former Jordanian administration still exist in the Water Department of the Civil Administration. It is true that functions of the Water Department have been limited, as described in Chapter 3, and it has been removed from policy functions for more than 25 years; however, staff of that organization (very possibly in collaboration with elements of the water technical committee) could, and perhaps should, become the core of a central operating authority. Certainly, these people are most likely to be able to fill the administrative responsibilities that, as we have indicated, should not dominate but would, nevertheless, represent an essential component of the PWA's work.

If the Water Department is viewed as a nascent national water-management agency, so too should existing municipal authorities be viewed as important collaborating institutions in the rebuilding of an integrated water-management system for the Occupied Palestinian Territories. A number of cities in the West Bank and Gaza have their own water-management agencies that can participate directly in the management processes. The largest is the Jerusalem Water Undertaking (JWU), which serves seven municipalities and 40 villages (containing about one-quarter of the population of the West Bank) and which is organized as a public utility. The JWU is both administratively well-run and technically efficient (losses of only 26%), and it comes close to being self-supporting. Other companies, such as those for Nablus, Hebron, Gaza City, and Khan Yunis, are municipally owned. In other places, such as Bethlehem, the companies are hybrids. Many of the water-management agencies serve not only the municipality, but surrounding villages and refugee camps as well. Although the competence (both technical and administrative) of these municipal agencies varies widely — the Jerusalem Water Undertaking seems to set the standard — they could, given time for training plus some equipment and more capital, be important participants in the water-management process in the West Bank and Gaza.

Nongovernmental organizations (NGOs) represent a third source for building institutional capacity for water management in the Occupied Palestinian Territories. Palestinian NGOs are quite competent and active in the field of water-supply assessment and monitoring. The Palestine Hydrology Group (PHG) focuses on monitoring the flow from springs and in wells, and also supports local, small-scale water-harvesting systems. It is building its own capacity to use remote-sensing data and, with funds from the United Kingdom, is working on a water resources management plan for the Territories. The Applied Research Institute of Jerusalem (ARIJ) is putting together a large water, land use, and environmental database, and has received a grant from Canada's IDRC to analyze alternative irrigation systems and their implications for water quantity and quality. To our knowledge, there is no comparable NGO based in the Gaza Strip (although both the PHG and ARIJ work throughout the Territories), but there are several environmental NGOs that monitor water quality and develop environmental protection plans. They worked closely with the Dutch team that produced a report on environmental conditions in the Gaza Strip (Bruins et al. 1991), which also deals with many water-related issues.

Finally, the seven universities of the West Bank and Gaza represent a store of social and natural science capacity that can serve as an independent source of information and analysis, particularly of less conventional options and alternative policies. Despite closure for many months during the *intifada*, the university system continued to operate, if at a minimal level. Engineering and physical science departments seem particularly strong; some of the research labs, for example, those at Birzeit's Centre for Environmental and Occupational Health Sciences, are well equipped and capable of providing a local but independent source of testing and analysis. University-affiliated groups, such as An-Najah's Rural Research Centre, can also be called upon for analyses of alternatives in specific sectors or regions.

All of these organizations have been utilized in the early stages of building capacity for the Palestinian Water Authority (PWA). Palestinian water experts have gone on study tours to other Middle Eastern and to European nations and, with the support of the technical committees, workshops have been arranged to consider alternative, institutional designs for the water sector. Broad recommendations were put together at a workshop at Birzeit University in April of 1994. According to this plan, the future institutional framework for the Palestinian water sector would have four main components.

The PWA would retain overall management responsibility, policy direction, and enforcement powers. Its primary objective would be the management and efficient allocation of all water to achieve social, economic, and environmental goals. This will include price regulation, pollution protection, conservation, waste minimization, setting standards, and protection from overexploitation. Retail water and wastewater services, however, would be provided by local, government-owned, regional water utilities (RWUs), responsive to regional concerns but operating within the standards set by the PWA.

It is expected that four regional water utilities would be formed, corresponding to the coastal, northern, central, and southern regions. All water abstraction and discharge will be licenced and monitored by the PWA. To complete the proposed institutional picture, the PWA would have two main subsidiaries: first, a national bulk utility to provide large-scale, wholesale water services and to design, build, and operate major components of infrastructure, for example, a West Ghor Canal; and second, a support-services company with capabilities in training, procurement, hydrogeology, and other activities that can be delivered more efficiently by a single body. Although these recommendations have yet to be acted upon, they appear to meet key criteria of efficiency, flexibility, and accountability. As well, they are notable for the emphasis on conservation and avoidance of waste (responsibility for which lies with the PWA itself) and on the comprehensive and integrated management, including wastewater.

In summary, more than most developing nations, and certainly more than most regions emerging from a quarter century of military occupation, the Occupied Palestinian Territories have adequate human resources for a rapid and complete transfer of powers and responsibilities in the field of water. The only exceptions to this statement are in the areas of resource economics, resource management, and demand management. Most of the water specialists in the Territories have engineering or physical science training, and there is a need for parallel expertise in the areas of water economics and water management and of that special set of skills necessary to establish a strong conservation program.

Key Roles of a Palestinian Water Authority

The new Palestinian Water Authority will have three immediate but general tasks: operating the existing system, managing an investment process, and planning for the future. For each task, it will have to make difficult choices between those things that must be done immediately, and those that can (or must) be put off until later. Water delivery must continue, breaks in the pipes must be repaired, and bills must go out while the PWA makes decisions about programs and investments that will take effect over the next 3–5 years, and also initiates a process of long-term planning.

The first task of the PWA will be to continue to operate the existing systems. This is a sizable undertaking, but, as suggested, likely not beyond the capability of the existing Palestinian public and private agencies. Clearly, it will require access to the information and data banks now held by the Israelis, which implies the need for computers. The computers may have to be supplied through international aid programs, but the absence of hardware is unlikely to be a problem for long. Operations will also require some immediate decisions about water pricing, decisions that will depend upon prior choices about the financing of the water system and about social objectives. For example, it must be determined to what extent the system will be expected to generate its own capital, and to what extent remote areas or poor people will be subsidized. Beyond the requirements that the pricing system promote efficiency in use and produce enough revenue for maintenance, a variety of pricing systems could be put in place.

There are two operational areas that will require new skills and new policies and programs in the near term: demand management and water quality. Conventional water authorities are supply oriented and

focused on water quantity. The Palestinian Council has the opportunity
to create the PWA in a modern mode, paying as much attention to
water demand as to supply and as much to water quality as to quantity.

A strong and enforceable program of demand management,
including everything from public awareness campaigns to end-use regulations and quotas, will be required regardless of how extensive the
water rights accorded to Palestinians. A well-designed pricing system is
essential but, in isolation, insufficient to maximize water efficiency and
conservation (Pearse et al. 1985; Brooks et al. 1990); information,
incentives, and regulations, among other things, are also required.
Fortunately, this is an area in which skills, materials and approaches
could be borrowed in large part from Israeli and Jordanian organizations.
Their cooperation could almost be assured by the prospect that attention to demand management would reduce pressure on limited water
resources. Water conservation has been a primary concern of the
experts delegated by the technical committees to look at water. All of
their statements emphasize the slogan that "waste is a misplaced
resource," and they have produced a report for the World Bank entitled
"Water Conservation in Palestine" (March 1994).

Expertise in water-quality management is the other area that will
need to be strengthened in the short term. All of the problems (with
possible exception of industrial wastes) that Israel is now experiencing
have already occurred — or shortly will — in the Occupied Palestinian
Territories. If either the PWA or the Palestinian Environmental
Protection Authority is not given a very clear mandate and enforceable
powers to limit degradation of water quality, it will not be long before
economic output and health conditions will begin to deteriorate. Here,
too, the Israelis have much to gain by cooperating with the PWA. As
indicated earlier, Israeli drinking water supplies are threatened at least
as much by the potential contamination in the recharge areas of the
Mountain Aquifer, which lie almost entirely within the West Bank, as
they are by the need to reallocate even sizable quantities of water from
the aquifer to the Palestinians.

The second main task of the PWA is more problematic than operating the existing system. Its staff will have to coordinate with other
departments and with an expected surfeit of external donor agencies to

manage new infrastructure investments that will be made in the water sector. There is even an Israeli proposal to establish a Middle Eastern development bank, which would operate much as do the other multilateral banks already established in other parts of the world.

The alternative to active involvement by the PWA is that donor agencies, rather than Palestinians, will determine when, where, and in what to invest. Competition for the funds will be strong among various sectors and within the water sector, and, even assuming that the productivity of new infrastructure investment in water can be demonstrated, management of the process will determine whether the capital is put to good use. Recent experiences in the cities of Bethlehem and of Gaza provide opposite cases in point. A new sewage system designed to serve a population of 100 thousand in Bethlehem and surrounding communities is nearing completion. Financed by Italian and German aid agencies at a total cost of about $18 million, the new system is evidently being incorporated into the existing one with a minimum of problems and disruption. In contrast, in Gaza City a well-intentioned investment of several million dollars by a group called American Near-East Refugee Aid to enhance the use of rainwater to recharge aquifers has failed to achieve any tangible result because of a lack of coordinated administrative infrastructure in the city.

There is nothing unique about the problems of managing water investments that will continue to challenge officials in the Occupied Palestinian Territories. Even well-established government agencies have difficulty coping with large projects. The record shows that water resource investments in developing countries typically yield net payoffs that fall below expectations and, commonly, are actually negative (Howe and Dixon 1993). The problems causing these poor results rarely originate from lack of technical or engineering competence. More typically, problems arise as a result of differing host country–donor agency priorities, design changes aimed at profile rather than efficiency, lack of input from local people or failure to allow for indigenous production patterns, and in some cases outright corruption (Howe and Dixon 1993). In addition, evidence from many years of experience has shown that funding for both training and institutional strengthening must be provided at the same time as, or even before, that provided for construction.

Finally, and most problematic of all because of the multidimensional nature of the issue, is the need to develop a water master plan for the West Bank and Gaza. To produce such a plan, the Palestinian Water Authority will have to work not just with other departments but with all other agencies and consult with the Palestinian people to initiate a decision-making process acceptable to all. Work of this kind is already under way within the technical committees. In mid-1993, the technical committees linked to the peace negotiations were given additional tasks that amounted to an exercise in national planning. Decisions about investments, management, and regulation in the water sector will have to be made before a final master plan is complete, but the very process of working toward the plan will help inform decisions such that investments and actions will be consistent with long-term planning. It is premature to discuss the details and dimensions of a water master plan for a new Palestinian entity, but it is not too soon to begin thinking about the process. Master plans are, by their very nature, political and, in terms of water, every resident of the Occupied Palestinian Territories will be vitally concerned and affected.

A Regional Water Authority

At least since Lowdermilk proposed a Jordan River version of the Tennessee Valley Authority, development of a formally organized, regional water management organization has been discussed. Whatever its theoretical merits, we believe that talk of creating a Jordan Valley Authority, much less an authority with even greater geographic scope, is premature. There has been too much bitterness and too little accommodation in recent history to believe than any of the parties would surrender the sovereignty necessary to permit such a supranational body. Moreover, it is not evident to us that any of the key issues that must be resolved in the next few years would be made simpler if that supranational body existed. Finally, although those who advocate a regional water authority no doubt have the best interests of all in mind, for now and for several years into the future it would be perceived simply as a way for Israel to gain access to still more water than is currently the case.

Although it is too early to consider a regional water authority, it may not be too early to consider some form of regional database. Again, the notion of a single regional node into which all water data would flow and to which any analyst would have access, is premature. Partial integration, however, of water data with common definitions and common formatting, together with agreed protocols for data collection and management, could be useful in broadening areas of disagreement. Assuming all parties have appropriate software and hardware, parallel but linked databases are possible. Moreover, in contrast to a regional water authority, these databases can be built step by step, with early steps aimed at building confidence and only the later ones aimed at true integration. First steps might include linking time-series data on water held by Israeli, Palestinian, and Jordanian agencies; comparing flow data held by the Israeli Hydrological Service with those held by the Palestine Hydrology Group; and agreeing on mutual approaches to quality control of data.

In downplaying the potential for a regional water authority — at least in the short term — we do not mean to ignore the potential for joint management of specific water resources. On the one hand, there is remarkably little experience with joint management of complex water systems. On the other hand, the fact that, despite a formal state of war for many years, Israel and Jordan recognized the need to work together to manage the Jordan River is strong evidence that cooperative — if not joint — management can work. It is difficult to see how the Mountain Aquifer could be managed, much less managed efficiently and safely, without joint management by Palestinians and Israelis. Joint management of the Mountain Aquifer was in fact the subject of a series of workshops held in Jerusalem in 1994 under the joint sponsorship of the Truman Institute and the Palestine Consultancy Group. Discussion at the workshops focused on appropriate institutions and policies for joint management, and the general tenor of the meeting was that cooperation, rather than conflict, was the only way to manage effectively the groundwater resources of Israel and the West Bank–Gaza. Joint management can be as limited or extensive as the situation requires and the working agreement permits. Of course, joint management works best when each party to the agreement is reasonably equal in power and access to data and when both share perspectives about the goals of management. This will not be the case between Israelis and Palestinians for some time, but the very process of joint management can build both confidence and capacity.

Community Involvement and WRAP

A consultant's report (Fuller et al. 1993, p. viii) for UNWRA on technical and economic requirements to resolve water and sanitation problems in the cities and refugee camps of Gaza is explicit about the role of the community:

> *Virtually all of these interventions require community involvement, public education and worker training to be successful. Thus, a focused program of community awareness and participation, matched by health education, is a recommendation in itself.*

The authors go on to point out that such measures are low in cost, compared with construction, and that community awareness and participation are essential "to ensure the long-term and sustained development of the environmental health sector throughout the Gaza Strip."

This approach is rare among the stacks of reports on water in Israel and the Occupied Palestinian Territories. In spite of all the concern about water and the effects of shortages on economic development and on human well-being, one seldom reads about the need to involve communities from the start in the planning and assessment of new facilities and the implementation of new policies. Yet, it is the very shortage of water, and the range of options that must be considered on both the demand and the supply sides to cope with shortages, that makes community involvement so important.

Experience around the world has proven the value of community involvement (Brooks and Peters 1988; Sadler 1993). Indigenous populations, as with many rural Palestinians, have been coping with water shortages and with the seasonal and annual variations in flow for centuries. Their approaches may be instructive. In addition, even if new methods are deemed appropriate, they are unlikely to win wide acceptance without proactive programs that explain the options to the community and detail the reasons why a specific option was chosen, and that listen carefully to alternatives and objections that may be raised by the community. From the same perspective, water and sanitation policy will, from time to time, require changes in programs and new investments. Those changes and those investments will benefit some and adversely affect others. Although people will generally support a new incentive program to promote conservation, few people want a sewage treatment plant, or even a pumping station, in their community or neighbourhood. People are much more likely to participate in conservation programs or to accept adverse effects if they believe that the distribution of benefits and costs is equitable, and this is often a matter of perception. For example, economists tend to argue in favour of price mechanisms to keep supply and demand in balance, but Sadler (1993) reports that a majority of the citizens of several cities surveyed in Australia feel that it would be fairer to impose restrictions on water use each summer or in times of drought.

Finally, whether dealing with households, industrialists, or farmers, demand management is as much a matter of sound information coupled with greater awareness as it is of economics and technology. Government and NGO files are filled with education and awareness programs that failed for lack of community involvement in their design and delivery. Sadler (1993, p. 4–2) sums up the situation as follows (emphasis as in original):

> In such a strategic approach [to water planning], business as usual will not be acceptable in the public processes, and the conservation and supply strategies will need to be forward looking, innovative and complementary.... The need for the strategic planning to be highly participative is three-fold:
>
> ≈ evaluation of options will involve public values and tradeoffs, and public input is essential to determining these;
> ≈ for such strategic decisions it is essential that there is public credibility in the conduct of the process;
> ≈ it is the public who, by their individual decisions, will implement water conservation and decide the intensity of behavioural change.

There are no prescriptions for extending community involvement. Some efforts can be general, as with Israel's Year of the Environment in 1993–94; others must be much more specific. Difficult choices have to be made among types of programs and among possible audiences. Some programs do exist; just as with water efficiency itself, the problem is not that such programs are entirely absent in Israel or the Occupied Palestinian Territories but rather, to paraphrase Naff (1990, p. 170), that community involvement programs are not so vigorous and extensive as the crisis and the scarcity requires them to be.

Public involvement will be made easier because of the large number of NGOs in the Occupied Palestinian Territories. NGOs played a remarkable role, particularly during the latter years of the occupation. Dealing with the difficulties of living under occupation and the imbalances in the economy created by dependency on Israel, NGOs sprang up to deal not merely with health, education, and social services, where they might have been expected, but also with economic issues, such as farmer cooperatives, credit bodies, and research and statistical institutions. In effect, the NGOs were engaged in governance, which suggests that they could also play a strong role in water resource management from both the supply and the demand sides.

Given the general need for centralization in urban water delivery and wastewater collection and the control currently exercised over pumping and irrigation by the Water Commission within Israel and the Civil Administration in the Occupied Territories, NGOs have to now been somewhat less active at the community level and in working with consumers of water than they have been in many other sectors. As well, Palestinians are, at present, understandably reluctant to conserve as much water as they can, or to protect watercourses as vigorously as they might, when the bulk of the benefits of their actions go to Israelis. At least, however, during the transition period after self-government is achieved, some form of farmer-managed water systems and locally controlled village water systems may be appropriate and reduce the management and regulatory burdens on the new water authority. Over time, NGOs could establish self-supporting (perhaps cooperative) forms of irrigation development, including management, training, and information dissemination. Although somewhat more difficult, similar kinds of decentralized systems could be established to manage and distribute water for domestic and municipal uses at the village level. Certainly, NGOs can be presumed to be more sensitive than government agencies to, and more capable of building upon, indigenous technology, something that will likely be critical — and not just in the transition phase.

Relationships between the technical committees and the NGOs that had, in many cases, been managing affairs and delivering services in the West Bank and Gaza during the period of occupation, have not always been amicable. The technical committees have a certain legitimacy, but they are not as well connected with, or so sensitive to the needs of, grass-roots representatives (or of women) as should be the case. The relationships may prove to be even more difficult in the future, particularly in villages, where the need for some forms of centralized control on agricultural practices may come to be resented. Villagers, however, recognize as no others the limitations of water, and they have historically been willing to associate for the purposes of managing and sharing water resources.

In response to both the pressing need to begin working on the technical issues facing the water sector in Gaza–Jericho before the establishment and full staffing of the PWA and the need for a community focus in water management, the UNDP and the Canadian International Development Agency (CIDA) provided funding for a small team of experts to initiate key studies. The group, known as the Water Resources Action Program (WRAP) for Palestine, consists of six professional staff with backgrounds in hydrogeology, engineering, economics, and sociology, and is coordinated by a steering committee (the chair of which is Professor El-Khodary, the head of the Palestinian delegation to the Working Group on Water Resources). WRAP has identified seven priority areas for immediate study: a survey of water resources in Gaza, a public awareness campaign, a survey of water resources in the West Bank, the international legal framework, the national legal framework, tariffs and pricing, and data archives for water. It is expected that these studies will provide the basis for the work of the PWA once it is established.

Next Steps

There is no shortage of capable and trained people resident in the Occupied Palestinian Territories who can work in the water sector. There are also existing institutions, some public and some private, that are well placed either to become components of the Palestinian Water Authority or to offer it support. Unfortunately, people do not necessarily talk to one another, and institutions do not necessarily communicate well. Indeed, given the advent of more normal relationships and structures within the Occupied Palestinian Territories, it would be surprising if some of these gaps were not deliberate as groups and individuals vie with one another for leadership roles in Palestinian water resource management.

The needs described in this chapter arise partly because of recent Palestinian political history, but also because the Occupied Palestinian Territories are part of the developing world. The Territories resemble countries emerging from colonialism, or at least from those forms of colonialism that allowed some social and economic development but stifled political development. Priorities for the future must be set, and setting such priorities is inherently a political process. Some of those priorities involve water directly, as with allocation decisions and mechanisms that, for whatever reasons, favour one sector over another. Priorities will also have to be set in the allocation of human resources to the water sector rather than to others (even other natural resource sectors), and in the purchase of modern tools for data processing, remote sensing and the like. Furthermore, there will be nearer term and longer term priorities, and some initiatives that Palestinians can address on their own and others that will require an acceptance of outside technical or financial assistance.

The key task is the creation of a sound institutional structure for water resources management. Issues associated with this requirement are already under study by the water technical committee and WRAP and involve the identification of tasks that a future central Palestinian authority would have to carry out in the water sector, organizational structures that would be needed by central authorities, and the capabilities required of such structures. If work is to advance, an active program of capacity building should be established. Although capacity building has been limited by the occupation, it would be naive to think that it will occur naturally once Israeli troops withdraw. Training is required in at least two senses: in the narrow sense of providing specific technical skills and specific pieces of software or hardware, and in the broader sense of the kind of policy development that will lead to a water master plan for the Occupied Palestinian Territories.

Given that the water technical committee began a study of reorganizing water management in mid-1993, it is evident that the Palestinians were building embryonic institutions well in advance of the announcement of the Peace Accord. In our view, it would be far more productive in the immediate future for donor agencies to support this capacity-building process, as Canada is doing with WRAP, than to provide large amounts of dollars (or yen or francs or riyals) to build new water supply infrastructure.

CHAPTER 11

MAINTAINING THE MOMENTUM

*The current Middle East peace process provides Israel, for the
first time in its history, with a real opportunity for the recognition
of its entitlements to both existence and land by the Arabs. Of
course, a by-product of this would be the acknowledgement by
Israel's neighbours of its entitlement to a fair proportion of the
area's waters. On equal footing, the peace process provides the
Palestinians, too, with their first opportunity for national recognition by Israel. Among national rights, of course, are entitlements to natural resources such as water. The sticky point comes
in deciding who is entitled to how much of the area's limited
water resources. Obviously this question is not limited in scope to
Israel and the anticipated Palestinian entity, but applies further
to the other involved countries in the area.*

— Zarour and Isaac (1992, p. 3)

THIS CONCLUDING CHAPTER brings together thoughts, ideas,
and proposals that have been explicit or implicit in the preceding
chapters. In effect, it provides a set of recommendations that are
intended as steps toward alleviating the water crisis in Israel and in the
Occupied Palestinian Territories and, by so doing, alleviating their
mutual and interrelated water and political problems. Many of these
recommendations, as with those for improved pricing systems for water,
could apply to many countries in the world; others, however, are unique
to the situation in which Israelis and Palestinians find themselves and
to the history and geography that they share.

To some degree, the weight of our recommendations bears most
heavily on Israel. That is neither accidental nor the result of bias.

Rather, it reflects that fact that Israel exists as a state with formal institutions and as the dominant economic and military power in the region. This policy emphasis, however, should not be misconstrued. **In no way do we deny the need for Israel — or any other nation — to be secure in its water supply.** Rather, we wish to emphasize the inefficiencies — economic, environmental, political, and institutional — that play such an important role in the region's water crisis and that, therefore, serve to reduce, not promote, water security. To the extent that Palestinians move toward statehood, or, at a minimum, to the extent that the Palestinian Water Authority gains control over water resources in the Occupied Palestinian Territories, the same sorts of recommendations and the same concern for security will apply. As Lowi (1991) insists, the concept of "security" must be defined in a sense that is broader than direct control over sources of supply.

Establishing Priorities

Before considering recommendations that can begin to deal with the quantity, quality, and geopolitical dimensions of the water crisis facing Israel and the Palestinians, it is necessary to establish priorities for action. In setting out such priorities, we place domestic considerations (activities within Israel and the Occupied Palestinian Territories) before regional ones. We believe that Israelis and Palestinians, along with each of the other peoples in the region, can and should take the initial steps toward mitigating the water crises in areas clearly within their own jurisdictions. Regional agreements for sharing water and joint responsibility for water management are probably the best long-term solutions, but they are unlikely to be acceptable, and even less likely to be stable, if participating nations do not have their own water-resource and water-use systems in order.

We propose, therefore, the following priorities toward resolution of water problems in Israel and the Occupied Palestinian Territories. We advance them with considerable confidence that they apply as well to other countries in the Jordan River Basin and, we suspect, although with less confidence, throughout the Middle East.

≈ **Priority 1: Moderating Water Demand** — First, priority must be accorded to policies and programs for attaining greater efficiency in the use of water, including both micro options aimed at the point of use and macro options in selecting among uses for water. Support of this priority includes not only formal regulations and improved technology, but also education and awareness campaigns. Support of this priority also includes what is perhaps the most important change in the short run: higher prices, particularly for water used in agriculture, and better designed pricing systems that not only cover costs but build in incentives to conserve

≈ **Priority 2: Improved Water Institutions** — The second priority must be the development of local and national institutions that can deal with both water supply and water demand, and both water quantity and water quality. Such institutions must have enough authority to make policy, but not enough power to allow them to ignore the claims of other parts or levels of government or of less powerful stakeholders. This priority is closely linked to the first. As stated by the former Executive Director of UNEP: "The major constraint on efficent water management [is] the weakness of the institutions concerned" (Tolba 1994, p. 2). Such weakness is all the more a threat because water management involves every individual, firm, and government agency in society, and all of them must collaborate in the management plan.

≈ **Priority 3: Augmenting Local Water Supply** — The third priority should be to promote measures to identify, develop, and manage alternative, local sources of water supply, including rainwater harvesting, brackish water, and recycled water. Sources of both potable water for drinking, cooking, and washing and of lower quality water for other household uses, gardening, and irrigation should be investigated. As with efficiency and conservation, this, too, should be a responsibility of whatever water institutions are created.

≈ **Priority 4: Building Regional Water Institutions** — The fourth priority focuses on international, but still intraregional, agreements and institutions for managing water, for sharing supplies, for creating markets to exchange or sell water, and for avoiding or mitigating water quality problems. This recommendation extends beyond the individual political entities that have been the focus of the first three priorities, but only to those nations sharing a river basin or an aquifer.

≈ **Priority 5: Augmenting Regional Water Supply** — Only fifth should consideration be given to interbasin transfers of water or water imports and to capital-intensive megaprojects such as large-scale desalination. We acknowledge that water imports may be an appropriate response to drought, and desalination may be an appropriate technology for small desert communities (at research stations, for example). These short-term or small-scale options are not the focus of our recommendation.

We do not maintain that this order of priorities must be followed in every case or every locale. The Gaza Strip, for example, may already be experiencing such excessive demands on its water resources that only the fourth and fifth options have any significant potential. Many analysts would accept our ordering of priorities, but they would argue that we should move sooner rather than later toward options lower down the list (for example, Shuval 1992). Nevertheless, we believe that the given order represents a starting point from which any nation in the region, and indeed each village, neighbourhood, and sector, can begin taking control of water management. Moreover, the proposed ordering is generally consistent with three principles: to focus first on options that are small in scale and locale-specific, as suggested by Falkenmark et al. (1989); to start with options that are less capital intensive, and only later move toward those that are more so; and to start with options that involve less complex (if no less bitterly contested) and lower level political considerations, and only later move to those that are more complex and involve regional or international considerations. We do not maintain that any of the needed steps is easy or inexpensive, but we do insist that some are easier and less expensive than others.

Several other points must be made before proffering our recommendations. First, because we wish to focus on what could be accomplished in the nearer rather than the more distant future, we have avoided recommending new studies or further research. Clearly, many studies and a substantial amount of research are going to be needed to achieve a better water future for the peoples of this region. In many cases, however, enough is already known to take some action in the absence of new research results. For the rest, we can only urge that research be initiated as soon as possible — and add the suggestion that the priorities for new studies are not different from those we have proposed in the foregoing for more immediate actions.

Second, many of the recommendations that follow have financial implications. They would require either reallocation of internal budgets or outside support from international aid or foreign investment. We are not unmindful of the financial implications and, to some extent, they have been taken implicitly into account. To explore the financing of a more efficient water sector, however, would have taken us well beyond the scope of this book.

Third, each priority level above and each recommendation below contains both technical and institutional dimensions. Emphasis here is placed on the latter. In part, this emphasis is intended to offset the tendency of most literature on water to focus on technical solutions. In larger part, it reflects our conviction that attention to institutional issues cannot be left until after a final peace settlement is in place. Moreover, technology is not as independent a variable as is commonly supposed. Technologies are often developed in response to a need that has emerged through social and economic institutions. As Homer-Dixon et al. (1993, p. 45) note: "The role of social ingenuity as a precursor to technical ingenuity is often overlooked."

Fourth, although we are intrigued by the tentative conclusion of the Harvard Middle East Water Project to the effect that the total value of the water in dispute between Israelis and Palestinians is not very large, nothing in this chapter depends upon that conclusion. It is reassuring that the values appear to be so modest, probably around $200 million per year, but, regardless of the true value of water, or of the premiums that governments may choose to place on the price of water at the border, the recommendations that follow remain (we believe) valid.

Finally, in the rapidly changing world of Israeli–Palestinian politics, it may well be that some of what we have listed as recommendations will have moved from the possible to the actual by the time this book appears in print. If this is the case (as indeed it is; see Afterword), we will be pleased that in this troubled part of the world politics will have proven faster than publication.

Domestic Recommendations

Conservation and Efficiency Programs

The following steps are, in our view, fundamental for both Israel and the Occupied Palestinian Territories, but primarily for Israel because the country's water use is so much greater both relatively and absolutely. The recommendations would, if adopted, orient the Israeli and Palestinian people toward a water strategy that would leave them both economically more stable and politically more secure, while offering a path that is considerably less environmentally damaging than the one that is now being followed.

≈ Develop a broad and enforceable strategy for water conservation as the first step toward reducing water scarcity. This strategy should, as appropriate for sector and end-use, include information programs, financial incentives, minimum efficiency standards, and regulation. Much of this structure already exists; states in this region already have some strong conservation measures in place, although not for all sectors. Those policies and programs, however, are simply not adequate given the growing pressure of demand on water resources — pressure that can only grow with increases in population, income, and human expectations.

≈ Gradually introduce appropriate (probably marginal-cost) pricing of water to encourage efficiency in allocation and use in all sectors, together with the reduction or elimination of subsidies (notably to farming, horticulture, and animal husbandry). Low prices for initial quantities of fresh water to all households can be justified on grounds of equity, as can water delivered to refugee camps. Moreover, given the long history of agriculture in the region and the sizable, if declining, agricultural sector, it would be neither equitable nor efficient to move too rapidly with pricing reform. What does need to be implemented immediately is a program with a fixed timetable to make the pricing system more effective in promoting end-use efficiency and to permit only those subsidies with wide support to remain.

≈ Initiate a major information program to promote awareness of the growing water shortage and of the parallel importance of protecting water quality. As with measures to promote greater water efficiency, such programs are already in place, but they fall short of what will be needed if the populations in question are both to act responsibly in their own use of water and to urge (or at least accept) the policy and pricing changes that governments need to enact and enforce over coming years.

≈ Encourage a shift in agricultural production patterns to reduce emphasis on water-intensive crops and increase productivity of drought-resistant and salt-tolerant crops. Grants or loans of various kinds would be appropriate to assist farmers in the transition to less water-intensive agriculture. Equally forceful encouragement, and possibly incentives, should be used to change production patterns with the objective of reducing the current excessive rates of water pollution originating from farm operations of all types.

≈ Encourage a shift to less water-intensive activities. Most notably this recommendation implies a shift from agriculture to light industry. Other shifts, however, are also necessary. Within industry, not only should shifts be encouraged from sectors that are more consumptive of water to those that are less, but possibly even more strongly, shifts should be encouraged from sectors that are responsible for significantly degrading the water they use to sectors that cause less environmental damage. Again, grants or loans to promote all of these shifts may be appropriate for an interim period.

≈ Restrict water use and control water degradation by the tourism sector. Tourism is among the strongest economic sectors in Israel, and it represents a major opportunity for the Occupied Palestinian Territories. The hospitality industry, as some prefer to call it, tends to be water intensive. Special efforts should be made to control water use and water degradation by the industry, as well as to make tourists aware of the constraints under which the region they are visiting must exist. Signs in washrooms to turn off the taps and extinguish lights are hardly sufficient given the nature of the problem, but even these small reminders are lacking in many facilities.

Institutional Structures: Israel

Israel already has an existing and reasonably well-functioning system for managing its water resources. Problems lie not in the efficiency of that system itself, but rather in its excessive focus on one sector (agriculture), in its relative neglect of water quality, and in the use of water by Israelis at the expense of Palestinians. The following changes would help to create a better balance in the management of water in Israel.

≈ Remove the Water Commission from the authority of the Ministry of Agriculture and give the Commission the independence, status, and structure it needs to design and implement a more sectorally neutral water system. Responsibilities of the new Commission should include, inter alia, water planning, water pricing, and water efficiency standards.

≈ Establish clear working relationships with and lines of authority between the Water Commission and the Ministry of Environment. Work toward the enforcement of tough pollution-control laws, likely under the control of the Ministry of Environment, with particular attention to agricultural runoff and industrial wastewater.

≈ In the interim, even before a final settlement, allocate more water to Palestinians in the Occupied Territories, partly as a gesture of good will and partly because it will force some cooperation between Israeli authorities and the new Palestinian Water Authority. This water should be released for agricultural or other economic developments, not simply for household and urban use. As indicated earlier, the Israelis have generally made water available as needed for the latter uses, but have not permitted the former to expand since 1967. Immediate allocation of additional water (which is to say, reallocation of existing water) is particularly critical to relieve the deteriorating situation in the Gaza Strip.

≈ Israeli officials, notably in the Hydrological Service, should reduce the level of security associated with water data and make them more widely available. Since the start of the peace process, steps have been taken to this effect, but bureaucratic obstacles continue to hinder Palestinian researchers and water managers. To the greatest extent possible, data should be released in both processed and unprocessed form so that managers and researchers have the option to conduct their own analyses and make their own interpretations.

≈ Israeli officials should work with their Palestinian counterparts to reach common definitions for water supply and demand, compatible systems for the collection and processing of water data, and appropriate quality standards for data. This recommendation is well short of a proposal for a regional database, but it does make the creation of such a database a possibility in the future.

≈ Occupation authorities outside Jericho and Gaza (where we assume Palestinian authorities will have full control) should explicitly recognize a joint concern for water use between the two peoples, and they should accept some degree of joint planning for and management of shared water resources, including both surface water and underground water. Implicitly, this would amount to a statement of Israeli dependency on water originating in lands that are predominantly occupied by, if not formally under the jurisdiction of, Palestinians. So be it. The current situation is a reflection of recent history, and the proposed change in approach would establish a basis from which discussions about sharing, likely with some form of compensation, could begin.

≈ Israel should indicate that those aquifers on the West Bank that rise on the West Bank and flow eastward will, henceforth, be managed by and for the Palestinian community.

≈ Because the Israeli wells immediately to the west of the Gaza Strip are so contentious, Israel should either cease pumping from them or provide clear evidence to the Palestinians that these wells are, in fact, tapping saline water, not fresh water.

Institutional Structures: Occupied Palestinian Territories

A nascent Palestinian Water Authority has emerged. How it will
develop, what powers it will have, and how effectively it will manage
those responsibilities remain to be seen. Although Palestinians will
have to define the nature, size, and political status of the organization
that will emerge, some of the needed dimensions are already clear.

≈ The new Palestinian Water Authority should be staffed and
funded as quickly as possible, and provided with the intellectual
and technical capacity to take full responsibility for managing
water resources. Such responsibility should be aimed at achieving
sustainability of water resources and high end-use efficiency. The
PWA should be directed to act in the best interests of the
Palestinian people and should be free of direct political influence,
except where that influence is effected through the democratic
process and conveyed openly through senior bodies in the
Palestinian political system.

≈ The Palestinian Water Authority will, almost inevitably, be preoccupied in its early stages with improving the delivery of potable
and irrigation water to its community. The PWA should not
become so preoccupied with supply that it fails to initiate programs and policies for demand management. In this respect, it
should review with great care the demand management measures
that have been taken (also those that have not been taken) in
Israel, Jordan, and other countries that have similar ecologies and
economic structures.

≈ The Palestinian Environmental Protection Agency should be
staffed, funded, and provided with capacity in exactly the same
manner as the PWA. In particular, the two authorities must
develop clear working relationships and lines of responsibility so
that water quality is protected as vigorously as water quantity.
Much can be learned by looking at those sectors, such as greenhouses and poultry, that have high potential in the Occupied
Palestinian Territories but have caused grievous water-pollution
problems in Israel. Ideally, they should be converted from sources
of problems to sources of water — potable water by rooftop harvesting and irrigation water by recycling wastewater.

≈ A computer-based, data-management capability for water must be established as soon as possible. Immediate linkages must be made with the Israeli water and environment databases, and the capacity to extract data from and contribute data to this system must be developed.

≈ Effort must be made to work with Israeli officials to make existing databases and data-collection systems compatible. Israeli records can be compared with those held by Palestinian NGOs (such as the Palestine Hydrology Group) to select the best estimates. In addition, historical records of water supply and demand can be examined, as can reports on hydrogeology, such as those held by Egyptian and Jordanian authorities in the Gaza Strip and the West Bank respectively.

≈ Formal, but flexible, criteria must be developed for the acceptance or rejection of proffered bilateral or multilateral international aid as well as direct foreign investment in the water sector. All aid or investment proposals, regardless of the sector, should be evaluated in terms of their demands for water and their likely effects on water quality. In effect, proposals should be subject to a "water-impact analysis." In this respect, water in place may be as valuable as water in use, and adequate consideration should be given to protection of natural areas and water-based recreation when evaluating alternative uses for water.

≈ A system of nature reserves should be established in which no development or a very restricted form of development is permitted. The reserves should be aimed jointly at protecting the water heritage of the region and at preserving ecological services of water. If the reserves can also support tourism and recreation, so much the better.

≈ Special forms of technical and financial assistance will likely be needed to assist with Palestinian agriculture. Farmers in the Occupied Palestinian Territories will have to adopt improved irrigation practices that will ensure that more of the water applied reaches the plants. They may need new sales cooperatives and other institutions as international markets again become open to them. They may also need quality-control mechanisms to meet international grading standards (such as that for olive oil) and to ensure low levels of pesticide residues.

≈ Steps should be taken to improve the quality of water in the Lower Jordan (below Lake Kinneret), which Palestinian farmers currently find too saline for most crops.

≈ Delivery and sewage systems must be planned for and constructed throughout the West Bank and the Gaza Strip, with most, if not all, of the sewage reclaimed for use within the Territories. This general position is not intended to preclude exchanges of either water or reclaimed sewage when that is more efficient than totally independent systems. Given population densities, only the most rural Palestinian communities should have stand-alone or private systems.

≈ The Palestinian Water Authority should take advantage of the existing human resource base in the municipal water companies and nongovernmental organizations that are found throughout the Occupied Territories. In part, this will relieve the heavy load under which the PWA will inevitably labour. In part, it will also provide stakeholder input for — ideally participation in — decisions about the management of water resources. Centralized planning is essential for both water supply and wastewater disposal, but the Palestinian Water Authority must resist the temptation to do everything itself. Planning will be improved if carried out in collaboration with the people most directly affected, and implementation of some decisions can more effectively be delegated to local groups and organizations.

≈ The Palestinian Water Authority will have to take special and immediate steps to deal with the water situation in the Gaza Strip. We urge that every attempt be made to look at local alternatives before turning to international pipelines or desalination. Obviously, the most stringent demand management measures, including shifts to crops that are tolerant to drought and to saline water, must be enacted — though enforcement is unlikely to be successful if such measures are adopted without careful consultation with local people. Local wastewater should be treated and recycled; as well, the possibility that recycled water might be imported from Israel should be investigated. Excessive leakage in the distribution system should be reduced. In the nearest term, however, the most feasible and possibly the cheapest option may well be to increase imports from Mekorot. The capacity of the lines feeding the Gaza Strip with external sources is said to be 15 Mm^3/year, of which less than 20% is currently utilized. We can understand the reluctance to make Gaza dependent on an Israeli pipeline, but the new willingness to work together and the desperate situation might overcome this attitude.

Alternative, Local Sources of Supply

The following recommendations are appropriate for both Israelis and Palestinians but, because of the strictures of the past quarter century, they will find their major application within the Occupied Palestinian Territories.

≈ Work toward reducing water loss in supply systems throughout the Territories. As we noted earlier, water loss is greater than 50% in most regions (the exception being the Jerusalem Water Undertaking). Faulty infrastructure, faulty metering, inadequate monitoring, and water theft are problems that must be addressed.

≈ Continue the trend toward full use of recycled water for agriculture or for recharging aquifers in parallel with investing in modern sewage systems wherever they do not now exist, repairing existing systems, and establishing clear standards for the treatment and use of recycled water. As sewer lines are improved or extended, prevent industrial wastes from mixing with domestic wastes.

≈ Establish rainwater-catchment systems at the appropriate scale wherever conditions and economics permit. Objections to these systems arise partly because of a lack of information and partly because of failures with some early and admittedly inadequate designs. Rooftop catchment from houses, greenhouses, and small buildings seems particularly appropriate as it is relatively inexpensive and produces potable water.

≈ Design with the intention of using saline water wherever this source is available and can be economically substituted for fresh water. As always with the use of saline water, measures should be instituted to ensure that the runoff does not cause environmental disruption.

Regional Recommendations

The conflict-management literature distinguishes four main causes of conflict: conflicts over data, conflicts over incompatible interests, conflicts generated by different values (for example, incompatible religious or cultural values), and conflicts over relationships (such as struggles for dominance between individuals, groups, or states whose values may be otherwise compatible). Conflicts over data (for example, over "facts" of resource use or current resource availability) are clearly amenable to resolution by research. Conflicts between stakeholders who believe their interests to be incompatible may be mitigated by research that demonstrates the existence or viability of alternatives not previously taken into account. The other forms of conflict are less susceptible to resolution by a search for greater knowledge; for them, resolution depends more on a search for acceptable political options.

The conflicts over water in the Jordan River Basin stem from the interaction of all of the causes outlined in the foregoing, and only when institutions designed to deal with each are put into place will reasonable solutions be achieved. Current institutional means for resolving these disputes in the Jordan River Basin are simply inadequate to meet the needs of reducing the water problems in the long term. Given the complexity of water problems in this region and, before September 1993, the political unwillingness to grant, even implicitly, political recognition, it is not surprising that, before the Israel–Jordan Peace Treaty (see Afterword), there had never been any official agreement on water between any Arab country and the State of Israel (Al-Khatib 1992).

As a way of furthering the progress at long last being made toward regional negotiation and cooperation, it is worth looking at some of the recommendations on transboundary waters that emerged from the International Conference on Water and the Environment held in Dublin in 1992 (Dublin Statement 1993). The Dublin Conference was one in a series of recent meetings on water and is described at greater length in Appendix 2. Three relevant recommended actions were:

≈ That countries evaluate the experience gained with existing transboundary basin water authorities, committees, and commissions;

≈ That countries support the further development of...institutional mechanisms for the coordination of water management within transboundary basins; and

≈ That nonriparian nations promote and support the cooperation of riparian countries within a transboundary basin in the establishment of appropriate legal, institutional, and operational mechanisms.

The types of institutional mechanisms that could be proposed vary widely — from institutes that promote data sharing and joint monitoring (the simplest to develop), to water policy development agencies, to river basin management committees (the most complex, particularly if they include provisions for joint action).

In addition to the committees and institutions that have been established in various jurisdictions to address transboundary river basin issues, numerous management agreements have been signed to address specific aspects of river management. These agreements generally fall into one of two categories: those aimed at an **equitable apportionment of water supplies** (such as the 1959 agreement between the then United Arab Republic and the Republic of Sudan, and the Indus Waters Treaty of 1960) and those that **promote joint management or exploitation of a river basin** (such as the Columbia River Treaty of 1961 between the United States and Canada).

In the future, as the various parties build enough confidence in their own abilities and those of their neighbours to think about substantive cooperation, a regional water institution for the Jordan River Basin will have to be established. It should, as a start, have a limited mandate, acting largely as an information clearinghouse. The same institution, however, could eventually evolve toward a river basin management authority. This would set the stage for a trilateral (or multilateral) agreement for sharing water resources, as was apparently included in the Camp David accords. It would also allow for the reestablishment of international negotiations to design a water system for the region (as with, for example, the Johnston Plan) and also permit the extension of such a design from surface to underground flows.

A useful point of departure for such an agreement might be found in the renewal of efforts to rebuild the dam on the Yarmouk that was destroyed by Israeli bombers in the 1967 war. Naff (1990) provides ample evidence of the potential benefits of that dam. Alternatively, and at considerably less expense according to Kally (1993), the winter flows of the Yarmouk River could be diverted to, and stored in, Lake Kinneret. If the height of the lake were raised somewhat, this stored water could be returned not only to Jordan but also to Palestinians during the summer months. Either option could provide the basis for construction of the long-proposed West Ghor Canal, which would provide a more stable water regime to West Bank farmers and communities (Shuval 1992). More importantly, either option would require some degree of mutual trust and joint management — more than "some" in the case of the Kinneret option — and this would present the opportunity, if not the requirement, for yet more trust and more joint management.

If trust has reached a point where shared research can be considered, a joint regional research institute on water could be developed. There is a need for a regional institute that would emphasize alternatives to the use of fresh water in agriculture, including studies of the long-term implications of greater use of recycled water and of brackish water. Although many water issues deserve study, these two are particularly important to the region and could represent a unique international contribution. If such an institute is considered, it would be essential that it incorporate teams working from both technical and socioeconomic perspectives.

Finally, we wish to support the views of those who have stated that some broadly based evaluation is needed to compare and contrast the range of water megaprojects proposed for the region. Each megaproject option has merits and problems, benefits and costs, and each may be viewed differently by Israelis and Palestinians — to say nothing of the perspective of the donor community. Thus, a single, all-encompassing ranking system is not reasonable to expect. If a set of unambiguous criteria is designed, however, it should be possible to compare each

proposal based upon criteria chosen by each party and, therefore, to
move toward an informed choice.

Conclusions

In this book we have examined the economic, ecological, and political
dimensions of the water — both surface and underground water —
shared by Israelis and Palestinians. We have also developed a set of
alternatives for resolving, or reducing the extent of, the mutual problems that exist between these two peoples. What is clear from the discussion of these issues is that the water "crisis" is actually a set of three
problems: water quantity, water quality, and the geopolitics of water —
or four problems if the lack of shared data is included. What is also clear
is that these problems are interrelated; proposed solutions must address
all of them. To complicate matters further, some of the least costly
alternatives are also the least palatable. Economic efficiency often conflicts with security objectives or with Zionist ideology and history. The
need to work out shared management through cooperation with former
occupiers is likely to conflict with Palestinian desires to be "masters in
their own house."

In areas of water stress, which is clearly the situation for the riparians of the Jordan River, only those approaches that treat quantity and
quality issues together, and that avoid economy–ecology conflicts, can
be taken seriously. Even if the countries and territories of the region are
relatively careful by international standards in their use of water, they
are far short of either the technical or the economic potential. Given
expected levels of population growth and aspirations for economic
development, conservation and efficiency in the delivery and use of
water are likely to be the most important "sources of supply" in the
Middle East. They are also likely to be the cheapest and the least environmentally damaging sources.

Some people view today's water problems in Israel (indeed
throughout the Jordan River Valley) as reaching crisis proportions;
others argue that those problems are merely the latest version of a
chronic situation. Depending upon the particular aspect of the problem
under question, either perspective is justified. It is clear, however, that,

for different reasons, **Israelis and Palestinians both face a crisis in water management.** That crisis has both internal and external dimensions, and it can be resolved only if both Israelis and Palestinians put their own water-management "houses" in order and if each accepts the concept of (indeed, explicit measures to achieve) equitable sharing and joint management of water resources with one another and with the Jordanians, Lebanese, and Syrians. If one had to identify the need in a single phrase, that phrase would be: **better governance.**

Finally, one cannot ignore that the politics of water in the region are being played out in an international context. With only a few exceptions, every nation in the Middle East depends upon water supplies in which at least one other nation — commonly an upstream nation on a river or an up-flow nation on an aquifer — has a significant interest. This explains in part why some nations that are usually antagonistic toward Israel are more moderate in the case of water. For example, whatever Syria may claim about limiting Israeli rights to Jordan River water could, later, be applied by Turkey to limit Syria's rights to Euphrates River water. Both Israel and Syria are downstream riparians.

In a recent review of economic and institutional issues on international river basins, Rogers (1992) evaluates various political bases for sharing water, and concludes that the most important is what he calls "the climate for agreement." He goes on to say that the following conditions are favourable for successful international agreements concerning water:

≈ Countries with the same technical perception of a problem;

≈ Similar consumption of goods and services;

≈ When water quality is an issue, the use of similar industrial production technologies;

≈ An extensive network of transnational and transgovernmental contacts between countries;

≈ The participation of a small number of countries;

≈ The desire of one large country to have an agreement; and

≈ The necessary development by one country of a good or service for its own use that may benefit other countries.

Unless one counts the United States as the "one large country" that desires an agreement, it is hard to argue that any one of these conditions is satisfied in the Jordan River Basin. Yet today some form of accommodation, if not an agreement, appears to be in the making.

In our view, the quotation from Zarour and Isaac (1992) that is cited at the beginning of this final chapter is the best single statement of the importance of water for Israel and the Occupied Palestinian Territories, both in the present and for the future. We share their perspective, and we share the statement's implicit optimism. Around the world, water use is growing faster than population. That scenario is simply not an option in the Middle East and, most certainly, not for the peoples who share the Jordan River Basin. In terms of the peace process, therefore, water resources must be both means and ends. In the words of Kenneth Boulding (1964):

> Water is far from a simple commodity;
> Water's a sociological oddity.
> Water's a pasture for science to forage in;
> Water's a mark of our dubious origin.
> Water's a link with a distant futurity;
> Water's a symbol of ritual purity.
> Water is politics, water's religion;
> Water is just about anyone's pigeon.
> Water is frightening, water's endearing;
> Water is more than mere engineering.
> Water is tragical, water is comical;
> Water is far from the Pure Economical.
> So studies of water, though free from aridity;
> Are apt to produce a good deal of turbidity.

WATER IN THE JORDAN–ISRAEL PEACE TREATY

T HE IMPORTANCE OF WATER to the peoples of the Jordan River Valley is illustrated in the recent signing of the Jordan–Israel Peace Treaty on 26 October 1994. The Treaty contains 30 articles of agreement; key in those 30 are agreements on international boundaries, security, economic relations, refugees, and, of course, water.

Article 6 of the Treaty is entitled simply "Water." It is devoted "to achieving a comprehensive and lasting settlement of all the water problems between [Israel and Jordan]." As such, it constitutes the first such agreement between Israel and any of its neighbours. Article 6 contains five paragraphs, none of which is exceptional in itself, except when one recalls that these two nations have been formally at war for nearly half a century.

Paragraph 1 provides for the mutual recognition of "rightful allocations" in the surface waters of the Jordan and Yarmouk rivers and the underground water of the Arava Valley. (The Arava, or Araba, Valley lies on either side of the Rift Valley, south of the Dead Sea; according to borders established in the Peace Treaty, about one-third of the valley lies in Israel and two-thirds in Jordan.)

Paragraph 2 states that each nation will ensure that its water management and development does not "in any way harm the water resources of the other party."

Paragraph 3 states that neither country has enough water to meet its needs and that they must both look to regional and international cooperation to increase supplies.

This rather ambiguous statement takes on meaning in Paragraph 4, where it is stated: "water issues along their entire boundary must be dealt with in their totality, including the possibility of trans-boundary water transfers...." This paragraph then provides for cooperation in developing water resources, preventing pollution, dealing with shortages, and, significantly, "minimizing wastage of water resources through the chain of their uses" — in a word, **conservation**. The same paragraph also covers data sharing and joint research.

Finally, Paragraph 5 makes reference to Annex II, where "undertakings" for implementation are detailed.

Pursuant to Article 6 of the Treaty is a detailed discussion of "water-related matters," which is set out as Annex II and, itself, contains seven articles of agreement. If Article 6 of the Treaty is unremarkable as a water agreement, the same cannot be said of Annex II. It is not merely an important step in terms of politics but also an important demonstration of how to incorporate both equity and efficiency into a water agreement — at least between Israel and Jordan: the place of Palestine is totally ignored. Water quality is mentioned almost as often as water quantity; and efficiency almost as much as additional water resources. Compared with other articles and annexes on related subjects (such as environment, energy, and rift-valley development), the provisions of Annex II are far more detailed and explicit.

Articles 1 through 4 of Annex II deal, respectively, with detailed allocation of water from the Yarmouk and the Jordan, storage and diversion structures, protection of water quality, and allocation of groundwater in the Arava Valley. The specifics of these provisions are, for our purposes, less important than their implications. Among other things, they provide at least 100 Mm^3 of water for Jordan, and more in the long term, much of it "to drinkable standards." This is enough, according to some reports, to eliminate Jordan's annual water deficit. The provisions also include joint measures to monitor water quality and to protect water sources by, among other things, prohibiting the dumping of municipal and industrial wastewater into either the Yarmouk or the Jordan "before they are treated to standards allowing their unrestricted agricultural use." Actions to implement this provision must be completed within 3 years. Further, saline water (carrying about 2 000 ppm of salts) that Israel has diverted to the Lower Jordan will be desalinated within 4 years and shared roughly equally by the two countries.

Other provisions reflect agreements that one might expect between good neighbours. For example, water balances shift between winter and summer, and each side agrees to allow "easy unhindered access of personnel and equipment" to facilities across the border. Israel also acknowledges Jordan's sovereignty over many of the wells it has drilled in the Arava Valley, and Jordan concedes that Israel can continue to use these wells.

The remaining three articles of Annex II are more general than the first four but are equally important. Article 5 requires 6 months notification of proposed changes to the quantity or quality of shared rivers and provides that any such change can be made only after mutual agreement. Article 6 provides for exchanging "relevant data" and for cooperation in both increasing water supply and improving efficiency of use. And, potentially most important of all, Article 7 formalizes and extends the role of the "picnic table summits" by establishing a joint water committee composed of three members from each country with broad, if still only vaguely defined, authority for the implementation of everything in the Annex. In effect, a body has been established that seems rather like the International Joint Commission that manages water along the United States–Canada border (see Chapter 7).

At several points in this book, we have argued that, if water can easily provide a pretext for conflict or even for war, it can equally well provide an impetus for cooperation or even peace. Events over the past 50 years demonstrate the former; the water provisions of the Jordan–Israel Peace Treaty reveal the latter. If the water issue can be settled peacefully in the Jordan Valley, it can be settled peacefully anywhere. At the same time, the silence of the Treaty on water rights for the Palestinians is evidence that peace has not yet arrived.

CLAIMS, COUNTERCLAIMS, FEARS, AND CONCERNS: FRESH WATER AS A REGIONAL ISSUE

SHUVAL (1992) DETAILS some of the claims and counterclaims as well as the real and perceived fears and concerns of the two sides in the dispute over fresh water.

Palestinian Claims and Concerns

1.   The Palestinians claim that the flow of the Mountain Aquifer, which is fed by rainfall over the West Bank (and 90% of which is currently extracted from deep wells mainly within Israel), should be allocated for their use, and that Israel's much-criticized, long-term overpumping of the aquifer is a serious threat to the Palestinians' future essential water reserves.

2.   The Palestinians are concerned that Israel, because of increased demands for development from the mass immigration of Jews from Russia and other countries, will extract more water from the Mountain Aquifer, depriving the Palestinians of an equitable share. Some Arab leaders have requested that authorities in these countries stop the emigration of Jews to Israel.

3.   The Palestinians claim that Israel's Civil Administration has effectively frozen Palestinian utilization of water sources in the Occupied Palestinian Territories, allocating insufficient amounts for urban and industrial use and practically no water for increased agricultural development or to meet the needs of a growing population. They claim that during the period of occupation, Israeli authorities have developed new water supplies in the Occupied Palestinian Territories and have allocated significant amounts of

water for agricultural and urban use for new Jewish settlements in the area. The Palestinians claim that this violates the Geneva Convention and that Israel misuses its authority as the "belligerent occupier." Particularly aggravating to Palestinian villagers is the perception of wasteful Israeli water use and landscape practices that often include the irrigation of lawns and the construction of swimming pools.

4. The Palestinians claim that the process of drilling new deep wells within the Occupied Palestinian Territories is depleting the aquifer, and traditional springs and shallow wells used for domestic and agricultural purposes in neighbouring Palestinian communities are drying up. They claim that Israel's pumping of groundwater near the Gaza Strip has caused severe salination of wells in Gaza. Even when the Israeli authorities supply water to the communities that lost their original wells or springs, the cost to the villagers is increased, which is viewed by Israelis as an appropriate method of controlling demand.

5. The Palestinians claim that in all new water projects developed by Israel in the Territories and that serve Palestinian communities, key controlling elements, such as regional reservoirs, valves, and control points, are located within Jewish settlements, which is viewed as a method of domination.

6. The Palestinians fear that, even if a peace settlement is achieved, and an appropriate Palestinian entity established, the division of the very limited shared water resources will leave them with insufficient amounts of water to accommodate population growth and the resettlement of the Palestinian diaspora with the required urban, industrial, and agricultural development.

7. In the event of major regional projects to import water to the region, there is concern and fear that Israel will retain practical and political control over all water supplied to the Palestinians and Jordan. There is equal concern that other nations of the region, which may supply additional water or allow water pipelines to pass through their territory, will use the water supply

lines for purposes of political control, as Turkey did in the case of the Iraqi oil pipelines during the Gulf War of 1990–91.

8.   In general, the Palestinians claim the priority rights to complete and total control of "Palestinian" water (the Mountain Aquifer) and suggest that complicated schemes to import water from other nations or to desalinate seawater focus on Israel which, in return, should forgo claims to the local, easily accessible, "Arab" water sources.

Israel's Claims and Concerns

1.   Israel claims that it has legitimate historical riparian rights to the Mountain Aquifer, based on the principle of prior use. Major portions of this aquifer flow naturally into its territory and have been developed at great expense and fully utilized over the past 60 years.

2.   Israel is concerned that, if the Palestinians achieve autonomy or independence, they will gain physical control of the Territory, and carry out their claim that all of the water of the shared Yarkon–Tanninim Aquifer (Mountain Aquifer) that is derived from rainfall within the West Bank (estimated to be about 80% of the total flow of the aquifer) be allocated exclusively for their own use. This fear is compounded in Israel's eyes by Palestinian goals of returning the Palestinian diaspora to any independent entity that is established.

Some Israelis claim that, if there is a major increase in pumping from the aquifer, it would mean a drastic reduction of Israel's most important, high-quality source of drinking water. It might mean a reduction in Israel's current utilization of that aquifer by some 300 Mm^3/year, cutting off the drinking water supplies for some 3 million people. Needless to say, this would be totally unacceptable to Israel.

3.   Even if an equitable agreement is achieved on the division of the waters of the Mountain Aquifer between Israel and any future Palestinian entity, there is serious concern about the possible

degradation of the quality of the water of the shared Mountain Aquifer as a result of inadequate monitoring and control of urban pollution, wastewater, and toxic agricultural and industrial wastes in the West Bank. This could cause serious pollution in the highly susceptible karstic limestone aquifer, making the water unfit for human consumption.

In 1990, General (Reserves) Raphael Eitan, at that time the Minister of Agriculture of Israel, published a full-page ad in the Israel press (*Jerusalem Post*, 10 August 1990) expressing many of the foregoing concerns and declaring that, because of the water issue alone, Israel can never give up the physical control of any of the Occupied Palestinian Territories. He cited both the threat of the diversion and overpumping of water vital to Israel and the danger of environmental pollution of the shared aquifer.

4.   There is also concern that unregulated overpumping of the Mountain Aquifer in the West Bank could lead to a serious lowering of the water table, with the resulting danger of salt-water intrusion and irreversible damage to the shared aquifer that could be a real threat to both partners.

5.   Palestinian calls for ending immigration to Israel from Russia and other countries is seen as unacceptable interference in Israel's internal affairs. Israel views unrestricted immigration of Jewish refugees as the cornerstone and raison d'être of the country, and any demand to restrict immigration is seen as unacceptable.

6.   Israeli officials maintain that Palestinians have not been deprived of the use of needed water. They cite the construction of new water supply pipes, introduced by Israel since the end of Jordanian rule in 1967; the granting of permits to the Palestinians to drill some 40 new deep wells; and the importation of water from the National Water Carrier to increase the water supplies to Palestinian cities and villages in the Occupied Palestinian Territories. According to Israeli claims, total water supply and per-capita use in the Occupied Palestinian Territories has increased significantly during the period of the Israeli administration. Israeli hydrologists say there is limited connection between

the groundwater in Gaza and Israel and that salination of wells in Gaza is solely the result of years of overpumping by the Palestinians prior to 1967. Israel also points out that many Palestinian claims of wells and springs drying up coincided with the 1988–91 drought period and may have nothing to do with Israel's water-development projects.

DECLARATIONS, DOCUMENTS, RULES, AND RHETORIC: FRESH WATER AS A GLOBAL ISSUE

FRESH WATER HAS BEEN a central focus of almost every international meeting on the environment and economics as far back as, and even before, World War II. In 1931, Prof. H.A. Smith reviewed 100 treaties on international rivers — and there are many hundreds of international rivers and lakes in the world with basins extending to nearly half the land area of the globe (Biswas 1993). Modern approaches to management of international waters began in 1956 when the International Law Association (ILA), a professional association similar to bar associations but grouping lawyers interested in and working on international law, issued the Dubrovnik rules that, among many other things, stated that river basins should be treated as an integrated whole, regardless of national borders. A decade later in 1966, the association adopted what have come to be called "the Helsinki Rules" for rivers and lakes that cross or form borders but for which there is no formal bilateral or multilateral agreement. For complex reasons, more related to concerns for sovereignty than either North–South or East–West politics, the Helsinki Rules were not adopted by the United Nations (Biswas 1993) and are, therefore, not binding. (Among other things, the Helsinki Rules were based on drainage basins rather than river channels.) The rules, however, have considerable influence in determining the equitable apportionment of water from international river basins. Specifically, the Helsinki Rules state that for international rivers and lakes, each riparian state gets a "reasonable and equitable share in the beneficial use of the water." Not surprisingly, the problems have come in defining "reasonable and equitable." In addition, states are expected to avoid actions that lead to "appreciable harm" to downstream or downflow states. Here, too, the words "appreciable harm"

have created definitional problems. In both cases, however, geographic, economic, demographic, social, and historic factors are all included in the original formulation — and this in an era before much consideration was given to water quality and the environment.

The Helsinki Rules were further developed by the International Law Commission (ILC), an organization created by the United Nations to focus on specific international legal issues, during the 1970s and 1980s, and particularly in the 1989 Bellagio Draft Treaty, which extended the rules to underground water. Thus, there exists a long history of international legal attention to the division of shared water resources. According to Elmusa (1993b), one can derive five key common factors from the numerous documents prepared by the ILA, ILC, and other bodies, all of which are used to define, or at least give more meaning to, the concepts of "equitable apportionment" and "appreciable harm."

- ≈ Natural attributes of that portion of a watershed within a state,
- ≈ Prior or existing use of the water,
- ≈ Social and economic needs of the population,
- ≈ Alternative resources and comparative costs to serve those needs, and
- ≈ Avoidance of damage to downstream states.

Each of these factors in turn begs definition, and nothing a priori defines the weighting among them. (Perhaps this is why the water flowing over Niagara Falls is divided **equally** rather than equitably between Canada and the United States; the Prairie Provinces Water Agreement in Canada also invokes equal sharing.) Still, as a guide for negotiations, they are the best available, at least if coupled with the widely accepted principles of prior notification of changes in use patterns and of accidents plus nondiscrimination among states in negotiations.

The fifth factor, avoidance of transboundary damage, finally brings environmental considerations explicitly into account. Unfortunately, just as environmental damages gain a place at the table, the definition of damage is becoming more complex. As originally conceived for surface water, it was always the upstream riparian that could cause harm to the downstream riparian; with aquifers, however, either the upflow or downflow riparian can be the source of damage.

Water and the environment were more explicitly joined as issues at the 1972 United Nations conference in Stockholm on the Human Environment. The emphasis at that conference was on sovereign rights to use and develop natural resources, including water, provided that environmental damages did not cross international borders. Although stronger on potential harm and on compensation than the Helsinki Rules, the principles established by the United Nations conference were still vague. A more focused discussion followed a few years later with the United Nations Conference on Water, held in Mara del Plata, Argentina, in 1977. The Mara del Plata conference maintained the emphasis on sovereignty but urged that more attention be payed to sharing and cooperation, and, in addition, gave more attention than the Stockholm conference to defining harm to other nations in terms of water quality and social impacts. For the first time at an international conference, the concept of water development as an exclusively engineering issue began to be questioned. Substantive progress, however, was slow and, as documented by Biswas (1993), the question of how to share natural resources (not just water) that cross international boundaries has continued to trouble the United Nations and international agencies to the present day.

Fresh water is referred to innumerable times in the report from the World Commission on Environment and Development (WCED 1987; also known as the "Bruntland Report"). Because the report is organized along thematic lines, however, there is no single focal point for water. Indeed, some analysts have criticized the Brundtland Report for its "water blindness." For present purposes, therefore, it is of special interest that fresh water is the subject of one of the longest chapters in Agenda 21, the general plan of action to emerge from UNCED (the United Nations Conference on Environment and Development, more popularly called the Earth Summit), held in Rio de Janiero in June 1992.

Although water is discussed at many points in the 600-odd pages and 40 chapters of Agenda 21, it is in Chapter 18, entitled "Freshwater Resources," that the most important statements are made. After a review of water resources and water problems around the world (based on Carroll-Foster 1993a,b), seven priority areas for action were set out.

≈ **Integrated water resources development and management** — aimed at stimulating holistic approaches to managing water;

≈ **Water resources assessment** — aimed as assessing and projecting the quantity and quality of water within a database as conceived at the Mara del Plata conference;

≈ **Protection of water resources, water quality, and aquatic ecosystems** — aimed at a preventative management approach to water use to protect human health along with flora and fauna;

≈ **Drinking-water supply and sanitation** — aimed at establishing rights to drinking water, equity in the distribution of supplies, and support for community management;

≈ **Water and sustainable urban management** — aimed at the linkages among urbanization, water use, and wastewater disposal;

≈ **Water for sustainable food production and rural development** — aimed at water as an input with special value in agriculture and fisheries and with a unique role, particularly for women, in rural communities; and

≈ **Impacts of climatic change on water resources** — aimed at research needs to define the impacts of global climatic change on freshwater resources.

Controversies over the wording that eventually appeared in Agenda 21 were evident at many of the preparatory committee meetings that were held before the Earth Summit. Various parties were concerned that placing less emphasis on water as an economic good might imply that it was also less important as a social good. In the end, both words were used. Other nations, mainly developing countries, were concerned about what they saw as excessive emphasis on international management and transboundary issues; they preferred a local or national management focus with emphasis on sovereignty. Developing countries were also concerned about retaining a focus on water quantity in contrast to the water-quality concerns of most industrialized nations. Again, compromises were eventually worked out. Everyone agreed on the need for capacity building, training and education, better data, and more research.

In the end, Agenda 21 reflected the enormous variety of political forces that went into drafting every chapter. Chapter 18, on Freshwater Resources, was certainly no exception. As emphasized in Carroll-Foster (1993a), the chapter lacks substance and is especially short of quantitative detail (except with regard to modeling). Despite its laudable goals, the chapter assumes rather than demonstrates that water contributes to social and economic well-being, and similarly assumes rather than demonstrates that the resource acts as a key constraint to future development. Apart from a statement that, by the year 2000, all states should achieve targets of 40 L of water per urban resident (presumably strictly for drinking, cooking, and sanitation), with 75% of those residents having access to on-site or community sanitation facilities and solid-waste disposal, Chapter 18 lacks targets. It is even shorter on commitments.

Given the high expectations for UNCED, which were no doubt unachievable from the start, it is perhaps more instructive to review results from the International Conference on Water and the Environment that was held in Dublin, Ireland, in January 1992, just 5 months before UNCED. This was much less a conference of politicians than one of experts — some 500 of them from over 100 countries and 80 intergovernmental and nongovernmental agencies. Although hardly free of competing interests (after all, everyone saw the Dublin meeting as a lead-up to UNCED), it did have more time to focus on the issue of water alone, and the inevitable trade-offs among social, economic, and cultural values (all within technical and resource constraints) could be aired without the same media attention and acute political sensibilities of a United Nations global conference.

The Guiding Principles from the Dublin Statement (1993) on water and sustainable development (see text box) were followed by sections entitled Action Agenda, Enabling Environment, and Follow-Up, all of which were supported by a conference report whose chapter headings were clearly the source for the Priority Areas for Action as they appeared in Chapter 18 of Agenda 21. Although the Dublin Conference report also lacks targets — as a report of experts, it could hardly impose them or undertake commitments — it is much more explicit

Guiding Principles

Concerted action is needed to reverse the present trends of overconsumption, pollution, and rising threats from drought and floods. The Conference Report sets out recommendations for action at local, national, and international levels based on four guiding principles.

Principle No. 1 — Fresh water is a finite and vulnerable resource, essential to sustain life, development, and the environment.
Because water sustains life, effective management of water resources demands a holistic approach, linking social and economic development with protection of natural ecosystems. Effective management links land and water uses across the whole of a catchment area or groundwater aquifer.

Principle No. 2 — Water development and management should be based on a participatory approach, involving users, planners, and policymakers at all levels.
The participatory approach involves raising awareness of the importance of water among policymakers and the general public. It means that decisions are taken at the lowest appropriate level, with full public consultation and involvement of users in the planning and implementation of water projects.

Principle No. 3 — Women play a central part in the provision, management, and safeguarding of water.
This pivotal role of women as providers and users of water and guardians of the living environment has seldom been reflected in institutional arrangements for the development and management of water resources. Acceptance and implementation of this principle require positive policies to address women's specific needs and to equip and empower women to participate at all levels in water-resources programs, including decision-making and implementation, in ways defined by them.

Principle No. 4 — Water has an economic value in all its competing uses and should be recognized as an economic good.
Within this principle, it is vital to recognize first the basic right of all human beings to have access to clean water and sanitation at an affordable price. Past failure to recognize the economic value of water has led to wasteful and environmentally damaging uses of the resource. Managing water as an economic good is an important way of achieving efficient and equitable use and of encouraging conservation and protection of water resources.

Source: Dublin Statement (1993).

about the waste of water in irrigation systems and urban distribution networks around the world (quantity), about the continuing degradation of water and of water-based habitats (quality), and about the excessive use of water of some countries while others face penury (equity). Differences between most industrialized countries, for which adverse weather patterns generally exert but a minor influence on the economy, and some developing nations, for which they can be disastrous, were clearly recognized. In many ways, the organization of the Dublin Statement is parallel with that of this book. For the moment, the Dublin Statement, together with the supporting documentation, is probably the most succinct overview of our daunting global water problems, and of the urgency of dealing with them, for deal with them we must. Being somewhat freer of political constraints, it could be much more explicit than Agenda 21 about the need to resolve conflicts — indeed, to resolve them soon and to resolve them by management based on river basins (or aquifers) rather than national (or other jurisdictional) boundaries. If the result from Rio fell short of the challenge from Dublin, that merely indicates how simultaneously fundamental and immediate are our global water problems, and how many disciplines and interests will be touched by any move toward their resolution.

GLOSSARY

Aquifer: An underground stratum capable of storing water and transmitting it to wells, springs, or surface water bodies.

Artesian: An aquifer that is under pressure.

Brackish water: Water containing more than 500 ppm of dissolved solids, but less than 35 000 ppm (the salinity of seawater).

Comprehensive water resources framework: An analytic framework for water-resources management that views water as a single resource with many uses and interlinkages with the ecological and socioeconomic systems.

Conjunctive use: Use of both surface and underground water for a single purpose, most commonly irrigation.

Consumptive water use: Water withdrawn from a surface or groundwater body that, because of absorption, transpiration, evaporation, or incorporation into a manufactured product, is not returned directly to a water body.

Demand management: Use of measures and practices, including education and awareness programs, metering, water pricing, quantitative restrictions, and other devices, to manage and control the demand for water.

Depletion: The withdrawal of water from surface or underground water bodies at a rate greater than the rate of replenishment (recharge rate).

Drip irrigation: Localized drop-by-drop application of water using pipes, tubes, filters, emitters, and ancillary devices to deliver water to specific sites at a point or grid on the soil surface.

Elasticity: A measure of the effect of price changes on the amount of any good or service purchased. The good or service (such as water) is said to have an elastic demand if the change in quantity purchased is proportionately greater than the change in price; it is inelastic if the change in quantity purchased is proportionately less.

Evapotranspiration: Evaporative water loss from plant surfaces.

Externality: The side effect of one party's actions on another party or parties, including both the general public and specific entities.

Fossil aquifer: A term sometimes used to refer to large, contained aquifers dating from a long time in the past. In practice, few such aquifers are true fossils because they continue to be recharged even though the recharge rate is typically very small relative to total storage.

Groundwater mining: The condition when withdrawals are made from an aquifer at rates in excess of recharge.

Instream water use: Use of water that does not require withdrawal or diversion from its natural watercourse.

Interbasin transfer: The physical transfer of water from one drainage basin to another.

Leakage: Physical losses of water from the delivery system, generally because of cracks in pipes or incomplete sealing of joints.

Market failure: A divergence between the (prevailing) market solution and the economically efficient solution.

Mining: See "groundwater mining".

Multipurpose development: Development of a particular water resource to serve two or more purposes simultaneously.

NIS: New Israel Shekel, the unit of currency in Israel.

Recycling process: Withdrawal of water for use in cooling or processing and subsequent reconditioning and reuse of the same water over and over, usually with relatively small additions of "make-up" water required to compensate for losses through evaporation or otherwise.

Riparian state: A state through or along which a portion of a river flows or a lake lies.

River basin: The land area from which water drains into a river.

Runoff: That part of precipitation that appears in surface streams. Alternatively, that part of irrigation water that is not consumed by plants or absorbed into the soil and is returned to some water body.

Salinity: The content of salts dissolved in water, generally measured in parts per million (ppm).

Storage: The impoundment of water in surface reservoirs or accumulation in underground reservoirs.

Sweet water: Fresh water.

Unaccounted-for water: The difference between the volume of water delivered into a supply system and the volume of water accounted for by legitimate consumption, whether metered or not.

User charges: A charge imposed upon direct users of water for water withdrawal, instream use, or assimilation of waste.

BIBLIOGRAPHY

Aboukhaled, A. 1992. Wastewater for crop production in the Near East: towards safe and efficient management. International Journal of Water Resources Development, 8(3), 204–215.

Abu-Sheikha. 1984. Far'a irrigation project: a feasibility study. An-Najah National University Publications, Nablus, West Bank, Israel.

Al-Khatib, N. 1992. Palestinian water rights. In Buskin, G., ed., Water: cooperation or conflict. Israel/Palestine Centre for Research and Information, Jerusalem, Israel. pp. 9–15.

Al-Khatib, N.; Assaf, K. 1994. Palestine water supplies and demands. In Proceedings of the First Israeli–Palestinian International Academic Conference on Water, Zurich, Switzerland, 10–13 December 1992. Elsevier Science Publishers BV, Amsterdam, Netherlands.

Amery, H.; Kubursi, A. 1992. Water scarcity in the Middle East: misallocation or real shortages? Paper presented at the Conference on the Middle East Water Crisis: Creative Perspectives and Solutions, 8–9 May 1992. University of Waterloo, Waterloo, ON, Canada.

Anderson, E.W. 1988. Water: the next strategic resource. In Starr, J.R.; Stoll, D.C., ed., The politics of scarcity: water in the Middle East. Westview Press, London, UK. pp. 1–21.

Anton, D. 1993. Thirsty cities: urban environment and water supply in Latin America. IDRC Books, International Development Research Centre, Ottawa, ON, Canada.

Assaf, K. 1994. Replenishment of Palestinian waters by artificial recharge as a non-controversial option in water resource management. In Isaac, J.; Shuval, H., ed., Water and peace in the Middle East. Elsevier Science Publishers BV, Amsterdam, Netherlands.

Avineri, S. 1994. Sidestepping dependency. Foreign Affairs, 73(4), 12–15.

Avnimelech, Y.; Klein, D.; Walach, R. 1992. Irrigation with sewage effluents: the Israeli experience. Israel Environment Bulletin, 15(2), 18–24.

Awartani, H. 1994. The demand for water in the Occupied Territories: estimates for 1992–2005. In Isaac, J.; Shuval, H., ed., Water and peace in the Middle East. Elsevier Science Publishers BV, Amsterdam, Netherlands.

Bakour, Y.; Kolars, J. 1994. The Arab Mashrek: hydrologic history, problems and perspectives. In Rogers, P.; Lydon, P., ed., Water in the Arab world: perspectives and prognoses. Harvard University Press, Cambridge, MA, USA. pp. 121–146.

Ball, G.W.; Ball, D.B. 1992. The passionate attachment: America's involvement with Israel 1947 to the present. W.W. Norton, New York, NY, USA.

Barberis, J. 1991. The development of the International Law of Transboundary Groundwater. Natural Resources Journal, 31(1), 167–186.

Baskin, G. 1992. The West Bank and Israel's water crisis. In Baskin, G., ed., Water: conflict or cooperation. Israel/Palestine Centre for Research and Information, Jerusalem, Israel. pp. 1–8.

Beaumont, P. 1989. Environmental management and development in drylands. Routledge, Chapman & Hall, London, UK.

———— 1994. The myth of water wars and the future of irrigated agriculture in the Middle East. Water Resources Development, 10(1), 10–21.

Beaumont, P.; Blake, G.H.; Wagstaff, J.M. 1988. The Middle East: a geographical study. 2nd ed. David Fulton Publishers, London, UK.

Bedeski, R.E. 1992. Unconventional security threats: an overview. North Pacific Cooperative Security Dialogue Research Programme, York University, North York, ON, Canada. Working Paper No. 11.

Benjamini, Y.; Harpaz, Y. 1986. Observational rainfall–runoff analysis for estimating effects of cloud seeding on water resources in northern Israel. Journal of Hydrology, 83, 3–4.

Benvenisti, E.; Gvirtzman, H. 1993. Harnessing international law to determine Israeli–Palestinian water rights: the Mountain Aquifer. Natural Resources Journal, 33, 544–567.

Beschorner, N. 1992. Water and instability in the Middle East. International Institute for Strategic Studies, London, UK. Adelphi Paper No. 273.

Biswas, A.K. 1993. Management of international waters: problems and perspective. International Journal of Water Resources Development, 9(2), 167–188.

Boulding, K. 1964. The economist and the engineer. In Smith, S.; Castle, E., ed., Economics and public policy in water resources development. Iowa State University Press, Ames, IA, USA. pp. 82–92.

Brachya, V. 1993. Environmental assessment in land use planning in Israel. Landscape and Urban Architecture, 23, 167–181.

Brooks, D.B.; Lonergan, S.C. 1992. Israel's newest problem. Voice of the Trees, 2(2), 3–4.

Brooks, D.B.; Peters, R. 1988. Water: the potential for demand management in Canada. Science Council of Canada, Ottawa, ON, Canada.

Brooks, D.B.; Peters, R.; Robillard, P. 1990. Pricing: a neglected tool for demand management. Alternatives, 17(3), 40–48.

Bruins, H.J.; Tuinhof, A.; Keller, R. 1991. Water in the Gaza Strip. Ministry of Foreign Affairs, Government of the Netherlands, The Hague, Netherlands.

Bulloch, J.; Darwish, A. 1993. Water wars: coming conflicts in the Middle East. Victor Gollancz, London, UK.

Calleigh, A.S. 1983. Middle East water: vital resource, conflict and cooperation. In Starr, J.R., ed., A shared destiny. Praeger Publishers, New York, NY, USA. pp. 121–135.

Caponera, D. 1985. Patterns of cooperation in international water law: principles and institutions. Natural Resources Journal, 25, 563–587.

Carroll-Foster, T., ed. 1993a. Agenda 21: abstracts, reviews, commentaries. IDRC Books, International Development Research Centre, Ottawa, ON, Canada.

———— 1993b. A guide to Agenda 21: issues, debates and Canadian initiatives. IDRC Books, International Development Research Centre, Ottawa, ON, Canada.

Choucri, N. 1991. Resource constraints as causes of conflict. Ecodecision, 2, 52–55.

Cooley, J.K. 1984. The war over water. Foreign Policy, 54 (Spring), 3–26.

Cran, J. 1992. The Medusa bag and Middle East water projects. Paper presented at the Conference on the Middle East Water Crisis: Creative Perspectives and Solutions, 8–9 May 1992. University of Waterloo, Waterloo, ON, Canada.

Daniell, Z. 1993. Lessons from Jerusalem. People and the Planet, 2(2), 14–15.

Davis, U.; Maks, A.; Richardson, J. 1980. Israel's water policies. Journal of Palestine Studies, 9(34), 3–32.

de Laet, C. 1992. La nature de l'eau: orthodoxe, hétérodoxe ou paradoxe? Ecodecision, 6, 18–20.

Deudney, D. 1991. Muddled thinking. Bulletin of the Atomic Scientists, 47(3), 22–28.

Doherty, K.B. 1965. Jordan waters conflict. International Conciliation, 553 (May), 2–66.

Dublin Statement. 1993. Report of the International Conference on Water and the Environment: Development Issue for the 21st Century.

Dudley, N.J.; Musgrave, W.F. 1993. Economics of water allocation under certain conditions. In Biswas, A.K.; et al., ed. Water for sustainable development in the twenty-first century. Oxford University Press, Delhi.

El-Ashry, M.T. 1991. Policies for water resource management in semiarid regions. Water Resources Development, 7(4), 230–234.

Elmusa, S. 1993a. The water issue and the Palestinian–Israeli conflict. The Center for Policy Analysis on Palestine, Washington, DC, USA. Information Paper No. 2.

———— 1993b. Dividing the common Palestinian–Israeli waters: an international water law approach. Journal of Palestinian Studies, 22, 3.

Elon, A. 1993. The peacemakers. The New Yorker, 20 December 1993, pp. 77–85.

EPA (US Environmental Protection Agency). 1992. Manual: guidelines for water reuse. EPA, Washington, DC, USA. EPA/625/2-92/004.

Esco Foundation. 1947. Palestine: a study of Jewish, Arab and British policies. Yale University Press, New Haven, CT, USA.

ESCWA (United Nations Economic and Social Commission for Western Asia). 1994. Report on cooperation among ESCWA countries in the field of shared water resources. ESCWA, Amman, Jordan. E/ESCWA/17/4(Part I)/Add.3.

Evenari, M.; Shanan, L.; Tadmor, N. 1982. The Negev: the challenge of a desert. 2nd ed. Harvard University Press, Cambridge, MA, USA.

Falkenmark, M.; Lundqvist, J.; Widstrand, C. 1989. Macro-scale water scarcity requires micro-scale approaches. Natural Resources Forum, 13(4), 258–267.

Fishelson, G. 1989. The Middle East conflict viewed through water: a historical view. The Armand Hammer Fund for Economic Cooperation in the Middle East, Tel Aviv University, Tel Aviv, Israel.

——— 1992a. Changes in water supply: impacts upon the Israeli economy. The Armand Hammer Fund for Economic Cooperation in the Middle East, Tel Aviv University, Tel Aviv, Israel.

——— 1992b. Solutions for the scarcity of water in the Middle East in times of peace. The Armand Hammer Fund for Economic Cooperation in the Middle East, Tel Aviv University, Tel Aviv, Israel.

——— 1994. Marginal value product of water in Israeli agriculture. In Isaac, J.; Shuval, H., ed., Water and peace in the Middle East. Elsevier Science Publishers BV, Amsterdam, Netherlands.

Fisher, F. 1994a. The Harvard Middle East water project: brief summary. Institute for Social and Economic Policy in the Middle East, John F. Kennedy School of Government, Harvard University, Cambridge, MA, USA.

——— 1994b. An economic framework for water negotiation and management. Institute for Social and Economic Policy in the Middle East, John F. Kennedy School of Government, Harvard University, Cambridge, MA, USA.

Foster, H.D.; Sewell, W.R.D. 1981. Water: the emerging crisis in Canada. Canadian Institute for Economic Policy, Ottawa, ON, Canada.

Frey, F.W.; Naff, T. 1985. Water: an emerging issue in the Middle East. Annals of the American Academy of Political Scientists, 482, 65–84.

Fuller, C.E.; Gemmell, J.S.; Wilson, R.W. 1993. Strategic action for development of the environmental health sector of the Gaza Strip. United Nations Relief and Works Agency for Palestine and Refugees in the Near East, New York, NY, USA.

Gabbay, S., ed. 1992. The environment in Israel. National report to the United Nations Conference on Environment and Development. Ministry of Environment, Jerusalem, Israel.

Galnoor, I. 1980. Water policymaking in Israel. Policy Analysis, 4, 339–365.

Garbell, M.A. 1965. The Jordan Valley plan. Scientific American, 212(3), 23–31.

Gleick, P.H. 1989. Climate change and international politics: problems facing developing countries. Ambio, 18(6), 333–339.

——— 1992. Water and conflict. Peace and Conflict Studies Program, University of Toronto, Toronto, ON, Canada. Project on Environmental Change and Acute Conflict, Occasional Paper No. 1. pp. 3–27.

Glueckstern, P. 1991. Cost estimates of large reverse osmosis systems. In Balaban, M., ed., Desalination and water re-use. Proceedings of the 12th International Symposium, Volume 1. Hemisphere Publishing, New York, NY, USA. pp. 49–56.

Goldenberg, L.C.; Melloul, L.C. 1992. Restoration of polluted groundwater: is it possible? Israel Environment Bulletin, 15(1), 16–24.

Gruen, G.E. 1994. Contribution of water imports to Israeli–Palestinian peace. In Isaac, J.; Shuval, H., ed., Water and peace in the Middle East. Elsevier Science Publishers BV, Amsterdam, Netherlands.

Gur, S. 1985. The Jordan Rift Valley: a challenge for development 1991. Revised edition. Prime Minister's Office, Government of Israel, Tel Aviv, Israel.

Hausman, L.J.; Karasik, A.D. 1993. Securing peace in the Middle East: project on economic transition. John F. Kennedy School of Government, Harvard University, Cambridge, MA, USA.

Hays, J.B. 1948. T.V.A. on the Jordan: proposals for irrigation and hydro-electric development in Palestine. Public Affairs Press, Washington, DC, USA.

Hayton, R.D.; Utton, A.E. 1989. Transboundary groundwaters: the Bellagio Draft Treaty. Natural Resources Journal, 29(3), 664–722.

Heathcote, R.L. 1983. The arid lands: their use and abuse. Longman Inc., New York, NY, USA.

Heller, M.A.; Nusseibah, S. 1991. No trumpets, no drums: a two-state solution of the Israeli–Palestinian conflict. Hill and Wang, New York, NY, USA.

Hillel, D.J. 1991. Out of the Earth: civilization and the life of the soil. The Free Press, New York, NY, USA.

Hillel, D.J.; Rosenzweig, C. 1992. The greenhouse effect and its implications regarding global agriculture. Massachusetts Agricultural Experiment Station, University of Massachusetts, Amherst, MA, USA. Research Bulletin No. 74.

Hirschberg, P. 1991. Pollution hot-spots. The Jerusalem Report, 2, 16–17.

Hoffman, D. 1992. The application of solar energy for large scale sea water desalination. Desalination, 89(2), 115–184.

——— 1994. Potential applications for desalination in the area. In Isaac, J.; Shuval, H., ed., Water and peace in the Middle East. Elsevier Science Publishers BV, Amsterdam, Netherlands.

Homer-Dixon, T.F. 1991. On the threshold: environmental changes as causes of acute conflict. International Security, 16(2), 76–116.

Homer-Dixon, T.F.; Boutwell, J.; Rathjens, G. 1993. Environmental change and violent conflict. Scientific American, 268(2), 38–45.

Hosh, L.; Isaac, J. 1992. Roots of the water conflict in the Middle East. Paper presented at the Conference on the Middle East Water Crisis: Creative Perspectives and Solutions, 8–9 May 1992. University of Waterloo, Waterloo, ON, Canada.

Howe, C.W.; Dixon, J. 1993. Inefficiencies in water project design and operation in the Third World: an economic perspective. Water Resources Research, 29, 7.

ILC (International Law Commission). 1983. Report to the UN General Assembly at its 34th Session. United Nations, New York, NY, USA.

Inbar, M.; Maos, J. 1984. Water planning and development in the northern Jordan Valley. Water International, 9, 20–28.

Israel, Central Bureau of Statistics. 1985. Statistical abstract of Israel. Central Bureau of Statistics, Jerusalem, Israel.

———— 1988. Statistical abstract of Israel. Central Bureau of Statistics, Jerusalem, Israel.

———— 1992. Statistical abstract of Israel. Central Bureau of Statistics, Jerusalem, Israel.

Issar, A.S. 1994. Water under the deserts of the Middle East. In Isaac, J.; Shuval, H., ed., Water and peace in the Middle East. Elsevier Science Publishers BV, Amsterdam, Netherlands.

IWEC (International Water Engineering Centre). 1993. Enhancement of Middle East water supply: a literature review of technologies and applications. University of Ottawa, Ottawa, ON, Canada.

Kally, E. 1993. Water and peace: water resources and the Arab–Israeli peace process (with G. Fishelson). Praeger, Westport, CT, USA.

Keller, P.; Canessa, R. 1993. Information taxonomy and data requirements for coastal GIS to support coastal planning and management. In Murphy, P., ed., Eyes on the future. Proceedings of the 1993 International Symposium on GIS. Polaris Publishing, Vancouver, BC, Canada. pp. 455–460.

Khatib, N. 1992. Palestinian water rights. In Baskin, G., ed., Water: conflict or cooperation. Israel/Palestine Center for Research and Information, Jerusalem, Israel. pp. 9–15.

Khouri, F. 1985. The Arab–Israeli dilemma. Syracuse University Press, Syracuse, NY, USA.

Khouri, N. 1992. Wastewater reuse implementation in selected countries of the Middle-East and North-Africa. In Schiller, E.J., ed., Sustainable water resources management in arid countries. Canadian Journal of Development Studies, Special Issue, 131–144.

Kneese, A.V. 1976. Report on Israel's water policy. World Health Organization, Geneva, Switzerland.

Kolars, J. 1990. The course of water in the Arab Middle East. American–Arab Affairs, 33 (Summer).

————— 1992a. Water resources of the Middle East. *In* Schiller, E.J., ed., Sustainable water resources management in arid countries. Canadian Journal of Development Studies, Special Issue, 103–119.

————— 1992b. A brief history of water in the modern Middle East. Paper presented at the Conference on the Middle East Water Crisis: Creative Perspectives and Solutions, 8–9 May 1992. University of Waterloo, Waterloo, ON, Canada.

————— 1993. The Litani River in the context of Middle Eastern water resources. The Centre for Lebanese Studies, Oxford, UK.

Laster, R. 1993. Right to know in Israel environmental law. Israel Environment Bulletin, 16(4), 21–24.

Leitner, G.F. 1991. Total water costs on a standard basis for three large, operating SWRO plants. *In* Balaban, M., ed., Desalination and water re-use. Proceedings of the 12th International Symposium, Volume 1. Hemisphere Publishing, New York, NY, USA. pp. 39–48.

Leopold, L.B.; Langbein, W.B. 1960. A primer on water. US Government Printing Office, Washington, DC, USA.

Lesch, A.M. 1992. Transition to Palestinian self-government: practical steps toward Israeli Palestinian peace. Indiana University Press, Bloomington, IN, USA.

Lonergan, S.; Brooks, D.B. 1994. The economics of water in the Middle East. Paper presented at the Annual Meeting of the American Association of Geographers, San Francisco, CA, USA, 31 March–4 April 1994. American Association of Geographers, Washington, DC, USA.

Lonergan, S.; Kavanagh, B. 1991. Climate change, water resources and security in the Middle East. Global Environmental Change, 1(4), 272–290.

Lovins, A.B. 1977. Soft energy paths: toward a durable peace. Ballinger Publishing Co., Cambridge, MA, USA.

Lowdermilk, W.C. 1944. Palestine: land of promise. Greenwood Press, New York, NY, USA.

Lowi, M. 1992. West Bank water resources and the resolution of conflict in the Middle East. Peace and Conflict Studies Program, University of Toronto, Toronto, ON, Canada. Project on Environmental Change and Acute Conflict, Occasional Paper No. 1. pp. 29–60.

————— 1994. Water and power: the politics of a scarce resource in the Jordan River Basin. Cambridge University Press, Cambridge, UK.

McDonald, A.T.; Kay, D. 1988. Water resources: issues and strategies. Longman Group Ltd, Harlow, Essex, UK.

Mekorot. 1944. The water resources of Palestine. Mekorot Water Co. Ltd, Tel Aviv, Israel.

Moore, J.W. 1992. Water-sharing regimes in Israel and the Occupied Territories — a technical analysis. Department of National Defence, Ottawa, ON, Canada. Operational Research and Analysis Establishment Project Report No. 609.

————— 1993. Parting the waters: calculating Israeli and Palestinian entitlements to the West Bank aquifers and the Jordan River Basin. Middle East Policy, 3, 1.

Muller, R.A. 1985. The value of water in Canada. Canadian Water Resources Journal, 10(4), 12–20.

Myers, N. 1986. The environmental dimension to security issues. The Environmentalist, 6(4), 251–257.

Naff, T. 1990. Testimony before the Sub-committee on Europe and the Middle East, Committee on Foreign Affairs, US House of Representatives: the Middle East in the 1990's: Middle East water issues. US Government Printing Office, Washington, DC, USA.

————— 1994. Demand-side water management: some implications. In Isaac, J.; Shuval, H., ed., Water and peace in the Middle East. Elsevier Science Publishers BV, Amsterdam, Netherlands.

Naff, T.; Matson, R.C., ed. 1984. Water in the Middle East: conflict or cooperation? Westview Press, Boulder, CO, USA.

Okun, D. 1991. Use of recycled water for non-potable urban uses. Water Science and Technology, 24, 9.

Paredes, C.R. 1993. El regreso de una ceramica necesaria. Universidad de la serena, La Serena, Chile.

Peabody, N.S., ed. 1992. Water policy innovations in California. World Bank, Washington, DC, USA. World Bank Working Paper.

Pearce, F. 1991. Wells of conflict on the West Bank. New Scientist, 1771, 36–40.

Pearse, P.H.; Bertrand, F.; MacLaren, J.W. 1985. Currents of change: final report of the inquiry on federal water policy. Environment Canada, Ottawa, ON, Canada.

Postel, S. 1991. The end of an era? International Agricultural Development, 11(6), 7–9.

————— 1992. Last oasis: facing water scarcity. W.W. Norton & Co., New York, NY, USA.

————— 1993. Facing water scarcity. In Brown, L., ed., State of the world: 1993. W.W. Norton & Co., New York, NY, USA. pp. 22–41.

Rabushka, A. 1993. The truth about Israel's economy. Jewish Post & Opinion, 15 December 1993, pp. 8–9.

Reifenberg, A. 1955. The struggle between the desert and the sown: the rise and fall of agriculture in the Levant. Jewish Agency Publishing Department, Jerusalem, Israel.

Renner, M. 1989. National security: the economic and environmental dimensions. Worldwatch Institute, Washington, DC, USA. Worldwatch Paper No. 89.

Robinson, J.B. 1988. Unlearning and backcasting: rethinking some of the questions we ask about the future. Technological Forecasting and Social Change, 33, 325–338.

———— 1990. Futures under glass: a recipe for people who hate to predict. Futures, 22, 820–842.

Rogers, P. 1986. Water — not as cheap as you think. Technology Review, 88, 31–43.

———— 1992. Economic and institutional issues: international river basins. In Le Moigne, G.; Barghouti, S.; Feder, G.; Garbus, L.; Mei, X., ed., Country experiences with water resources management: economic, institutional, technological and environmental issues. World Bank, Washington, DC, USA. Technical Paper No. 175. pp. 63–69.

———— 1994. The agenda for the next thirty years. In Rogers, P.; Lydon, P., ed., Water in the Arab world: perspectives and prognoses. Harvard University Press, Cambridge, MA, USA. pp. 285–316.

Roots, F. 1992. International agreements to prohibit or control modification of the environment for military purposes. In Schiefer, H.B., ed., Verifying obligations respecting arms control and the environment: a post Gulf War assessment. University of Saskatchewan Press, Saskatoon, SK, Canada.

Rothman, J.; Lowi, M. 1992. Culture, conflict and cooperation: the Jordan River Basin. In Baskin, G., ed., Water: conflict or cooperation. Israel/Palestine Center for Research and Information, Jerusalem, Israel. pp. 54–71.

Salem, O.S. 1994. EIA in the Arab states: an uneasy take-off. Centre for Environment and Development for the Arab Region and Europe, Cairo, Egypt.

Savage, C. 1994. Book review: Alaska water exports: a discussion paper by Ric Davidge. Water Resources Development, 10(1), 91–93.

Sbeih, M. 1994. The reuse of wastewater for irrigation: some aspects on the West Bank. In Isaac, J.; Shuval, H., ed., Water and peace in the Middle East. Elsevier Science Publishers BV, Amsterdam, Netherlands.

Schiff, Z. 1993. Israel's water security lines. Policywatch, 75, 1–3.

Schrijvet, N. 1989. International organization for environmental security. Bulletin of Peace Proposals, 20(2), 115–122.

Seckler, D. 1993. Designing water resources strategies for the twenty-first century. Winrock International Center for Economic Policy Studies, Arlington, VA, USA. Discussion Paper No. 16.

Shady, A.M., ed. 1989. Irrigation drainage and flood control in Canada. Canadian International Development Agency, Ottawa, ON, Canada.

Shawwa, I.R. 1992. The water situation in the Gaza Strip. In Baskin, G., ed., Water: conflict or cooperation. Israel/Palestine Center for Research and Information, Jerusalem, Israel. pp. 16–25.

Shelef, G. 1991. Wastewater reclamation and water resources management. Water Science and Technology, 24, 9.

Shuval, H. 1992. Approaches to finding an equitable solution to the water resources shared by Israel and the Palestinians over use of the mountain aquifer. In Baskins, G., ed., Water: conflict or cooperation. Israel/Palestine Center for Research and Information, Jerusalem, Israel. pp. 26–53.

Smith, C.G. 1966. The disputed waters of the Jordan. Transactions of the Institute of British Geographers, 40, 11–128.

Starr, J.R. 1992. Water security, the missing link in our Middle East strategy. In Schiller, E.J., ed., Sustainable water resources management in arid countries. Canadian Journal of Development Studies, Special Issue, 35–48.

Starr, J.R.; Stoll, D.C. 1988. Water in the year 2000. In Starr, J.R.; Stoll, D.C., ed., The politics of scarcity: water in the Middle East. Westview Press, London, UK.

Tahal Consulting Engineers Ltd. 1989. Supply of water by sea from Turkey to Israel: pre-feasibility study. Tahal Consulting Engineers Ltd, Tel Aviv, Israel.

Tahboub, I.K. 1992. Status of the precipitation enhancement program in Jordan. Jordan Meteorological Service, Amman, Jordan.

Teclaff, L. 1967. The river basin in history and law. Nijhoff Publishers, The Hague, Netherlands.

Tolba, M.K. 1994. Middle East water issues: action and political will. In Biswas, A.K., ed., International waters of the Middle East from Euphrates–Tigris to Nile. Oxford University Press, Bombay, India. pp. 1–4.

Ullman, R.H. 1983. Redefining security. International Security, 8(1), 129–153.

UNDP (United Nations Development Programme). 1993. Report of the mission to review UNDP's programme in the Occupied Palestinian Territories. Chapter 5: The water problems in Gaza. UNDP, New York, NY, USA.

United Nations. 1983. First report on the law of non-navigable use of international waters. United Nations, New York, NY, USA. UN Doc. A/CN.4/367.

————— 1992. Water resources of the Occupied Palestinian Territories. United Nations, New York, NY, USA.

US National Academy of Science. 1991. Policy implications of global warming. US National Academy of Science, Washington, DC, USA.

Vesilind, P.J. 1993. Water: the Middle East's critical resource. National Geographic, 183, 5.

Wade, N.M. 1991. The effect of the recent energy cost increase on the relative water costs from RO and distillation plant. In Balaban, M., ed., Desalination and water re-use. Proceedings of the 12th International Symposium, Volume 1. Hemisphere Publishing, New York, NY, USA. pp. 3–18.

Wangnick, K. 1991. 1990 Worldwide desalting plants inventory: the development of the desalination market. In Balaban, M., ed., Desalination and water re-use. Proceedings of the 12th International Symposium, Volume 1. Hemisphere Publishing, New York, NY, USA. pp. 19–37.

WCED (World Commission on Environment and Development). 1987. Our common future. Oxford University Press, Oxford, UK.

Westing, A.H. 1986. Environmental factors in strategic policy and action: an overview. In Westing, A.H., ed., Global resources and international conflict: environmental factors in strategic policy and action. Oxford University Press, New York, NY, USA. pp. 1–20.

———— 1989. The environmental component of comprehensive security. Bulletin of Peace Proposals, 20(2), 129–134.

Whitman, J. 1988. The environment in Israel. 4th ed. Ministry of the Interior, Environmental Protection Service, Jerusalem, Israel.

Whittington, D. 1992. Possible adverse effects of increasing block water tariffs in developing countries. Economic Development and Cultural Change, 41(1), 75–87.

Wishart, D. 1989. An economic approach to understanding Jordan Valley water disputes. Middle East Review, 21(4), 45–53.

———— 1990. The breakdown of the Johnston negotiations over the Jordan waters. Middle Eastern Studies, 26(4), 536–546.

Wolf, A. 1995. Hydropolitics along the Jordan River: scarce water and its impact on the Arab–Israeli conflict. United Nation University Press, Tokyo, Japan. (In press)

Wolf, A.; Lonergan, S.C. 1994. Hydropolitics in the context of environmental change: the dispute over water in the Jordan River Basin. In Dinar, A.; Lochman, E., ed., Water quantity/quality disputes and their resolution. Greenwood (Praeger) Press, Westport, CT, USA.

World Bank. 1993a. Developing the Occupied Territories: an investment in peace. World Bank, WA, USA. IBRD Staff Report.

———— 1993b. Gains that might be made from water conservation in the Middle East. Multilateral Working Group on Water Resources of the Middle East Peace Process, World Bank, Washington, DC, USa. Informal Staff Paper.

WRI (World Resources Institute). 1989. World resources: 1988–1989. Oxford University Press, New York, NY, USA.

———— 1993. World resources: 1992–1993. Oxford University Press, New York, NY, USA.

Zarour, H.; Isaac, J. 1991. The water crisis in the Occupied Territories. Paper presented at the 7th World Congress on Water Resources, Rabat, Morocco, 12–16 May 1991. International Water Resources Association, Champaign, IL, USA.

———— 1992. Nature's apportionment and the open market: a promising solution convergence to the Arab–Israeli water conflict. Paper presented at the Conference on the Middle East Water Crisis: Creative Perspectives and Solutions, 8–9 May 1992. University of Waterloo, Waterloo, ON, Canada.

———— 1993. Nature's apportionment and the open market: a promising solution to the Arab–Israeli water conflict. Water International, 18(1), 40–53.

Zeitouni, N.; Becker, N.; Shechter, M.; Luk-zilberman, E. 1991. Two models of water market mechanisms with an illustrative application to the Middle East. Natural Resource and Environmental Research Center, University of Haifa, Haifa, Israel.

INDEX

ABOUT THE AUTHORS

Stephen C. Lonergan is Professor of Geography at the University of Victoria in British Columbia, Director of the University's Centre for Sustainable Regional Development, and Chair of the Environment and Security Panel of the Canadian Global Change Program. Dr Lonergan received his PhD in regional science from the University of Pennsylvannia in 1981. Since then, he has taught in the geography departments of McMaster University (Hamilton, Ontario), the University of Aukland (Aukland, New Zealand), and, in his current position, the University of Victoria. His principal areas of research include the social and economic impacts of climatic change, strategies to reduce CO_2 emissions, and poverty and environmental degradation. Dr Lonergan has authored many journal articles and book chapters on regional development and environmental issues.

David B. Brooks is Director of the Environmental Policy Program in the Environment and Natural Resources Division of IDRC. Dr Brooks received an MS in geology from the California Institute of Technology in 1956 and a PhD in economics from the University of Colorado in 1963. For the past 30 years, he has applied his expertise in natural resource economics and policy development at a number of institutions, including Resources for the Future Inc.; the Bureau of Mines of the US Department of the Interior; Energy, Mines, and Resources Canada; and Energy Probe. His professional experience has focused on energy and materials conservation, renewable energy, energy and minerals policy, and environmental issues, and has extended across many industrialized and developing nations. Since 1988, Dr Brooks has served as honourary president of Friends of the Earth Canada, which he helped to found in 1978. He is the author of many articles and books on the sustainable management of our natural resources.

About the Institution

The International Development Research Centre (IDRC) is a public corporation created by the Parliament of Canada in 1970 to support technical and policy research to help meet the needs of developing countries. The Centre is active in the fields of environment and natural resources, social sciences, health sciences, and information sciences and systems. Regional offices are located in Africa, Asia, Latin America, and the Middle East.

About the Publisher

IDRC Books publishes research results and scholarly studies on global and regional issues related to sustainable and equitable development. As a specialist in development literature, IDRC Books contributes to the body of knowledge on these issues to further the cause of global understanding and equity. IDRC publications are sold through its head office in Ottawa, Canada, as well as by IDRC's agents and distributors around the world.